Welcome to

2004

This edition has been researched and written
by
Wendy Lockett

Thank you for helping Great Ormond Street Hospital Children's Charity in 2004, the centenary of the first ever production of Peter Pan.

Celebrating 100 *Years of Peter Pan* The rights of Peter Pan were bequeathed by JM Barrie to GOSH. The value of this fantastic legacy remains a secret, at Barrie's request, in keeping with the magic and mystery of Peter Pan.

Through the sales of these guides we will have raised over £30,600. Since 1998 we have contributed to the funding of a mobile X-ray unit, syringe pumps, infusion pumps and a hoist, but this year we are committed to helping with a much bigger project tackling the hospital infrastructure. This 10-year redevelopment programme will upgrade the Hospital and increase its overall size enabling treatment for over 20% more patients. In the pursuit of excellence, the plan will bring the hospital right up to date with modern day medical practices and clinical care.

Funds contributed in 2004 will go towards the first stage of the re-development. A brand new Patient and Accommodation Centre, opening in 2004, will include 30 rooms for children who require short-stay treatments, along with their families. It will also contain eight transitional care flats for children who are well enough to leave their wards but need some care before they are allowed to return home.

We are proud to announce that a 6p contribution to the above charity will be made for each 'Let's Go with the Children' book sold this season. Thank you for your support. Registered charity No. 235825 ©1989 GOSHCC. 🌟 2003 GOSHCC

Getting yourself involved

Great Ormond Street Hospital Children's Charity needs everyone's support as they aim to raise over £20 million each year. There are many ways to get involved from trekking in Namibia to attending musical concerts. Log on to www.gosh.org or call 0207 916 5678 for an up to date listing of planned events, some of which can involve the whole family. Look out particularly for special Peter Pan themed events throughout the year.

Published by **Cube Publications**, 290 Lymington Road,
Highcliffe, Christchurch, Dorset BH23 5ET
Telephone: 01425 279001 Fax: 01425 279002
www.cubepublications.co.uk
Email: enquiries@cubepublications.co.uk
2nd edition
ISBN 1 903594 41 3

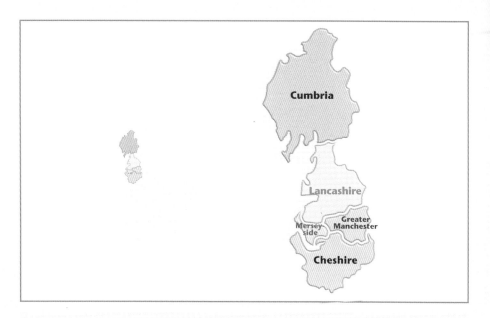

Cumbria

Lancashire

Mersey side | Greater Manchester

Cheshire

How to use this guide

This guide is one of a set of 13 covering all the counties of England and each county in this edition is colour coded as shown on the map above.

There are several chapters of subject interest as listed in the Contents opposite enabling you to choose something specific for you and your children to do or somewhere for you all to go.

If you have young children who love animals, dip into the Farms, Wildlife & Nature Parks chapter, or, if you have active teenagers, take a look at the Sports & Leisure chapter where you will find something to keep them busy.

Check out History, Art & Science and widen young horizons or choose a nearby venue from the Free Places chapter. A surprising number of things are free.

Whatever your budget, plan a day out to include a variety of activities. You may like to hire a boat, take a train ride, visit a really interesting museum, go bowling, stop off at a soft play centre, try snow sports, visit a zoo or go for a hike. Whatever interests you and your family, there is information included within the following chapters to help you occupy a wet afternoon, a long weekend or the whole school holidays.

We have highlighted price bands, facilities for school trips, places that are open all year and places that cater for birthday parties, but please call in advance if you have special needs or want particular information.

Whether you live locally or you are just visiting, you will find an amazing wealth of diverse interests, entertainments and activities in this area for children of all ages. We hope you will discover more about the area than you thought you already knew.

Please write to us with any constructive comments on the guide. We shall be delighted to hear from you. Our address is on page 1.

Use this guide with a good geographical map to help you find your way.
Discover somewhere new, plan your route and keep the children busy by
encouraging them to help with the navigating.

Contents

Key

Price codes are given as a maximum entry cost for a family of four, (2 Adults, 2 children):
A: £10 **B**: £20 **C**: £30 **D**: £40 **E**: £50 **F**: FREE **G**: Over £50 **P**: Pay as you go

Schools	School party facilities, visits by arrangement
Birthdays	Birthday parties are organised here
NT	National Trust property - www.nationaltrust.org.uk
EH	English Heritage property - www.english-heritage.org.uk

Telephone Numbers are provided for most entries.

Should you require special facilities for someone with a disability, please call before your visit to check suitability.

Opening Times

LAST ADMISSIONS
Many last admission times are an hour before the quoted closing time. If in any doubt, phone and ask if you know you will be arriving late. Don't get caught out and be disappointed!

WINTER AND CHRISTMAS OPENING
Many attractions close earlier in Winter and most are closed over Christmas and New Year. If you want to visit in this period, call in advance to check! At the time of going to print not all opening times were decided. We have suggested you phone for opening times if this was the case!

Please mention this guide when visiting attractions

USEFUL INFORMATION

LOCAL COUNCILS

The Local Councils have Leisure Services Departments looking after a wide range of leisure facilities, many of which are featured within this guide, from the best parks and open spaces to sports facilities and museums. They may be able to provide further information on special events and playschemes organised for children, particularly in the school holidays.

CHESHIRE: Cheshire County Council 01244 602424. Chester City Council 01244 324324. Congleton Borough Council 01270 763231. Crewe and Nantwich Borough Council 01270 537777. Halton Borough Council 0151 424 2061. Macclesfield Borough Council 01625 500500. Vale Royal Borough Council 01606 862862. Warrington Borough Council 01925 444400.

CUMBRIA: Allerdale Borough Council 01900 326333. Barrow-in-Furness Borough Council 01229 894900. Carlisle City Council 01228 817000. Copeland Borough Council 01946 852585. Cumbria County Council 01228 606060. Eden District Council 01768 864671. South Lakeland District Council 01539 733333.

GREATER MANCHESTER: Bolton Metropolitan Borough Council 01204 333333. Bury Metropolitan Borough Council 0161 253 5000. Manchester City Council 0161 234 5000. Oldham Metropolitan Borough Council 0161 911 3000. Rochdale Metropolitan Borough Council 01706 647474. Salford City Council 0161 794 4711. Stockport Metropolitan Borough Council 0161 480 4949. Tameside Metropolitan Borough Council 0161 342 8355. Trafford Metropolitan Borough Council 0161 912 1212. Wigan Metropolitan Borough Council 01942 828508.

LANCASHIRE: Blackburn with Darwen Borough Council 01254 585585. Blackpool Borough Council 01253 477477. Burnley Borough Council 01282 425011. Chorley Borough Council 01257 515151. Fylde Borough Council 01253 721222. Lancashire County Council 01772 254868. Lancaster City Council 01524 582000. Pendle Borough Council 01282 661661. Preston City Council 01772 906000. Ribble Valley Borough Council 01200 425111. Rossendale Borough Council 01706 217777. South Ribble Borough Council 01772 421491. West Lancashire District Council 01695 577177. Wyre Borough Council 01253 891000.

MERSEYSIDE: Ellesmere Port and Neston Borough Council 0151 356 6789. Knowsley Metropolitan Borough Council 0151 489 6000. Liverpool City Council 0151 233 3000. St Helens Metropolitan Borough Council 01744 456000. Sefton Metropolitan Borough Council 01704 533133. Wirral Metropolitan Borough Council 0151 638 7070.

TOURIST INFORMATION CENTRES

Tourist Information Centres are a great complement to this guide and can provide advice and detail on the many interesting local events that take place and local accommodation for visitors, as well as stocking colour leaflets about many of the attractions featured in this guide.

CHESHIRE: Chester: 01244 402111. Congleton: 01260 271095. Crewe & Nantwich: 01270 610983. Knutsford: 01565 632611. Macclesfield: 01625 504114. Northwich: 01606 353534. Runcorn: 01928 576776. Warrington: 01925 632571. Wilmslow: 01625 522275.

CUMBRIA: Alston Moor: 01434 382244. Ambleside: 01539 432582. Appleby: 017683 51177. Barrow-in-Furness: 01229 894784. Carlisle: 01228 625600. Cockermouth: 01900 822634. Coniston: 015394 41533. Kendal: 01539 725758. Keswick: 017687 72645. Kirby Lonsdale: 01524 271437. Maryport: 01900 813738. Penrith: 01768 867466. Sedbergh: 01539 620125. Sellafield: 019467 76510. Silloth: 01697 331944. Ulverston: 01229 587120. Whitehaven: 01946 852939. Windermere: 01539 446499. Workington: 01900 606699.

GREATER MANCHESTER: Altrincham: 0161 912 5931. Ashton-under-Lyne: 0161 343 4343. Bolton: 01204 334400. Bury: 0161 253 5111. Manchester: 0161 234 3157. Oldham: 0161 627 1024. Rochdale: 01706 864928. Saddleworth: 01457 870336. Salford: 0161 848 8601. Stockport: 0161 474 4444. Wigan: 01942 825677.

LANCASHIRE: Accrington: 01254 872595. Barnoldswick: 01282 666704. Blackburn: 01254 53277. Blackpool: 01253 478222. Burnley: 01282 664421. Cleveleys: 01253 583378. Clitheroe: 01200 425566. Fleetwood: 01253 773953. Lancaster: 01524 32878. Lytham St Anne's: 01253 725610. Morecambe: 01524 582808. Nelson: 01282 661701. Preston: 01772 253731. Rawtenstall: 01706 229828.

MERSEYSIDE: Birkenhead: 0151 647 6780. Liverpool: 09066 806886. St Helens: 01744 456951. Southport: 01704 533333.

Adventure & Fun

Quite a medley here, with a strong emphasis on fun and play, rides and thrills. This chapter includes theme parks, play centres, other fun activities and unusual themed venues such as laser game centres, water fun parks, maize mazes and model villages.

There are numerous soft play centres in the North West and listed here are a selection of the larger venues. Age or height restrictions apply at most soft play and laser game centres and opening times vary, so please ring before visiting.

Also check out the many 'fun pubs' and family restaurants with soft play or adventure playgrounds such as Brewsters or Wacky Warehouse.

CHESHIRE

Chester, Amazon Play Experience, 2 Overleigh Road, Handbridge, 01244 659700. Soft play with ball pools, bridges and slides. Schools Birthdays **Open all year** Price A.
Laser Quest, Volunteer Street, 01244 400500. Enjoy indoor sci-fi adventure games with sound and special effects. Schools Birthdays **Open all year** Price P.

Crewe, Funsters, Stalbridge Road, 01270 500525, is an indoor play centre with slides, ball pools and dressing-up clothes. Also GT racing slot-car circuit to hire, ring first to book. Schools Birthdays **Open all year** Price A.

Frodsham, Cocos Play Barn, Lady Heyes Craft & Antique Centre, Kingsley Road, 01928 789028. A large and exciting three-level soft play area for all ages. Schools Birthdays **Open all year** Price A.

Nantwich, Reaseheath Maize Maze, www.reaseheath.ac.uk 01270 625131. Find your way out of the dinosaur maze. Open mid Jul-early Sept, daily, 11am-6pm (allow enough time to get out!). Schools Birthdays **Price A.**

Northwich, Joe Crow's Play Stacks, Blakemere Craft Centre, Chester Road, Sandiway, www.playstacks.co.uk 01606 301321. Explore the soft play area and then visit the computer games 'Zapper Zone'. Schools Birthdays **Open all year** Price A.

Warrington, Giggles Playmill, Evans House, Norman Street, 01925 445753. Indoor adventure play and soft room for the under 5s. Schools Birthdays **Open all year** Price A.
Gulliver's World, www.gulliversfun.co.uk 01925 444888, is designed for families with children between the ages of 2 and 13. From the whoosh of the roller coaster to the splash of the log flume, children will have a great day out. Special rides for younger children. Telephone for opening times and prices. Schools Birthdays.

Waverton, Crocky Trail, Guy Lane, www.crockytrail.co.uk 01244 335753. A large outdoor adventure park where you can try the vertical roundabout, walk the plank or get caught in the spider trap! New for 2004 is the Titanic Slide. Open daily, 10am-5pm. Schools **Open all year** Price B.

CUMBRIA

Ambleside, Bonkers and Bobbies Den, Piano Café, 5 Market Cross, 015394 31198. Relax with a drink while the children have fun on the slides and in the ball pool. Schools Birthdays **Open all year** Price A.

Barrow-in-Furness, LazerZone, The Custom House, 1 Abbey Road, www.1abbeyroad.co.uk 01229 823823. Advanced laser tag interactive arena where you can zap your friends and enemies! Schools Birthdays **Open all year** Price P.

Carlisle, Laser Quest, Bush Bow, Victoria Viaduct, 01228 511155. Space age fun with laser guns. Schools Birthdays **Open all year** Price P.

Magic Castle Adventure Playground, 1st Floor, Atlas Works, Nelson Street, 01228 401095. There is a separate area for under 5s at this indoor play area. Schools Birthdays **Open all year** Price P.

Grange-over-Sands, Lakeland Miniature Village, Winder Lane, Flookburgh, www.lakelandminiaturevillage.com 015395 58500. Enjoy the Lakeland landscape in miniature, made from local slate. New Japanese tree house opening in 2004. Play area. Open daily, 10am-dusk. Schools Birthdays **Open all year** Price A.

Grizedale, Go Ape!, Grizedale Forest Visitor Centre, www.goape.cc 0870 444 5562. This new extreme outdoor adventure course has rope bridges, tarzan swings and zip slides. Wear suitable clothing. Advance booking essential, age and height restrictions apply, and adult supervision required. Open Apr-Oct, daily, 9am-dusk; Nov and Mar, Sat-Sun. Schools Birthdays **Price E.**

Maryport, Clown-A-Round, Station Street, 01900 818811. Coco's corner for the under 4s and climbing frames, ball pools, tunnels and slides for older children at this adventure play centre. Schools Birthdays **Open all year** Price A.

Penrith, Noah's Ark Soft Play Centre, 1st Floor, 36-40 Burrowgate, 01768 890640. A bouncy castle, ball pools and slides to use up all that surplus energy. Schools Birthdays **Open all year** Price A.

Silloth-on-Solway, The Sunset Leisure Centre, Stanwix Park Holiday Centre, www.stanwix.com 016973 32666. Buy a day pass and get access to the Leisure Centre, swimming pools, amusement arcade and soft play area. Pass also includes evening entertainment. Open daily, 9am-9pm. Schools Birthdays **Open all year** Price B.

Whitehaven, Billy Bears Fun Centre, Unit B1, Haig Enterprise Park, Kells, 01946 690003, has a ball pool, slides and bouncy castle for under 6s. Schools Birthdays **Open all year** Price P.

Workington, Funky Monkeys Fun Factory, Derwent Howe Industrial Estate, Peart Road, 01900 64222. Let off steam in this indoor adventure play centre. Special area for under 4s. Schools Birthdays **Open all year** Price P.

GREATER MANCHESTER

Bolton, Laser Quest, 101 Bradshawgate, 01204 388308. Stalk your opponents in a sci-fi adventure game. Schools Birthdays **Open all year** Price P.

Chadderton, Fun Bay 1, Unit 3, 16 Watts Street, 0161 620 5955. Try out the ball pools, slides and bouncy castle at this indoor adventure play centre with separate toddler village. Schools Birthdays **Open all year** Price A.

Dunham Massey, Redhouse Farm Maize Maze, Redhouse Lane, www.redhousefarm.co.uk 0161 941 3480. Get lost in the maize! Open daily, mid Jul-mid Sept, 10am-4.30pm. Schools Birthdays **Price B.**

Hyde, Hyde Leisure Pool, Walker Lane, 061 368 4057. Dare you try the white water ride through the tunnel? Splash down the slide and jump in the waves. Schools Birthdays **Open all year** Price A.

Jumping Jacks Adventureland, Caxon works, Dukinfield Road, 0161 366 9366, is home to Turbo Jacks (go-karting for 5-13 year olds), Jumping Jacks soft play and Cactus Jacks Wild West Action Town. Open Tues-Sun, telephone for details. Schools Birthdays **Open all year** Price P.

Manchester, Laser Quest, Arch 58 Whitworth Street West, 0161 228 2231. Laser games for a space age adventure. Schools Birthdays **Open all year** Price P.

Oldham, Jolly Jungle, Featherstall Road, 0161 628 4411. Indoor adventure play centre with separate baby and toddler areas. Messy activities for pre-school children Mon-Fri, 10am-2pm. Schools Birthdays **Open all year Price P.**

Stockport, Alphabet Zoo Adventure Playcentre, King Street West, 0161 477 2225, has rollers, ball pools, slides and cargo nets together with a toddler area. Schools Birthdays **Open all year Price A.**

The Trafford Centre, The Adventures of Dreamieland, 203 The Dome, www.dreamieland.com 0161 749 7490. A short, interactive fantasy ride where your mission is to save Dreamieland. School holiday activity sessions. Open Mon-Fri, 10am-9pm, Sat, 10am-8pm, Sun, 12noon-6pm. Schools Birthdays **Open all year Price A.**
Laser Quest, The Dome, 0161 755 0600. Sci-fi adventure games with sound and special effects. Schools Birthdays **Open all year Price P.**

Wigan, Megazone, AMF Wigan, Wallgate, 01942 820225. Indoor adventure games of laser tag. Schools Birthdays **Open all year Price P.**

LANCASHIRE

Blackburn, Waves Water Fun Centre, Nab Lane, 01254 51111. Whizz down the flume, try a gentle slide, splash in the fountains or relax in the jacuzzi. Schools **Open all year Price B.**

Blackpool, Blackpool Model Village and Gardens, East Park Drive, Stanley Park, www.blackpoolmodelvillage.com 01253 763827. Admire a miniature world which includes a model railway. All set in beautiful gardens. Open Feb-mid Mar, Sat-Sun, 10am-5pm; mid Mar-Oct, daily. Schools **Price A.**
Blackpool Tower, www.theblackpooltower.com 01253 622242, includes the Tower Circus, Tower Top with the Walk of Faith, an indoor adventure playground with Zap Zone and an aquarium. A full day out for all the family. Phone for opening times. Schools Birthdays **Open all year Price D.**
Louis Tussauds Waxworks, 87/89 Central Promenade, 01253 292029. Famous rock stars, great sportsmen and even Harry Potter are all immortalised in wax. The Chamber of Horrors now includes the Lancashire Witches. Open daily, Easter-Oct, 10am-5pm (8pm in Summer school hols), Nov-Mar, 11am-5pm. Schools **Open all year Price B.**
Pleasure Beach, Ocean Boulevard, www.blackpoolpleasurebeach.co.uk 0870 444 5566. From white knuckle rides to a special area for younger children, this is an attraction for all ages. Many rides are indoor. Free entry to the park, price band applies to unlimited ride ticket. Telephone for opening times. Schools Birthdays **Price G.**
Sandcastle Waterworld, South Promenade, www.sandcastle-waterworld.co.uk 01253 343602, has white knuckle water chutes and 90m water slides! New for 2004, giant interactive water play area. Telephone for opening times and prices. Schools Birthdays.

Chorley, Playmates, Unit F26-28 Coppull Enterprise Centre, Mill Lane, Coppull, 01257 470288. Discover a spooky hole, slides and bridges at this indoor adventure play centre. Soft centre for under 5s, bookshop and story time. Schools Birthdays **Open all year Price A.**

Chorley(near), Camelot Theme Park, Charnock Richard, www.camelotthemepark.co.uk 01257 452100, offers a variety of white knuckle rides including the spinning roller coaster, The Whirwind. Daily jousting tournament, juggling and magic displays. Animal kingdom and soft play area. Open Easter-mid Oct, telephone for details and prices. Schools Birthdays.

Horwich, Tumble Jungle, 168 Chorley New Road, 01204 696158. Aerial walkways, rope bridges and ball pools mean lots of excitement. Schools Birthdays **Open all year Price A.**

Morecambe, Megazone Laser Adventure, The Megazone Building, 94-96 Marine Road, www.megazonemorecambe.co.uk 01524 410224. A laser adventure full of excitement and fun. Schools Birthdays **Open all year Price P.**

Nelson, **Pendle Wavelengths,** Leeds Road, 01282 661717, is where it's always Summertime! Brave the roof-high waterslide, jump above the waves or have fun in the beachside playland. Schools Birthdays **Open all year** Price A.

Oswaldtwistle, **Bubbles Play Centre,** Oswaldtwistle Mills, 01254 770752. Squeeze between rollers, wade through ball pools and check out the slides at this indoor soft play centre. Separate areas for under 5s and babies. Schools Birthdays **Open all year** Price A.

St Anne's, **The Island,** South Promenade, www.the-island.ws Leisure facilities at the beach include family rides, swimming pool, pitch and putt and Surfside indoor family amusement centre with ten-pin bowling.

MERSEYSIDE

Birkenhead, **Europa Pools,** Conway Street, 0151 647 4182. Splash down the flumes or relax in the jacuzzi. There is a children's lagoon and a wave machine every 30 minutes. Schools Birthdays **Open all year** Price B.

Bootle, **Liverpool Quasar,** Switch Island Leisure Park, Dunnings Bridge Road, 0151 525 5676. All the family can take part in a thrilling laser game. Birthdays **Open all year** Price P.

Brimstage, **Brimstage Hall Maize Maze,** www.brimstagehall.co.uk 07919 674977. When you get out of the maze, there are tractor and trailer rides, games and quiz trails. Open mid Jul-mid Sept, 10am-5pm. Schools Birthdays **Price B.**

Knowsley, **Heatwaves Leisure Centre,** Waterpark Drive, 0151 443 2750. Large flume and leisure pool with wave machine every 20 minutes. Small toddler pool. Schools Birthdays **Open all year** Price A.

Liverpool, **Happy Dayz,** 166 Townsend Lane, 0151 256 6663. Plenty of scope for soft play fun at this indoor centre with special area for under 5s. Schools Birthdays **Open all year** Price P.

New Brighton, **The New Palace,** Marine Promenade, 0151 639 6041, includes amusement arcades, adventureland indoor play and new 7m indoor climbing wall. Outdoor funfair open Easter-Sept, school hols and weekends. Schools Birthdays **Open all year** Price P.

Southport, **Lakeside Miniature Railway,** Marine Lake, 01772 745511, has been operating since 1911. Take a trip alongside the lake and down towards the beach. Open daily, Easter-end Oct, weather permitting. Schools **Price A.**
Model Railway Village, Lower Promenade, King Gardens, 01704 538001. A miniature railway layout within landscaped gardens. Open Easter-Sept, daily, 11am-4pm (5pm during Summer school hols). Schools **Price A.**
Pleasureland, Marine Drive, www.pleasureland.uk.com 0870 220 0204. Over 100 rides and attractions, including roller coasters, the Traumatizer Chaos ride and special junior area for younger children. Open Mar-Nov, days and times vary, phone for details and prices. Schools Birthdays.
Silcock's Funland, Southport Pier, www.silcock-leisure.co.uk 01704 536733. A large indoor family amusement centre with arcade and video games and mini rides for younger children. Open daily, times vary. **Open all year** Price P.
Turbo Ted's Play Centre, 23 Princes Street, 01704 530165. 'Bouncing Bears' inflatables for 5-9 year olds and adventure soft play for under 7s. Schools Birthdays **Open all year** Price P.

Can't find a babysitter?

SitterS
0800 38 900 38

For Evening Babysitters
www.sitters.co.uk

Evening Babysitters with Professional Childcare Experience

Now you can find mature, friendly and reliable evening babysitters, available at short notice. For your reassurance we interview each babysitter in person and check all references thoroughly.

All Sitters babysitters have professional childcare experience and most are local authority registered childminders or professionally qualified nursery nurses.

How does Sitters' service work

When you make a booking we arrange for a babysitter to attend at the appointed time. At the end of the evening you pay the babysitter for the hours they have worked. Babysitting rates start from £4.40 per hour and vary depending on your area. There are no additional charges for travelling costs and all bookings are for a minimum of 4 hours.

Each time you book a babysitter we charge a nominal £4 booking fee to your credit card. You can register with Sitters free! Membership of just £12.75 for 3 months will only be charged after your first sitting. Call us today - less than £1 per week is a small price to ensure your children are in experienced hands.

For more information, phone us FREE today or

0800 38 900 38
or visit us at www.sitters.co.uk
Please quote Ref: LET'S GO

Experienced Childcarers Needed

Sitters welcomes applications from suitable babysitters. You will need to be over 21, have professional childcare experience, your own transport and immaculate references. For more information and to register your interest phone 0800 38 900 38 or visit www.sitters.co.uk.

Recruitment & Employment Confederation

We're in  YELLOW PAGES

INVESTOR IN PE

It is a real adventure for children to go on a journey and to experience other forms of transport. Join an organised trip or let them try out other vehicles for themselves. In the North West you can hire boats or bikes, take bus and tram tours, ride steam trains, cruise waterways and get away from the family car!

BOAT HIRE

CHESHIRE

Bunbury, Anglo Welsh Holidays, 01829 260957, narrow boats available for day hire.
Crewe, Queens Park, Wistaston Road, rowing boats in Summer.
Nantwich, Nantwich Canal Centre, Basin End, 01270 625122, narrow boats.
Scholar Green, Heritage Narrow Boats, The Marina, 01782 785700, narrow boats for day hire.

CUMBRIA

Ambleside, Windermere Lake Cruises, 015394 32225, rowing boats.
Coniston, Coniston Boating Centre, Lake Road, 015394 41366, canadian canoes, motor, rowing and sailing boats.
Keswick, Derwent Water Marina, Portinscale, 017687 72912, canadian canoes, kayaks, rowing and sailing boats, windsurfing boards. Keswick Launch Company, Keswick Boat Landings, 017687 72263, motor and rowing boats.
Newby Bridge, Fell Foot Park, 015395 31273, rowing boats.
Windermere, Shepherds, Bowness Bay, 015394 45395, motor and sailing boats.

GREATER MANCHESTER

Littleborough, Hollingworth Lake Water Activity Centre, Lakebank, 01706 370499, rowing boats for hire at weekends and in school holidays.
Oldham, Alexandra Park, King's Road, rowing boats.
Prestwich, Heaton Park, Middleton Road, 0161 773 1085, pedaloes and rowing boats.

LANCASHIRE

Blackpool, Stanley Park, West Park Drive, motor boats, pedaloes and rowing boats.
Chorley, L and L Cruises, Heath Charnock, 01257 480825, narrow boats for day hire.
Garstang, Admiral Boat Hire, Cabus Nook Lane, Winmarleigh, 01995 603271, self-drive cruisers for day hire.
Lytham St Anne's, Fairhaven Lake, canoes, motor and rowing boats.

MERSEYSIDE

Southport, Marine Lake, The Promenade, 01704 539701, motor boats.

BOAT TRIPS

CHESHIRE

Chester, Bithell Boats, Boating Station, Souters Lane, www.showboatsofchester.co.uk 01244 325394. Regular 30-minute cruises on the River Dee and a two-hour cruise to Ironbridge. Private charter also. Operates Summer, daily, 11am-5.30pm; Winter, Sat-Sun, 11am-4pm. Schools Birthdays **Open all year.**

CUMBRIA

Coniston, Coniston Launch, www.conistonlaunch.co.uk 015394 36216. Departures from a number of points around the lake. Special interest cruises include 'Swallows and Amazons' on selected dates. Sailings all year with a limited service Nov-Mar. Schools Birthdays **Open all year** Price P.

Steam Yacht Gondola, NT, 015394 63850. This restored Victorian boat is also available for private charter. Sailings daily, Apr-Oct. Schools Birthdays **Price B.**

Derwentwater, Keswick Launch, www.keswick-launch.co.uk 017687 72263. A full timetable of trips around the lake from different stages. Private charter available. Sailings mid Mar-Nov, daily; Dec-mid Mar, Sat-Sun. Schools Birthdays **Open all year Price P.**

Ullswater, Ullswater Steamers, www.ullswater-steamers.co.uk 017684 82229. Cruises from various stages around the lake and with a selection of themes. Sailings throughout the year, times vary. Schools **Open all year Price P.**

Windermere, Windermere Lake Cruises, www.windermere-lakecruises.co.uk 015395 31188. Enjoy a variety of trips departing from Lakeside, Bowness or Ambleside. Combined cruise and attraction tickets available. Sailings all year, reduced service Nov-Easter. Schools **Open all year Price P.**

GREATER MANCHESTER

Ashton-under-Lyne, Tameside Canal Boat Trust, Portland Basin Museum, 0161 339 1332. The narrow boat 'Still Waters' takes you on a 40-minute trip along the Ashton Canal. Also available for private charter. Operates Easter-Oct, Sun, Bank Hols and museum event days, 12noon-4pm. Schools Birthdays **Price A.**

Littleborough, Hollingworth Lake, 01706 370499. Try a 30-minute trip aboard the 'Lady Alice' motor launch. Operates Easter-Sept, Sat-Sun and school hols, from 1pm, weather permitting. **Price A.**

Manchester, City Centre Cruises, Castlefield Basin, Liverpool Road, www.citycentrecruises.co.uk 0161 902 0222. Cruises aboard the 'Castlefield' on the Bridgewater Canal. Subject to weather conditions and water levels. Private charter also. Operates Easter-Oct, Sun, 1-4pm. Schools Birthdays **Price A.**

Saddleworth, Pennine Moonraker Canal Cruises, Uppermill, www.saddleworth-canal-cruises.co.uk 0161 652 6331. Enjoy an hourlong trip on a diesel-engine narrow boat along the Huddersfield Canal. Available for private charter. Operates Easter-mid Oct: Sat, from 1pm; Sun, 12noon-4pm; Wed, 1-2pm; daily in school hols. Schools Birthdays **Price A.**

Salford, Irwell & Mersey Packet Company, moors at the Lowry, Salford Quays, 0161 776 1657. An hourlong trip with commentary along the Manchester Ship Canal and the River Irwell. Private charter also. Operates Mar-Dec, Sun, 2.30pm and 3.30pm, weather permitting. Schools Birthdays **Price B.**

LANCASHIRE

Colne, Foulridge Canal Cruises, Foulridge Wharf, www.canaltrips.info 01282 844033. A cruise along the Leeds and Liverpool Canal aboard the 'Marton Emperor' narrow boat, which is also available for private charter. Operates May-Sept, Sun (Jul-Sept, Tues sailings also). **Price B.**

St Anne's, Fairhaven Lake, 01253 735439. The 'Jubilee' passenger launch takes you on a 20-minute trip around this pretty lake, Open Easter-Oct, Sat-Sun, and daily in Summer school hols. Schools **Price A.**

MERSEYSIDE

Liverpool, Mersey Ferries, River Explorer Cruises, Pier Head www.merseyferries.co.uk 0151 330 1444. Family cruises on the river Mersey with commentary telling the story of Liverpool's historic past. There is a free children's activity pack with child return Explorer tickets. This trip allows you to break your journey by stopping at Seacombe and Woodside Terminals and to rejoin and complete your cruise later that day. At Seacombe, visit the aquarium where you can learn about the underwater world of the River Mersey. The Pirates Paradise soft play area is a great treat for 2-9 year olds, or enjoy the fresh air with a walk along the promenade to New Brighton. At Woodside, why not stop for lunch or afternoon tea at the café and visit Birkenhead Priory or the Heritage Centre with its tram and other exhibits. Operates Mon-Fri, 10am-3pm, Sat-Sun, 10am-6pm. Schools Birthdays **Open all year** Price B **Check out inside front cover.**

Yellow Duck Marine, Anchor Courtyard, Albert Dock, 0151 708 7799. Try this amphibious tour of the city for a unique way to see Liverpool! Trips run daily, mid Feb-Christmas. Summer departures, 11am-5.15pm. Please ring for Winter times. Schools Birthdays **Price C.**

Southport, Marine Lake, 01704 539701. Two very different boat trips. Try a gentle cruise aboard the 'Southport Belle' with commentary and bar, or an exciting high-speed ride aboard the 'Southport Jetboat'. Sailings Easter–mid Sept. **Price P.**

BUS TRIPS

CHESHIRE
Chester, City Transport/City Sightseeing, www.city-sightseeing.com 01244 347457. An open-top bus tour with live commentary. Hop on or off at any of the 19 stopping points around the city. Departs every 10-30 minutes, depending on time of year. Schools Birthdays **Open all year** Price P.

MERSEYSIDE
Liverpool, City Sightseeing Tour, 0906 680 6886. A 50-minute tour on an open-top bus with commentary from a Blue Badge Guide. Times and frequency vary, ring for details. Schools **Open all year** Price C.

CYCLE HIRE

CUMBRIA
Ambleside, Biketreks, Compston Road, 015394 31505. Ghyllside Cycles, The Slack, 015394 33592.
Coniston, Summitreks, 14 Yewdale Road, 015394 41212.
Hawkshead, Grizedale Mountain Bikes, Grizedale Visitor Centre, Grizedale Forest Park, 01229 860369.
Kendal, Askew Cycles, Old Brewery, Wildman Street, 01539 728057.
Keswick, Keswick Motor Company, Fiat Garage, Lake Road, 017687 72064. Keswick Mountain Bikes, Southey Hill, 017687 75202.
Staveley, Millennium Cycles, Bankside Barn, Crook Road, 01539 821167. **Wheelbase,** Staveley Mill Yard, 01539 821443.
Ulverston, Gill Cycles, 1 The Gill, 01229 581116.
Windermere, Country Lanes Cycle Centre, The Railway Station, 01539 444544.

LANCASHIRE
Lancaster, Cyclepoint, Lancaster Railway Station, 01524 389410.

TRAIN TRIPS

CUMBRIA
Alston, South Tynedale Railway, www.strps.org.uk 01434 381696 (talking timetable 01434 382828). Travel by steam or diesel on a scenic 60-minute return journey to Kirkhaugh. Open Easter-Oct, Sat-Sun and school hols; steam season, mid Jul-Aug. Schools **Price B.**

Ravenglass, Ravenglass to Eskdale Railway, www.ravenglass-railway.co.uk 01229 717171. Venture seven miles into the heart of the Eskdale Valley on a 15" narrow-gauge train. Find out about 'La'al Ratty', the water vole stationmaster, and look for his quiz book. 'Santa Trains' before Christmas. Operates mid Mar-Oct, daily; Nov-Mar, limited service. Schools Birthdays **Open all year Price C.**

Settle, Settle to Carlisle Railway Line, 0870 602 3322. Regarded as one of the country's most scenic train journeys, this service runs daily, stopping at various stations in Cumbria and Yorkshire. Schools **Open all year Price P.**

Ulverston, Lakeside & Haverthwaite Railway, Haverthwaite Station, 015395 31594. A trip by steam locomotive along this steeply graded line running through beautiful countryside. Operates mid Apr-Oct, daily. Schools Birthdays **Price B.**

GREATER MANCHESTER

Bury, East Lancashire Steam Railway, www.east-lancs-rly.co.uk 0161 764 7790. Depart from Bury, Rawtenstall or Ramsbottom. There is a new extension to Heywood. Special events programme including 'Thomas the Tank Engine' and 'Santa Specials'. Operates Sat-Sun and Bank Hols, 10am-4pm; extended service in Summer school hols. Schools **Open all year Price B.**

LANCASHIRE

Blackpool, DalesRail, www.dalesrail.com 01200 429832. Escape from the car, with this special leisure service which runs from **Blackpool** to **Carlisle**, via **Preston** and **Blackburn**. A joint venture with Lancashire County Council, First North Western and the Rail Ramblers it offers a scenic train journey together with organised walks. The walks are designed to link with the Sunday DalesRail service and you can choose from three levels of difficulty, with the easy walk being most suitable for younger children. Alternatively, take the train and explore by yourself. With bus links at selected stations, this is a great way to get out and about. Operates Easter-Oct, Suns only. Telephone for details. Schools **Check out outside back cover.**

Preston(near), West Lancashire Light Railway, Station Road, Hesketh Bank, www.westlancs.org 01772 815881. One of the restored ex-industrial locomotives takes you on a short ride along this narrow-gauge steam railway. Special events during Summer and 'Santa Specials' in Dec. Open Easter-Oct, Suns and Bank Hols. Schools Birthdays **Price A.**

TRAM TRIPS

LANCASHIRE

Blackpool, Blackpool Tramway System, www.blackpooltransport.com 01253 473000. Take a trip on the first electric tramway in Britain. Some of the vehicles still in use today are more than 100 years old. Special tours during Blackpool Illuminations. Frequent daily service. Schools **Open all year Price P.**

MERSEYSIDE

Birkenhead, Birkenhead Tramway, 1 Taylor Street, 0151 647 2128. Take a trip in an Edwardian open-top tram and visit the Wirral Bus and Tram Heritage Centre. Operates Sat-Sun, Apr-Oct, 1-5pm, Nov-Mar, 12noon-4pm. Additional opening in school hols. Schools **Open all year Price A.**

Sports & Leisure

Sport is a great way for young people to channel surplus energy or occupy spare time. It can offer personal challenge, foster team spirit and generate an interest which can provide a pleasurable and necessary diversion in later life. Sport is a good way to have fun, make new friends, to be fit and feel good. Try climbing, snow sports or the many different activities on offer at your sports and leisure centre.

Leisure pursuits may lead to a new hobby or simply occupy leisure time in a relaxed and entertaining way. Try pottery painting, go to the theatre or have a go at ten-pin bowling.

ADVENTURE HOLIDAYS

PGL Activity Holidays, www.pgl.co.uk 08700 507 507, has ten UK residential centres, offering activity holidays for 7-10, 10-13 or 13-16 year olds covering football, drama, kayaking, 'Adrenaline Adventure', 'Learner Driver' and much more. There are also 'Family Active' holidays for all the family and centres in France. Winter snow sports are available in Austria. Telephone for free brochure. **Check out page 18.**

BOWLING (TEN PIN)

CHESHIRE: Chester: **Megabowl** Unit 33 The Greyhound Pk Sealand Rd 01244 383125. Ellesmere Port: **Megabowl Coliseum** Leisure Pk Coliseum Way 0151 356 5100. Macclesfield: **AMF Bowling** London Rd 01625 616438. Northwich: **Winnington Bowl** Winnington La 01606 786836. Warrington: **LA Bowl** Chetham Court Winwick Quay 01925 639222.
CUMBRIA: Barrow-in-Furness: **Superbowl** Hollywood Pk 01229 820444. Carlisle: **AMF Bowling** Currock Rd 01228 810310. Workington: **Miami Superbowl** 4 Derwent Howe Ind Est 01900 872207.
GREATER MANCHESTER: Bolton: **Hollywood Bowl** 25-27 The Linkway Middlebrook Leisure and Retail Pk 01204 692999. Bury: **Megabowl Park** 66 Pilsworth 0161 767 9150. Didsbury: **Megabowl** Wilmslow Rd 0161 446 4200. Leigh: **Superbowl** Windermere Rd 01942 606731. Stockport: **Megabowl** Grand Central Sq 0161 476 6624. Trafford Centre: **Namco Station** The Orient 0161 749 1111. Wigan: **AMF Premier Bowl** Miry La 01942 820225. Worsley: **XS Superbowl** 30 Shield Dri Wardley Ind Est 0161 794 3374.
LANCASHIRE: Accrington: **Superbowl** The Viaduct Hyndburn Rd 01254 875500. Blackpool: **AMF Premier Bowl** Mecca Buildings Central Dri 01253 295503, **Blackpool Superbowl** 29-37 Market St 01253 752020. Burnley: **AMF Bowling** Finsley Gate 01282 412548. Morecambe: **Superbowl** Central Dri 01524 400974. Preston: **Lakeside Superbowl** 50 Greenbank St 01772 555080, **Megabowl** Capitol Centre Walton-le-Dale 01772 884800. St Anne's: **Surfside Family Amusement Centre** The Island 01253 722666.
MERSEYSIDE: Bootle: **Megabowl** Switch Island Leisure Pk 0151 525 5676. Liverpool: **Hollywood Bowl** Edge Lane Retail Pk 0151 228 1048. Southport: **Premier Bowl** Ocean Plaza Marine Dri 01704 543569.

CINEMAS

CHESHIRE: Chester: **Odeon*** Northgate St, **UGC** Greyhound Retail Pk Sealand Rd 0870 155 5158. Crewe: **Apollo** High St 01270 255708. Ellesmere Port: **Warner****. Knutsford: **Studio** Knutsford Civic Centre Toft Rd 01565 633005. Northwich: **Regal** London Rd 01606 43130. Runcorn: **Cineworld** Trident Pk Halton Lea 01928 759812. Warrington: **UCI** Westbrook Centre 0870 010 2030.
CUMBRIA: Ambleside: **Zeffirellis** Compston Rd 01539 431771. Barrow-in-Furness: **Apollo** Hollywood Pk 01229 825354. Carlisle: **Lonsdale** Warwick Rd 01228 525586, **Warner**** 50 Botchergate. Cockermouth: **Kirkgate** 01900 826448. Kendal: **Brewery Arts Centre**

Highgate 01539 725133. Keswick: **Alhambra** 01768 772195. Penrith: **Alhambra** Middlegate 01768 862400. Ulverston: **Roxy** Brogden St 01229 582340. Windermere: **Royalty** Lake Rd Bowness 01539 443364. Workington: **Plaza** Maryport Rd Siddick 01900 870001.

GREATER MANCHESTER: Bolton: **UGC Megaplex** Eagley Brook Way 0870 907 0714, **Warner****. Bury: **Warner**** Park 66 Pilsworth Rd. Didsbury: **UGC** Wilmslow Rd 0870 907 0742. Heaton Moor: **Savoy** 0161 432 2114. Manchester: **AMC** 0161 817 3000, **Cornerhouse** 70 Oxford St 0161 200 1500, **thefilmworks** 0870 010 2030, **Odeon*** Oxford St, **Showcase** 0161 220 8765, **UCI Trafford Centre** The Dome 0870 010 2030. Marple: **Regent** Stockport Rd 0161 427 5951. Oldham: **Roxy** Hollins Rd Hollinwood 0161 681 6250. Rochdale: **Odeon*** Sandbrook Pk. Salford: **Warner**** The Quays. Stockport: **The Plaza** 0161 477 7779, **UGC** Grand Central Sq Wellington Rd South 0870 155 5173. Urmston: **Curzon** Princess Rd 0161 748 2929. Wigan: **UGC** Robin Pk 0870 155 5150.

LANCASHIRE: Accrington: **Premier** The Viaduct Hyndburn Rd 01254 306660. Blackburn: **Apollo** King William St 01254 695979. Blackpool: **Odeon*** Rigby Rd. Burnley: **Apollo** Manchester Rd Hollywood Pk 01282 456222. Clitheroe: **Grand** 01200 423278. Lancaster: **The Dukes** 01524 598500, Regal 71 King St 01524 64141. Morecambe: **Apollo** 4 Central Dri 01524 426642. Preston: **The Palace** Market Pl Longridge 01772 785600, **UCI** Port Way Ashton on Ribble 0870 010 2030, **Warner****. St Anne's: **Pleasure Island Cinema** South Promenade 01253 780085.

MERSEYSIDE: Allerton: **Odeon***. Birkenhead: **Warner**** Europa Boulevard Conway Pk. Bootle: **Odeon***. Bromborough: **Odeon*** Welton Rd. Liverpool: **FACT** 88 Wood St 0151 707 4450, **Odeon***, Plaza Crosby Rd North 0151 474 4076, **Showcase** 0151 549 2021, **UGC** Edge Lane Retail Pk 0870 155 5146, **Woolton** 0151 428 1919. St Helens: **Cineworld** Chalon Way West 01744 616576. Southport: **SBC** 0870 240 4442.

---

* ODEON CINEMAS Hotline: 0870 5050007

**UCI CINEMAS Hotline: 0870 0102030

CLIMBING WALLS

Also check out 'Outdoor Pursuits' in this chapter. Many of the centres offer outdoor rock climbing.

CHESHIRE: Chester: **The Walls** Unit 7 Chesterbank Business Pk River La Saltney 01244 682626. Warrington: **The North West Face** St Ann's Church Winwick Rd 01925 650022.

CUMBRIA: Barrow-in-Furness: **Park Leisure Centre** Greengate St 01229 871146. Cockermouth: **Cockermouth Sports Centre** Castlegate Dri 01900 823596. Kendal: **Kendal Climbing Wall** Lakeland Climbing Centre 01539 721766. Keswick: **Indoor Climbing Wall** Southey Ind Est 017687 72000. Penrith: **Eden Climbing Wall** Penrith Leisure Centre Southend Rd 01768 863450.

GREATER MANCHESTER: Oldham: **Oldham Sports Centre** Lord St 0161 911 4090. Rochdale: **Balderstone Community School** Queen Victoria St Balderstone 01706 751500. Salford: **Salford Watersports Centre** 15 The Quays 0161 877 7252. Stockport: **The Rope Race** Goyt Mill Upper Hibbert La Marple 0161 426 0226.

LANCASHIRE: Blackburn: **YMCA Climbing and Bouldering Wall** Clarence St 01254 51009. Clitheroe: **Roefield Leisure Centre** Edisford Rd 01200 442188. Lancaster: **Indoor Climbing Wall** Lancaster University Sports Centre 01524 594000.

MERSEYSIDE: Liverpool: **Awesome Walls Climbing Centre** St Albans Church Athol St 0151 298 2422.

ICE SKATING

LANCASHIRE: Blackburn: **Ice Arena** 01254 263063. Blackpool: **Pleasure Beach Arena** Ocean Boulevard 0870 444 5566.

CHESHIRE: Warrington: **Speed Karting** Unit 2 Bank Quay Trading Est 01925 234236.
CUMBRIA: Carlisle: **Carlisle Indoor Karting** Newtown Ind Est 01228 510061. Maryport: **West Coast Indoor Karting** Solway Trading Est 01900 816472.
GREATER MANCHESTER: Gorton: **Karting 2000** Froxmer St 0161 273 1100. Radcliffe: **Cat One Karting** The Mill Water St 0161 723 1010. Trafford Park: **Daytona** Unit 4 Circle South Trafford Park Rd 0161 876 0876. Wigan: **Three Sisters Country Park** 01942 270230, **Wigan Pier Indoor Karting** Swan Meadow Rd 01942 829697.
LANCASHIRE: Blackburn: **Blackburn Indoor Karting** East Lancs Warehouse Bridge St 01254 683684. Blackpool: **Kapitol Karting** Central Dri 01253 292600, **Karting 2000** New South Promenade Starrgate 01253 408068. Burscough: **Kartworld** Unit 4 Burscough Ind Est 01704 896633. Colne: **Prestige Indoor Karting** Holker Mill Burnley Rd 01282 865675. Lancaster: **Elite Karting** Lancaster Leisure Pk Wyresdale Rd 01524 33830. Preston: **Trax** Preston Docklands 01772 731832.
MERSEYSIDE: Liverpool: **Mersey Indoor Karting** Unit 1 Paragon Centre Picton Rd 0151 734 1736.

MUSIC AND MOVEMENT

Jo Jingles, www.jojingles.co.uk 01494 719360, is a leading music and singing experience with an educational slant for children aged 6 months to 7 years. Exciting and stimulating classes run at venues all over the country. For details on classes in your area or for information on the franchise opportunity please call 01494 719360, email: headoffice@jojingles.co.uk or visit the website. Birthdays **Check out page 18.**

Monkey Music, www.monkeymusic.co.uk 01582 766464, runs music classes for babies and children aged between 6 months and 4 years at venues all over the UK. Business franchise opportunities are available in this area. Please telephone for details. **Check out page 18.**

Rhythm Time, www.rtfg.co.uk 0121 711 4224, runs quality music classes for babies, toddlers and older children. Interesting new ideas and songs to help development and musical skills. Courses written by a music teacher. Classes opening all over the UK. For details or information about the exciting franchise opportunity please call or email kathy@rtfg.co.uk. **Check out inside back cover.**

OUTDOOR PURSUITS

For water-based activities check out 'Watersports' in this chapter.
CUMBRIA: Coniston: **Summitreks** 14 Yewdale Rd 015394 41212. Eskdale: **Outward Bound** Eskdale Green 0870 513 4227. Glenridding: **Patterdale Hall** 017684 82233. Grizebeck: **Adventures** The Old School 01229 889761. Grizedale: **Go Ape!** Grizedale Forest Visitor Centre 0870 444 5562. Kendal: **Adventure Days** 28 Finkle St 01539 720750. Keswick: **Keswick Climbing Wall & Activity Centre** 017687 72000, **Newlands Adventure Centre** Stair 017687 78463, **Vivid Events** 017687 75351. Penrith: **Greystoke Castle Estate** 01768 483722, **Rookin House Farm** Troutbeck 01768 483561. Portinscale: **Cumbria Outdoors** 017687 72816. Tebay: **Country Venture** 015396 24286. Torver: **The Rock Outdoor Adventures** 015394 41030. Ullswater: **Howtown Outdoor Centre** 01768 486508, **Outward Bound** Watermillock 0870 513 4227. Windermere: **Mere Mountains** 015394 88002, **Pleasure in Leisure Ltd** 015394 42324, **R & L Adventures** 015394 45104.
GREATER MANCHESTER: Bury: **Alternative Adventure** Seddons Farm House Newington Dri 0161 764 3612, **Burrs Activity Centre** Burrs Country Pk Woodhill Rd 0161 764 9649.
LANCASHIRE: Carnforth: Borwick Hall Borwick 01524 732508.

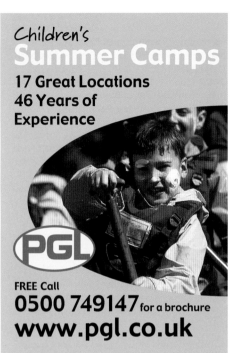

POTTERY ACTIVITIES

CHESHIRE: Hale Village: **The Art Café** Ashley Rd 0161 929 6886. Sandbach: **The Potters Barn** Roughwood La Hassall Green 01270 884080.
CUMBRIA: Penrith: **Greystoke Gill Studio Pottery** Greystoke Gill 017684 83123, **Wetheriggs Pottery** Clifton Dykes 01768 892733.
LANCASHIRE: Fleetwood: **The Pottery Studio** (Autism Initiative) Farmer Parrs Animal World Rossall La 01253 772664.

SNOW SPORTS

CHESHIRE: Runcorn: **Ski Centre** Town Pk 01928 701965.
CUMBRIA: Kendal: **Kendal Ski Slope** Canal Head North 01539 733031.
LANCASHIRE: Rawtenstall: **Ski Rossendale** Haslingden Old Rd 01706 226457.

SPECTATOR SPORTS

Abbreviation: T: Tours.
CHESHIRE: Macclesfield: **Macclesfield Town Football Club** 01625 264686. Tarporley: **Oulton Park Race Circuit** Little Budworth 01829 760301.
CUMBRIA: Carlisle: **Carlisle United Football Club** 01228 526237. Workington: **Speedway** Derwent Pk Stadium 01943 878448.
GREATER MANCHESTER: Bolton: **Bolton Wanderers Football Club** Reebok Stadium Middlebrook Leisure and Retail Pk 01204 673670 T. Bury: **Bury Football Club** Gigg La 0161 764 4881. Manchester: **Lancashire County Cricket Club** Warwick Rd 0161 282 4000, **Manchester City Football Club** City of Manchester Stadium Sports City 0161 231 3200 T, **Manchester Phoenix Ice Hockey Team** MEN Arena Hunt's Bank City Centre 0161 930 8000, **Manchester United Football Club** Sir Matt Busby Way Old Trafford 0870 442 1994 T. Oldham: **Oldham Athletic Football Club** Boundary Pk 0161 624 4972. Salford: **Salford City Reds Rugby League** The Willows Willows Rd 0161 736 6564. Stockport: **Stockport County Football Club** Edgeley Pk Hardcastle Rd Edgeley 0161 286 8888. Wigan: **Wigan Athletic Football Club** JJB Stadium Loire Dri 01942 774000, **Wigan Warriors Rugby League** JJB Stadium Loire Dri 01942 774000.
LANCASHIRE: Blackburn: **Blackburn Rovers Football Club** Ewood Pk 0870 111 3232 T. Blackpool: **Blackpool Football Club** Seasiders Way 0870 443 1953. Burnley: **Burnley Football Club** 0870 443 1882. Carnforth: **Warton Stock Car Club** 01524 416169. Preston: **Preston North End Football Club** 0870 442 1964.
MERSEYSIDE: Liverpool: **Everton Football Club** Goodison Pk 0151 330 2277 T, **Liverpool Football Club** Anfield Rd 0151 260 6677 T. St Helens: **St Helens Rugby League** Dunriding La 0870 756 5252. Widnes: **Widnes Rugby League** Autoquest Stadium Lowerhouse La 0151 510 6000.

SPORTS AND LEISURE CENTRES

Abbreviations: LC: Leisure Centre, LCx: Leisure Complex, SC: Sports Centre, SCx: Sports Complex. * indicates centre has a swimmimg pool.
CHESHIRE: Alsager: **Alsager LC*** Hassall Rd 01270 875704. Bollington: **Bollington LC*** Heath Rd 01625 574774. Chester: **Northgate Arena*** Victoria Rd 01244 380444. Congleton: **Congleton LC*** Worrall St 01260 271552. Crewe: **Copenhall LC** Coronation St 01270 585698, **Shavington LC** Rope La 01270 663221. Ellesmere Port: **EPIC LC*** McGarva Way 0151 355 6432. Frodsham: **Frodsham LC** Queensway 01928 733953. Holmes Chapel: **Holmes Chapel LC** Selkirk Dri 01477 534401. Knutsford: **Knutsford LC*** Westfield Dri 01565 653321. Macclesfield: **Macclesfield LC*** Priory La Upton Priory 01625 615602. Middlewich: **Middlewich LC** St Anne's Walk 01606 832193. Northwich: **Sir John Deane's LC*** 01606 353930. Poynton: **Poynton LC*** Yew Tree La 01625 876442. Rudheath: **Rudheath LC**

Shipbrook Rd 01606 41051. Runcorn: **Brookvale LC*** Barnfield Ave Murdishaw 01928 712051, **Halton SC** Murdishaw 01928 714815. Sandbach: **Sandbach LC*** Middlewich Rd 01270 767129. Warrington: **Birchwood LC** Benson Rd 01925 458130, **Broomfields LC*** Broomfields Rd Stockton Heath 01925 268768, **Fordton LC*** Chiltern Rd Orford 01925 572504, **Great Sankey LC*** Barrowhall La 01925 724411, **Woolston LC*** Hall Rd 01925 813939. Wilmslow: **Wilmslow LC*** Rectory Fields 01625 533789. Winsford: **Winsford SCx*** The Drumber 01606 552776.

CUMBRIA: Barrow-in-Furness: **Park LC*** Greengate St 01229 871146. Cockermouth: **Cockermouth SC*** Castle Gate Dri 01900 823596. Dalton-in-Furness: **Dalton LCx*** Chapel St 01229 463125. Kendal: **Kendal LC*** Burton Rd 01539 729777. Penrith: **Penrith LC*** Southend Rd 01768 863450. Ulverston: **Ulverston LC*** Priory Rd 01229 584110. Whitehaven: **Whitehaven SC** Flatt Walks 01946 695666. Workington: **Workington LCx*** Newlands La South 01900 61771.

GREATER MANCHESTER: Altrincham: **Altrincham LC*** Oakfield Rd 0161 912 5900. Ashton-under-Lyne: **The Broadoak Centre** off Broadoak Rd 0161 330 7975, **The Copley Centre*** Huddersfield Rd Stalybridge 0161 303 8118, **The Etherow Centre** Mottram Rd Broadbottom 01457 763165. Bolton: **Bolton Excel** Lower Bridgeman St 01204 334456, **Deane LC*** Junction Rd 01204 334432, **Farnworth LC*** Brackley St Farnworth 01204 334477, **Harper Green Community LC** Harper Green Rd Farnworth 01204 334234, **Horwich LC*** Victoria Rd 01204 334488, **Little Lever Community LC** Church St 01204 334177, **Sharples Community LC*** Hillcot Rd Astley Bridge 01204 334224, **Turton Community LC*** Bromley Cross Rd 01204 334440, **Westhoughton Community LC*** Bolton Rd 01942 634810, **Withins Community LC** Newby Rd Breightmet 01204 334133. Bury: **Castle LC*** Bolton St 0161 253 6506. Droylsden: **Medlock LC** Fold Ave 0161 370 3070. Manchester: **Abraham Moss LC*** Crescent Rd Crumpsall 0161 720 7622, **Belle Vue LC** Kirkmansulme La 0161 953 2470, **Broadway LC*** Broadway New Moston 0161 681 1060, **Chorlton LC*** Manchester Rd Chorlton-cum-Hardy 0161 881 2130, **George H Carnell LC** Kingsway Pk Davyhulme 0161 912 2980, **Moss Side LC*** Moss La East 0161 226 5015, **Partington LC*** Chapel La 0161 912 5430, **Sale LC*** Broad Rd Sale 0161 912 3361, **Sportcity Fitness and Health** Rowsley St Eastlands 0161 231 8602, **Stretford LC*** Great Stone Rd 0161 912 4800, **Urmston LC*** Bowfell Rd Flixton 0161 912 2960, **Walton Park LC** Raglan Rd Sale 0161 912 3400. Middleton: **Middleton LC*** Suffield St 0161 643 2894. Oldham: **Chadderton SC*** Middleton Rd 0161 911 3043, **Failsworth SC*** Brierley Ave 0161 911 5072, **Oldham SC*** Lord St 0161 911 4090, **Royton SC*** Park St 0161 911 3081. Rochdale: **Central LC*** Entwistle Rd 01706 639194, **Heywood SCx*** West Starkey St 01706 621040, **Oulder Hill LCx*** Hudsons Walk Greave 01706 645522. Salford: **Fit City Broughton Centre** Camp St 0161 792 2375, **Fit City Cadishead Centre** Lords St 0161 775 7928, **Fit City Clarendon Centre*** Liverpool St 0161 736 1494, **Fit City Ordsall Centre** Trafford St 0161 848 0646. Stockport: **Avondale Leisure and Target Fitness Centre*** Heathbank Rd Cheadle Heath 0161 477 4242, **Cheadle Hulme Recreation Centre*** Woods La Cheadle Hulme 0161 485 4299, **Hazel Grove Pools and Target Fitness Centre** Jacksons La 0161 439 5221, **Peel Moat Sports and Target Fitness Centre** Buckingham Rd Heaton Moor 0161 442 6416, **Ridge LC** Hibbert La Marple 0161 484 6688. Wigan: **Ashton LC*** Old Rd Ashton-in-Makerfield 01942 720826, **Hindley LC*** Mornington Rd 01942 253142, **Howe Bridge SC*** Eckersley Fold La Atherton 01942 870403, **Robin Park Arena and SC** Loire Dri Newtown 01942 828550.

LANCASHIRE: Bacup: **Bacup Leisure Hall** Burnley Rd 01706 875550. Bamber Bridge: **Bamber Bridge LC*** Brindle Rd 01772 322012. Banks: **North Meols Community LC** Greaves Hall La 01704 212970. Blackburn: **Audley Sports and Community Centre** Chester St 01254 680012, **Shadsworth LC*** Shadsworth Rd 01254 264561. Blackpool: **Blackpool LC** Westpark Dri 01253 478470. Burnley: **Padiham LC*** Park Rd Padiham 01282 664588, **Thompson Centre*** Red Lion St 01282 664444. Burscough: **Burscough SC** Bobby Langton Way 01704 895266. Chorley: **All Seasons LC*** Water St 01257 515000. Clitheroe: **Roefield LC** Edisford Rd Clitheroe. Colne: **Pendle LC*** Crown Way 01282 661166. Darwen: **Darwen LC*** Green St 01254 771511. Fleetwood: **Fleetwood LC*** The Esplanade 01253 771505. Fullwood:

Fullwood LC* Black Bull La 01772 716085. Garstang: **Garstang LC** Windsor Rd 01995 605410. Haslingden: **The Sports Centre** Helmshore Rd 01706 227016. Lancaster: **Lancaster University SC*** 01524 594000, **Salt Ayre SC*** Salt Ayre La 01524 847540. Leyland: **Leyland LC*** Lancastergate 01772 432285. Longridge: **Longridge LC** Preston Rd 01772 784474. Lostock Hall: **Lostock Hall SC** Todd La North 01772 628063. Penwortham: **Penwortham LC*** Crowshill Rd 01772 747272. Preston: **Westview LC*** Ribbleton La West View Ribbleton 01772 796788. Skelmersdale: **Skelmersdale SC** Digmoor Rd Digmoor. Thornton: **Thornton SC** Victoria Rd East 01253 824108.

MERSEYSIDE: Bebington: **The Oval*** Chester Rd 0151 645 0596. Birkenhead: **The Sports Centre** Grange Rd West 0151 652 9336. Bootle: **Bootle LC*** Washington Pde 0151 330 3301, **Fernhill SC** Fernhill Rd 0151 933 7232. Crosby: **Crosby LC*** Mariners Rd 0151 932 9080. Garston: **Garston LC*** Long La 0151 233 5701. Halewood: **Halewood LC*** Baileys La 0151 443 2124. Huyton: **Huyton LC*** Roby Rd 0151 443 3786. Kirkby: **Kirkby SC** Valley Rd Westvale 0151 443 4402. Knowsley: **Heatwaves LC*** Waterpark Dri Stockbridge Village 0151 443 2754. Leasowe: **Leasowe Recreation Centre*** Twickenham Dri 0151 678 5632. Liverpool: Cardinal **Heenan SC*** Honeys Green La 0151 233 2345, **Croxteth SC** Altcross Rd 0151 548 3421, **Greenbank Sports Academy** Greenbank La 0151 280 7757, **Norris Green LC*** Ellergreen Rd 0151 233 6295, **Park Road SC*** Steble St 0151 709 5395, **Picton SC*** Wellington Rd Wavertree 0151 734 2294, **Toxteth Sport & LC** Upper Hill St 0151 709 7229. Newton-le-Willows: **Selwyn Jones SC*** Ashton Rd 01744 677970. Prescot: **Prescot LC** Warrington Rd 0151 430 7202, **Scotchbarn SC*** Scotchbarn La 0151 443 4643. St Helens: **Haydock LC** Clipsley La Haydock 01744 677505, **Queens Park LC*** Boundary Rd 01744 677465, **Sutton LC*** Elton Head Rd 01744 677375. Southport: **Dunes*** Esplanade 01704 537160. Thingwall: **Thingwall LC*** Thingwall Hall La 0151 220 7173. Walton: **Walton SC** Walton Hall Ave 0151 523 3472. Widnes: **Kingsway LC*** Kingsway 0151 495 2200. Woodchurch: **Woodchurch LC*** Carr Bridge Rd 0151 677 9433.

LANCASHIRE: Burnley: **Padiham Leisure Centre,** Park Road, Padiham, 01282 664588, includes a swimming pool, Future Fitness gymnasium, aerobic studios, sauna and sun-beds. Why not take a crash course of swimming lessons or have a go at canoeing? Activities in the school holidays include sessions with a giant inflatable for children aged 8-13, telephone for details.

The Thompson Centre, Red Lion Street, 01282 664444. It has three pools, Future Fitness gymnasium, Lifters gymnasium, aerobic studios, sports halls and squash courts. You can try a new sport and there is a wide range of children's activities available during school holidays, including trampolining, football, basketball, badminton, unihoc and kwik cricket. The pool also holds disco fun sessions with inflatables for swimmers aged 8-13. You can book a crash course of swimming lessons, and there are crèche facilities for children aged 6 weeks-5 years. Why not let the staff organise a birthday party for you? Telephone for details. Schools Birthdays **Check out page 22.**

SWIMMING POOLS (INDOOR)

Please also check the list of Sports and Leisure Centres above. Those marked with an * have a pool.
CHESHIRE: Chester: **Chester City Baths** Union St 01244 320898. Crewe: **Crewe Swimming Pool** Flag La 01270 560052. Nantwich: **Nantwich Swimming Pool** Wall La 01270 610606. Northwich: **Northwich Pool** Moss Farm Firdale Rd Hartford 01606 783835. Runcorn: **Runcorn Swimming Pool** Bridge St 01928 572114.
CUMBRIA: Appleby: **Appleby Pool** Chapel St 01768 351212. Carlisle: **The Pools** James St 01228 625777. Keswick: **Keswick Leisure Pool** The Old Station Station Rd 01768 772760. Whitehaven: **Copeland Swimming Pool** Cleator Moor Rd 01946 695021. Windermere: **Troutbeck Swimming Pool** 015394 43243.
GREATER MANCHESTER: Ashton-under-Lyne: **Ashton Pool** Water St 0161 330 1179, **Denton Pools** Victoria St 0161 336 1900, **Droylsden Pool** Manchester Rd 0161 370 5509,

Dukinfield Pool Birch La 0161 330 5208, **Hyde Leisure Pool** Walker La 0161 368 4057. Bolton: **Jubilee Community Pool** Darley St 01204 334443. Manchester: **Levenshulme Pool** Barlow Rd 0161 224 4370, **Manchester Aquatics Centre** Oxford Rd 0161 275 9450, **Miles Platting Pool** Varley St 0161 205 8939, **Withington Pool** Burton Rd 0161 445 1046. Oldham: **Crompton Pool** Farrow St 01706 844751, **Glodwick Pool** Nugget St 0161 911 3040. Radcliffe: **Radcliffe Pool** Green St 0161 253 7814. Rochdale: **Castleton Swimming Pool** Manchester Rd Castleton 01706 632117. Saddleworth: **Saddleworth Pool** Station Rd 01457 876668. Salford: **Fit City Broughton Pool** Great Cheetham St West 0161 792 2847, **Fit City Irlam Pool** Liverpool Rd 0161 775 4134, **Fit City Worsley Pool** Bridgwater Rd 0161 790 2084. Stockport: **Cheadle Pool** Shiers Dri Cheadle 0161 428 3216, **Grand Central Pools** 12 Grand Central Sq Wellington Rd South 0161 474 7766, **Marple Swimming Pool** Stockport Rd Marple 0161 427 7070, **Reddish Swimming Pool** Gorton Rd Reddish 0161 432 4285, **Romiley Pool** Holehouse Fold Romiley 0161 430 3437. Wigan: **Atherton Baths** Mayfield St 01942 882454, **Hindley Pool** Boarsdane Ave 01942 255401, **Tyldesley Pool** Castle St 01942 882722, **Wigan International Pool** Library St 01942 243345.
LANCASHIRE: Blackburn: **D**aisyfield Swimming Pools Daisy La 01254 277300. Blackpool: **Lido Swimming Pool** Lytham Rd 01253 478482, **Moor Park Swimming Pool** Bristol Ave 01253 478487. Burnley: **Gannow Pool** Sycamore Ave 01282 664477. Carnforth: **Carnforth Community Swimming Pool** Kellett Rd 01524 734699. Clitheroe: **Ribblesdale Pool** Edisford Rd 01200 424825. Garstang: **Garstang Swimming Centre** Birch Rd 01995 604340. Haslingden: **Haslingden Swimming Pool** East Bank Ave 01706 215883. Heysham: **Community Swimming Pool** Melling Rd 015242 21119. Lancaster: **Capernwray Hall Swimming Pool** 01524 733908, **Ingleton Swimming Pool** 015242 21119. Nelson: **Pendle Wavelengths** Leeds Rd 01282 661717. Ormskirk: **Park Pool** Park Rd 01695 576325. Poulton: **Swimming & Fitness Centre** Breck Rd 01253 891629. Preston: **Kirkham Indoor Pool** Station Rd 01772 682989. Ramsbottom: **Ramsbottom Pool** Porritt Way 01706 824208. Rossendale: **Marl Pits Swimming Pool** Newchurch Rd 01706 226850. St Anne's: **St Anne's Pool** The Island 01253 721325. Skelmersdale: **Nye Bevan Pool** Southway 01695 727111.
MERSEYSIDE: Birkenhead: **Europa Pools** Conway St 0151 647 4182. Kirkby: **Kirkby Pool** Hall La 0151 443 4303. Maghull: **Deyes Lane Swimmimg Pool** Deyes La 0151 531 0933. Liverpool: **Breckside Park Swimmimg Pool** Breckside Pk 0151 260 8434, **Newhall Swimming Pool** Longmoor La 0151 530 1218. St Helens: **Parr Swimming Pool** Ashcroft St 01744 677236. Seacombe: **Guinea Gap Baths** Riverview Rd 0151 639 9792. Woolton: **Woolton Swimmimg Pool** Quarry St 0151 428 1804.

LANCASHIRE: Burnley: **Gannow Pool,** Sycamore Avenue, 01282 664477, offers swimming and snorkelling and has a special swimming programme for school holidays, which includes a giant slide inflatable and disco fun for children aged 8-13. Younger children must be accompanied by an adult. You can book a crash course of swimming lessons and there is a family area for parents with small children. Phone for details. Schools **Check out page 22.**

SWIMMIMNG POOLS (OUTDOOR)

CUMBRIA: Shap: **Shap Open Air Swimming Pool** Gayle Ave 01931 716572.
CHESHIRE: Nantwich: **Nantwich Brine Pool** Wall La 01270 610606.

THEATRES

Grease on Tour, www.greasethemusical.co.uk   Grease the Musical is on tour throughout the country this year and is going to be at a theatre near you! The show is packed with explosive energy, vibrant 1950s pop culture and lots of unforgettable songs. Take the family to this fabulous Rock'n'Roll musical filled with irresistible groovy and memorable moments. Don't miss it! For full information, casting details, competitions, special offers and full tour venues and dates log on to the website above. **Check out page 24.**

CHESHIRE: Chester: **Gateway Theatre** Hamilton Pl 01244 340392. Crewe: **Lyceum Theatre** Heath St 01270 537333.

family friendly museums

- Explore Lancashire's Family Friendly Museums
- Hours of fun from country to coast
- Twelve wonderful locations
- Discover grand country houses and working textile museums
- Exciting programme of events, activities and exhibitions for all the family
- Free on site parking & baby changing facilities at most museums
- Relaxing cafes and museums shops
- save £s with our family and friends season tickets
- **Kids Go Free** at most museums
- For more details see the history section under Lancashire County Museums

Lancashire
County Council

Tel: 01772 534061

Lancashire County Museums
www.lancsmuseums.gov.uk

History, Art & Science

Step back in time and find out about the past, explore the world of art and design or discover the mysteries of science and technology. The places listed here have admission charges, but there are many wonderful museums and places of interest which are free to visit. Check out the 'Free Places' chapter as well, so you don't miss anything.

Museums marked with * are Lancashire County Museums.
Check out editorial at top of Lancashire listing.

CHESHIRE

Alderley Edge, Nether Alderley Mill, NT, Congleton Road, 01625 584412. See this old water mill with its Victorian machinery in action (subject to repairs being completed, please call before visit). Open Apr-Oct, Wed-Fri, Sun and Bank Hol Mons, 1-4.30pm. Schools **Price A.**

Bunbury, Bunbury Watermill, Mill Lane, 01829 261422, is a restored Victorian water mill. Witness the power of water as it turns machinery used to grind grain into flour. Guided tours only. Open Apr-Sept, Sun, 1.30-4.30pm, and for organised groups all year. Schools **Price A.**

Chester, Cheshire Military Museum, The Castle, 01244 327617, uses computers and hands-on exhibits to guide visitors through the military history of Cheshire. Events and activities. Open daily, 10am-5pm. Schools **Open all year** **Price A.**
Dewa Roman Experience, Pierpoint Lane, Bridge Street, 01244 343407. Spend time in the hands-on studio and visit the reconstructed street to experience the smells and sounds of a Roman fortress. Open daily, Feb-Nov, 9am-5pm, Dec-Jan, 10am-4pm. Schools **Open all year** **Price B.**
Guided Tours. A number of historical tours are available to help the family explore and learn about the city. Don't miss the Ghost Tour which runs from June to October! Contact the Tourist Information Centre on 01244 351609 for more details.

Congleton, Congleton Museum, Market Square, www.congletonmuseum.co.uk 01260 276360, opened in 2002, with the emphasis on local history. Follow the time line and use touchscreen computers to discover more. Activities during school holidays. Open Tues-Fri and Sun, 12noon-4.30pm, Sat, 10am-4.30pm. Schools **Open all year** **Price A.**
Little Moreton Hall, NT, 01260 272018. Learn about life in Tudor times by taking a guided tour. Events programme includes living history weekends and family activities. Telephone for opening times. Schools **Price B.**

Crewe, The Railway Age, Vernon Way, www.therailwayage.co.uk 01270 212130, houses a collection ranging from steam trains to modern advanced passenger trains. Pull levers in the signal box or have a game of giant noughts and crosses. Open daily, mid Feb-end Oct, 10am-4pm. Schools Birthdays **Price B.**

Ellesmere Port, The Boat Museum, South Pier Road, www.boatmuseum.org.uk 0151 355 5017, follows the social and industrial history of Britain's canals. See working engines and board a narrow boat to find out what life was like. Open Apr-Oct, daily, 10am-5pm; Nov-Mar, Sat-Wed, 11am-4pm. Schools **Open all year** **Price B.**

Farndon(near), Stretton Watermill, 01606 41331. A small working water mill situated in lovely countryside with displays and picnic area. Open Apr and Sept, Sat-Sun, 1-5pm; May-Aug, Tues-Sun. Schools **Price A.**

Knutsford, Tabley House, www.tableyhouse.co.uk 01565 750151. This richly furnished Palladian house has a children's activity booklet, parklands and picnic area. Open Apr-Oct, Thurs-Sun and Bank Hol Mons, 2-5pm. Schools **Price B.**
Tatton Park, www.tattonpark.org.uk 01625 534400. An historic country estate with mansion, farm, parkland and gardens. Children will love the fallow deer in the park and the rare and traditional breeds on the farm. Special events and activities. Opening times vary. Schools **Open all year** **Price B.**

Macclesfield, Macclesfield Silk Museums, www.silk-macclesfield.org, include the Heritage Centre, 01625 613210, and Silk Museum, 01625 612045. Follow the town's industrial development and its links with China and the Far East. Guided mill tours available (telephone for times). Open Mon-Sat, 11am-5pm, Sun, 1-5pm. Schools **Open all year Price B.**

Mouldsworth, Mouldsworth Motor Museum, Smithy Lane, www.mouldsworthmotormuseum.com 01928 731781. See this collection of motor cars, motorcycles, early bicycles, pedal cars and associated memorabilia in a stunning Art-Deco setting. Children's quiz sheet with prizes and hands-on activities. Open Feb-Nov, Sun, 12noon-5pm (Jul-Aug Wed and Sun); additional opening during Bank Hols. Schools Birthdays **Price A.**

Nantwich, Hack Green Secret Nuclear Bunker, www.hackgreen.co.uk 01270 629219. Explore displays and re-created scenes in this former nuclear bunker. Send a Morse code message or try out a Home Office bed! Soviet Spy Mouse Trail for younger children. Open Apr-Oct, daily, 10.30am-5.30pm; Nov-Mar, Sat-Sun, 11am-4.30pm. Closed Dec. Schools **Price B.**

Northwich, Anderton Boat Lift, Lift Lane, Anderton, www.andertonboatlift.co.uk 01606 786777, is the world's first boat lift. Restoration work was completed in 2002 and an operations centre with exhibition area and interactive activities opened in 2003. Admission includes boat trip. Open end Mar-Oct, daily, 9.30am-5pm; Nov-end Mar (operations centre only, no boat trip), Wed-Sun, 10.30am-3.30pm. Schools Birthdays **Open all year Price B.**
The Salt Museum, 162 London Road, www.saltmuseum.org.uk 01606 41331. Follow the story of salt and the industry which has grown around it. Interactive gallery, free quiz sheets, exhibitions and special events. Open Tues-Fri, 10am-5pm, Sat-Sun, 2-5pm; also Bank Hol Mons and every Mon in Aug. Schools **Open all year Price A.**

Runcorn, Norton Priory Museum & Gardens, Tudor Road, Manor Park, www.nortonpriory.org 01928 569895. A family-friendly historic site with sculpture trail and displays of real objects depicting life in the monastery. Open Apr-Oct, Mon-Fri, 12noon-5pm, Sat-Sun, 12noon-6pm; Nov-Mar, daily, 12noon-4pm. Schools **Open all year Price A.**

Styal, Quarry Bank Mill & Styal Estate, NT, 01625 527468, has interactive power galleries, a working waterwheel and the Apprentice House, home to pauper children. Families can learn about the story of cotton from real spinners and weavers. Open Apr-Sept, daily, 10.30am-5.30pm; Oct-Mar, Tues-Sun, 10.30am-5pm. Schools **Open all year Price B.**

Tarporley(near), Beeston Castle, EH, 01829 260464. Imagine life as a soldier in this medieval fortress set high above the Cheshire plains. Special events throughout the year. Open daily, Apr-Sept, 10am-6pm, Oct-Mar, 10am-4pm. Schools **Open all year Price A.**

CUMBRIA

Alston, Alston Model Railway Centre, Station Yard Workshops, www.alstonmodelrailwaycentre.co.uk 01434 382100, displays a permanent exhibition of model railway layouts, which includes a hands-on layout for children. Open Easter-Oct, daily, 11am-5pm; Nov-Easter, Wed-Mon, 11am-4pm. Schools **Open all year Price A.**

Ambleside, Ambleside's Armitt Museum, Rydal Road, www.armitt.com 015394 31212. Discover history from Roman times to the present, together with Beatrix Potter's natural history water colours. Family events, children's guides, hands-on activities and work sheets. Open daily, 10am-4.30pm. Schools **Open all year Price A.**

Bowness–on–Windermere, The World of Beatrix Potter Attraction, The Old Laundry, www.hop-skip-jump.com 015394 88444. See the characters brought to life at this enchanting indoor re-creation of the tales of Beatrix Potter. Open daily, Apr-Sept, 9.30am-5.30pm, Oct-Mar, 9.30am-4.30pm. Schools Birthdays **Open all year Price B.**

Cark-in-Cartmel, Holker Hall and Gardens & The Lakeland Motor Museum, www.holker-hall.co.uk 015395 58328. Enjoy this stately home and award-winning gardens together with the Motor Museum and Campbell Bluebird Legend Exhibition. Picnic area, adventure playground, children's guides and family activities in school holidays. Open end Mar-Oct, Sun-Fri, times vary. Schools Birthdays **Price C.**

Carlisle, Carlisle Castle, EH, 01228 591922, is an impressive medieval fortress. Don't miss the dungeons! Activity sheets and exhibition area with guided tours during the Summer, ring for details. Ticket includes entry to the King's Own Royal Border Regimental Museum. Open daily, Apr-Sept, 9.30am-6pm, Oct, 10am-5pm, Nov-Mar, 10am-4pm. Schools **Open all year Price B.**
King's Own Royal Border Regimental Museum, Queen Mary's Tower, The Castle, www.armymuseums.org.uk 01228 532774. Wide-ranging displays include uniforms, equipment, anti-tank guns and other weapons. Look out for the 102-year-old box of chocolates. Entry included in admission to Carlisle Castle. Open daily, Apr-Sept, 9.30am-6pm, Oct-Mar, 10am-4pm. Schools **Open all year Price B.**
The Solway Aviation Museum, Aviation House, Carlisle Airport, Crosby-on-Eden, www.solway-aviation-museum.co.uk 01228 573823, with 'past and present' room, mock-up control tower and a chance to sit in the pilot's seat. A number of British jet aircraft are on display and new for 2004 is an original airfield fire tender. Open Apr-Oct, Sat-Sun, 10.30am-5pm (additional opening Jun-Sept, ring for details). **Price A.**
Tullie House Museum and Art Gallery, Castle Street, www.tulliehouse.co.uk 01228 534781. Discover the history of Carlisle and the Roman Empire. Exciting re-creations, hands-on activities and audiovisual displays. Events programme with family activities during school holidays. Opening times vary. Schools **Open all year Price B.**

Cockermouth, Cumberland Toy & Model Museum, Banks Court, Market Place, www.toymuseum.co.uk 01900 827606, evokes childhood memories for young and old with toys from the 1900s through to the present day. Press the buttons to see the toys work. Open daily, Feb and Nov, 10am-4pm, Mar-Oct 10am-5pm; limited opening Dec-Jan, phone first. Schools **Open all year Price A.**

Coniston, Brantwood, www.brantwood.org.uk 015394 41396. The home of John Ruskin, artist and writer, has quiz sheets, trails and a hands-on den with painting materials. Ruskin's boat and coach are on display and the original ice house can be seen. Open mid Mar-mid Nov, daily, 11am-5.30pm; Winter, Wed-Sun, 11am-4.30pm. Schools **Open all year Price B.**
The Ruskin Museum, www.ruskinmuseum.com 015394 41164. Find out about Donald Campbell's water speed record, Coniston Water, the geology of the area and local artist John Ruskin. Interactive computers and hands-on exhibitions. Open mid Mar-mid Nov, daily, 10am-5.30pm; Winter, Wed-Sun, 10.30am-3.30pm. Schools **Open all year Price A.**

Egremont, Florence Mine Heritage Centre, www.florencemine.co.uk 01946 825830. Visitors can take a tour round a working iron-ore mine. Learn about mining and miners' lives in the Heritage Centre. Suitable clothing and footwear required. Times for tours and Heritage Centre vary. Schools **Open all year Price C.**

Finsthwaite, Stott Park Bobbin Mill, EH, 01539 531087. A working museum, giving a taste of industrial life and working conditions for the bobbin makers. Watch bobbins being produced on restored machinery. Guided tours and events. Open daily, Apr-Sept, 10am-6pm, Oct, 10am-5pm. Schools **Price A.**

Gilsland, Birdoswald Roman Fort, www.birdoswaldromanfort.org 016977 47602, was once home to 1,000 Roman soldiers. A great chance to explore a well-preserved stretch of Hadrian's Wall. Interactive visitor centre and special events programme. Open Mar-Oct, daily, 10am-5.30pm. Schools **Price A.**

Holmbrook, Eskdale Mill, Boot Village, 019467 23335. Visit one of the last remaining two-wheel, water-powered corn mills and learn about Cumbrian life. Why not take a picnic to the impressive waterfalls which power the mill? Open Easter-Sept, phone for days and times. Schools Price A.

Kendal, Abbot Hall, www.abbothall.org.uk 01539 722464. This small independent art gallery displays both old and modern works. Changing programme of exhibitions and activities, with a Saturday art club and family boxes to help young children understand the exhibits. Open Feb-late Dec, Mon-Sat, 10.30am-5pm (4pm in Winter). Schools Price B.

Kendal Museum, Station Road, www.kendalmuseum.org.uk 01539 721374. With fossil rubbing and a computer interactive display of Kendal Castle, there is lots here to see and do. Activities include workshops during school holidays and 'Toddlers Treasure Chest' sessions on Wednesday mornings. Open Mon-Sat, mid Feb-Mar and Nov-Dec, 10.30am-4pm, Apr-Oct, 10.30am-5pm. Schools Price A.

Levens Hall, www.levenshall.co.uk 015395 60321. Historic Elizabethan family home with lovely gardens including a fabulous topiary. Children's quiz book and adventure playground. Steam engines and model traction engine on Sundays. Open early Apr-mid Oct, Sun-Thurs. Gardens, 10am-5pm. House, 12noon-5pm. Schools Price C.

Museum of Lakeland Life, Abbot Hall, www.lakelandmuseum.org.uk 01539 722464. Follow the development of the arts and crafts industry in the Lake District. Captain Flint's Locker is an activity room where children can enjoy nautical games. Events and activities programme. Open mid Feb- Christmas, Mon-Sat, 10.30am-5pm (4pm in Winter). Schools Price A.

Keswick, Cars of the Stars Museum, Standish Street, www.carsofthestars.com 017687 73757, features vehicles used in TV and film - Chitty Chitty Bang Bang, Mr Bean's Mini, Harry Potter's Ford Anglia and many, many more. Open Easter-Nov and Feb school hols, daily, 10am-5pm; Dec, Sat-Sun. Schools Price B.

Cumberland Pencil Museum, Southey Works, Greta Bridge, www.pencils.co.uk 017687 73626. Learn about the history of pencil making and see the world's longest pencil. Find out how the lead gets inside. Children's drawing corner and drawing competitions. Open daily, 9.30am-4pm. Schools **Open all year** Price A.

Keswick Museum and Art Gallery, Fitz Park, Station Road, 017687 73263, is set in the grounds of Fitz Park which has a playground and picnic area. Discover the 500-year-old cat. The museum is undergoing refurbishment in 2004, please ring first. Open Apr-Oct. Schools Price A.

Mirehouse, www.mirehouse.com 017687 72287. Award-winning historic home and gardens. Look out for the schoolroom and nursery, enjoy the Poetry Walk and the Bee Garden. Natural adventure playground, children's history trail and nature notes. Open Apr-Oct. Gardens daily, 10am-5.30pm. House, Sun, Wed (& Fri in Aug), 2-5pm. Schools Price B.

The Puzzling Place, Museum Square, www.puzzlingplace.co.uk 017687 75102, is where you will be fascinated! Anti-Gravity Room, Optical Illusions, Puzzle Area and much more. Open daily, 10am-6pm. Schools Birthdays **Open all year** Price A.

Threlkeld Quarry & Mining Museum, Threlkeld Quarry, www.threlkeld-mine.co.uk 017687 79747. Discover the history of mining, from hand chipping to huge modern earth-moving processes, and have a go at panning for gold! Underground tour not suitable for under 6s, dress sensibly. Open Mar-Oct, Tues-Sun, 10am-5pm. Schools Birthdays Price C.

Keswick(near), Honister Slate Mine, Honister Pass, www.honister-slate-mine.co.uk 017687 77230. Take the Big Mountain Mine Tour deep underground and learn about traditional skills of slate mining. Three tours daily, ring for times. Mountain buggies available for small children. Open Mon-Fri, 9am-5pm, Sat-Sun, 10am-5pm. Schools **Open all year** Price B.

Maryport, Senhouse Roman Museum, The Battery, Sea Brows, www.senhousemuseum.co.uk 01900 816168, is situated next to the Roman Fort and houses the Netherhall Collection of Roman artefacts. Follow 'Humphrey's Guide', dress up as a Roman or take part in an archaeological dig. Events programme with workshops during school holidays. Open

Apr-Jun, Tues, Thurs-Sun, 10am-5pm; Jul-Oct and Bank Hols, daily, 10am-5pm; Nov-Mar, Fri-Sun, 10.30am-4pm. Schools **Open all year** Price A.

Milnthorpe, Heron Corn Mill and the Museum of Paper Making, Beetham, 015395 65027. This restored working mill displays the mechanics of a water-powered corn mill. The museum explains the process of paper making with occasional demonstrations. Open Apr-Sept, Tues-Sun, 11am-5pm. Schools **Price A.**

Nenthead, Nenthead Mines Heritage Centre, www.npht.com 01434 382037. Experience 'The Power of Water and Darkness' at Nenthead. Underground tours, working water wheels and interactive displays. Height and age restrictions apply for mine visits. Open Easter-Oct, daily, 10.30am-5pm. Schools Birthdays **Price B.**

Penrith, Dalemain Historic House & Gardens, www.dalemain.com 017684 86450. A spectacular family home - look out for Mrs Mouse's House and the nursery. Outside, see the fallow deer, red squirrels and the children's garden. Open end Mar-21st Oct, Sun-Thurs. House, 11am-4pm (3pm Sept-Oct). Gardens, 10.30am-5pm (4pm Sept-Oct). Schools **Price B.**
Hutton-in-the-Forest, www.hutton-in-the-forest.co.uk 017684 84449. Explore this richly furnished historic house, using children's quiz sheets, available during school and Bank Holidays. Visit the walled gardens and enjoy the woodland walk. Gardens open Easter-end Oct, Sun-Fri, 11am-5pm. House open, 9th-18th Apr and 2nd May-3rd Oct, Thurs-Fri, Sun and Bank Hol Mons, 12.30-4pm. Schools **Price B.**

Penrith(near), Brougham Castle, EH, 01768 862488. See the ruins of this impressive 13th century historical site. Study the exhibition of relics from Roman times and imagine what life was like, living at the castle. Open daily, Apr-Sept, 10am-6pm, Oct, 10am-5pm. Schools **Price A.**

Ravenglass, The New Muncaster, www.muncaster.co.uk 01229 717614. This castle offers a great family day out. It is home to the World Owl Centre which holds a daily flying display at 2.30pm. Visit the Meadow Vole Maze, and maybe win a prize. Outdoor play area. Open Feb half term, then 21st Mar-7th Nov, times vary. Schools **Price C.**

Silloth-on-Solway, Solway Coast Discovery Centre, Liddell Street, 016973 33055. Meet 'Auld Michael' the monk and 'Oyk' the Oystercatcher and learn all about the area and its formation in the Ice Age. Time Machine exhibition. Open Apr-Oct, daily, 10am-4.30pm; Nov-Mar, Sun-Fri. Schools **Open all year** Price A.

Sizergh, Sizergh Castle, NT, 015395 60070, is a family home dating from medieval times and is noted for its interior decoration. The estate includes a rock garden and woodlands. Events programme and children's quiz sheet for both house and gardens. Open Apr-Oct, Sun-Thurs; Gardens from 12.30pm, House 1.30-5pm. Schools **Price B.**

Troutbeck, Townend, NT, 015394 32628. This 17th century family home contains books, furniture and domestic implements from the past. Children can help to make a rag rug and use the discovery sheet as a guide. Meet 'Mr Brown' as part of the living history programme most Thursdays. Open Apr-Oct, Tues-Fri and Sun, 1-4.30pm or dusk if earlier. Schools **Price A.**

Ulverston, Laurel and Hardy Museum, 4c Upper Brook Street, 01229 582292, is dedicated to the famous comedians. See the large collection of memorabilia. Cinema shows films and documentaries daily. Open Feb-Dec, daily, 10am-4.30pm. **Price A.**

Ulverston(near), Gleaston Water Mill, Gleaston, www.watermill.co.uk. 01229 869244. A restored, working water-powered corn mill with apiary and observation hive. Suitable clothing required. Small collection of farm animals. Events and activities throughout the year. Open Tues-Sun, 10.30am-5pm. Schools **Open all year** Price A.

Whitehaven, The Beacon, West Strand, www.thebeacon-whitehaven.co.uk 01946 592302, holds the Met Office Gallery where hands-on displays and interactive computers explain world weather systems. Have a go at being a TV weatherman! Programme of activities. Open Easter-Oct, Tues-Sun, 10am-5.30pm, and Mon in school hols and at Bank Hols; Nov-Mar, Tues-Sun, 10am-4.30pm. Schools **Open all year** Price B.

The Rum Story, Lowther Street, www.rumstory.co.uk 01946 592933. Learn about rum making and its history. Smuggling, prohibition and slavery are all part of the story. See the re-created rain forest and African village. Open daily, Apr-Sept, 10am-5pm, Oct-Mar, 10am-4pm. Schools Birthdays **Open all year** Price B.

Windermere, Windermere Steamboat and Museum, Rayrigg Road, www.steamboat.co.uk 015394 45565. Home to a special collection of steam and motor boats and set in a striking lakeside location. Model boat pond and picnic area. Special events, cruises and art exhibitions. Open daily, mid Mar-early Nov, 10am-5pm. Schools **Price A.**

GREATER MANCHESTER

Altrincham, Dunham Massey, NT, 0161 941 1025, offers stunning parkland with fallow deer and guided walks. Try the hands-on family tour of the mansion and explore life below stairs. See the recently restored, fully operational, water-powered sawmill. Picnic area. Special events. Deer park open daily. House, gardens and mill open Apr-Oct, days and times vary. Schools **Open all year** Price B.

Bolton, Hall i'th' Wood, Green Way, off Crompton Way, 01204 332370. Discover this historical home and learn all about life in Tudor and Stuart times. Dress up in Tudor costume and take part in the history trail. Special events and activities. Open Easter-Oct, Wed-Sun, 11am-5pm; Nov-Mar, Sat-Sun. Schools **Open all year** Price A.

Smithills Hall, Smithills Dean Road, www.smithills.org 01204 332377. Set in restored gardens, this listed building with medieval connections has quiz sheets for children and events and activities during school holidays. Opening times vary. Schools **Open all year** Price A.

Bramhall, Bramall Hall, Bramhall Park, 0161 485 3708, has medieval origins. Explore the Victorian kitchen, servants' quarters and look out for mysterious priests' hides. Children's play area and events programme. Opening times vary. Schools **Open all year** Price B.

Bury, Lancashire Fusiliers Museum, Wellington Barracks, Bolton Road, 0161 764 2208. Learn about the regiment and see the medals and uniforms. Open Mon-Tues and Thurs-Sat, 9.30am-4.30pm. Schools **Open all year** Price A.

Disley, Lyme Park, NT, 01663 762023. This estate and mansion with its deer park has been featured in TV and film productions. Tours of the house, trails in the park, play area and family events throughout the year. Park open daily. House and gardens, Easter-Oct, days and times vary. Schools **Open all year** Price B.

Manchester, Manchester United Museum and Tour Centre, Sir Matt Busby Way, Old Trafford, www.manutd.com 0870 442 1994. Follow the history of this famous club by going on a stadium tour and see the collection of memorabilia. Open daily, 9.30am-5pm (tours 9.40am-4.30pm). Times alter on match days, please ring first. Schools **Open all year** Price C.

Museum of Transport, Boyle Street, Cheetham Hill, 0161 205 2122, uncovers the history of public transport from a horse-drawn bus to Manchester's modern Metrolink. See the large collection of restored vehicles and a re-created workshop and ticket office. Themed weekends. Open Wed, Sat-Sun and Bank Hols, 10am-5pm (4pm in Winter). **Open all year** Price A.

People's History Museum, The Pump House, Bridge Street, www.peopleshistorymuseum.org.uk 0161 839 6061, is dedicated to the lives of ordinary people. Enjoy the 'play your part' interactive displays which guide you through the exhibits. Events programme and children's activities during school holidays. Open Tues-Sun and Bank Hol Mons, 11am-4.30pm. Free admission on Fri. Schools **Open all year** Price A/F.

Urbis, Cathedral Gardens, www.urbis.org.uk 0161 907 9099, opened in 2002. This state-of-the-art museum explores life in different cities around the world. Access is via the Glass Elevator Sky Glide. Many interactive displays. Open daily, 10am-6pm. Schools **Open all year** Price B.

Rochdale, Ellenroad Engine House, Elizabethan Way, Milnrow, www.ellenroad.org.uk 01706 881952. Explore the original 3,000-horsepower steam mill engines, saved and restored from a Lancashire cotton mill. Picnic area, special events and activities. Open first Sun of the month, 12noon-4pm. Closed Jan. Schools **Price A.**

Rochdale Pioneers Museum, 31 Toad Lane, museum.co-op.ac.uk 01706 524920, is home to the co-operative movement. Use the display, exhibition and re-created shop to learn about this retailing revolution and how the movement has evolved. Open Tues-Sat, 10am-4pm, Sun, 2-4pm. Schools **Open all year** Price A.

Saddleworth, Saddleworth Museum and Art Gallery, High Street, Uppermill, www.saddleworthmuseum.co.uk 01457 874093. A small museum exploring the local heritage, including the local Roman fort. Hands-on activity area, family boxes and school holiday 'boredom busters'. Open Apr-Oct, Mon-Sat, 10am-5pm, Sun, 12noon-5pm; Nov-Mar, 1-4pm. Schools Birthdays **Open all year** Price A.

Salford, The Lowry, Pier 8 Salford Quays, www.thelowry.com 0161 876 2000. Set in a stunning waterside location, this modern arts centre is home to the largest public collection of L S Lowry's pictures. Family activities and events at weekends and in school holidays. Open daily, telephone for times. Schools **Open all year** Price A.

Stockport, Hat Works, Wellington Mill, Wellington Road South, www.hatworks.org.uk 0161 355 7770. Learn all about the industry by using interactive demonstrations and restored working machinery. Story telling and feltmaking sessions (booking essential). Open Mon-Sat, 10am-5pm, Sun, 11am-5pm. Schools Birthdays **Open all year** Price B.

Stockport Air Raid Shelters, Chestergate, 0161 474 1940. Explore the passages in the largest purpose-built underground air-raid shelters, and experience wartime life. Guided tours available. Open Mon-Sat, 11am-5pm, Sun, 1-5pm. Schools **Open all year** Price B.

Wigan, The Wigan Pier Experience, Wigan Pier, Trencherfield Mill, www.wiganpier.net 01942 323666. A full day out. The Way We Were Museum is a trip back in time with re-creations of a coal mine and a Victorian classroom. Opie's Museum of Memories examines 100 years of domestic life in Britain. Next, take a short boat trip across the canal to visit Trencherfield Mill. Open Mon-Thurs, 10am-5pm, Sat-Sun, 11am-5pm. Schools **Open all year** Price C.

LANCASHIRE

Lancashire County Museums*, www.lancsmuseums.gov.uk, has family friendly events at 12 excellent locations throughout Lancashire and admission for accompanied children is free to most attractions (excludes the Maritime Museum, the Cottage Museum and Lancaster Castle). The stunning museums range from coast to countryside, from historic country houses to steam powered textile mills and offer family friendly displays, live events, activities and exhibitions, including the lively new exhibition `Grin up North', which captures the spirit of Northern comedy (www.grinupnorth.net). During school holidays, weekends and bank holidays there are many events designed for children and families. Why not go along, get involved and develop a new interest! Activities include quiz and adventure trails and seasonal themed craft workshops. Most museums also have cafes, gift shops and free car parking. You can also take advantage of one of the special ticket offers, giving unlimited visits and access to all events and activities for family and friends. Ask at any one of the museums for details. For more information see the individual entries (marked *) in this chapter. **Check out page 26.**

Burnley, Queen Street Textile Museum*, Harle Syke, www.lancsmuseums.gov.uk 01282 412555. Find out about Victorian factory life and why weavers learned to lip-read and use sign language. Follow the activities of Mill Mouse. Special events programme. Open mid Mar-Nov: Mar & Nov, Tues-Thurs, 12noon-4pm; Apr & Oct, Tues-Fri, 12noon-5pm; May-Sept, Tues–Sat, 12noon-5pm, and all Bank Hol Suns and Mons. Schools **Price A.**

Carnforth, Leighton Hall, www.leightonhall.co.uk 01524 734474. This historic family home has a caterpillar maze and aviaries housing birds of prey. Flying displays each afternoon, weather permitting. Play area, woodland trail and events programme. Open May-Sept, Tues-Fri, Sun and Bank Hol Mons, 2-5pm (12.30-5pm in Aug). Schools **Price B.**

Chorley, Astley Hall Museum and Art Gallery, Astley Park, www.astleyhall.co.uk 01257 515555. An Elizabethan building with a wealth of history. Free quizzes and rubbings. Events and activities programme all year. Open Apr-Oct, Tues-Sun and Bank Hol Mons, 12noon-5pm; Nov-Mar, Sat-Sun, 12noon-4pm. Please ring before visiting. Schools **Open all year Price A.**

Clitheroe, Clitheroe Castle Museum, Castle Hill, 01200 424635, has an exciting events programme during school holidays, which includes hands-on activities and workshops for all the family. Open Easter-Oct, daily, 11am-4.30pm; Nov-Easter, please ring for details. Closed mid Dec-Jan. Schools **Price A.**

Fleetwood, Fleetwood Museum*, Queens Terrace, www.nettingthebay.org.uk or www.lancsmuseums.gov.uk 01253 876621. Follow the story of Fleetwood from fishing and cargo port to holiday resort. Fishing quiz, roof-top camera and a chance to become a virtual fisherman! Open Apr-Nov, Mon-Sat, 10am-4pm, Sun, 1-4pm. Schools **Price A.**

Helmshore, Helmshore Mills Textile Museums*, Holcombe Road, www.lancsmuseums.gov.uk 01706 226459, tells the story of Lancashire's textile industry using family-friendly displays and hands-on activities. Follow the adventures of 'Cotton Cat'. Special events. Open Apr-Oct, Mon-Fri, 12noon-4pm, Sat-Sun, 12noon-5pm. Schools **Price A.**

Hoghton, Hoghton Tower, 01254 852986. A 16th century manor house with connections to William Shakespeare and the naming of beef sirloin. See underground passages, dungeons and gardens. Events programme. Open Jul-Sept, Mon-Thurs, 11am-4pm, Sun, 1-5pm, and some Bank Hols. Schools **Price B.**

Lancaster, Cottage Museum*, 15 Castle Hill, www.lancsmuseums.gov.uk 01524 64637. This small museum is an artisan house with low ceilings and narrow stairs dating from 1739 furnished as in Victorian times. Open Easter-end Sept, daily, 2-5pm. Schools **Price A.**
Judges' Lodgings*, Church Street, www.lancsmuseums.gov.uk 01524 32808. This house, once used by visiting judges, is now home to the Gillow Museum, displaying furniture in period rooms. See the playroom and visit the Victorian schoolroom. Events programme, ring for details. Open Easter-Oct, times vary. Schools **Price A.**
Lancaster Castle*, Castle Hill, www.lancsmuseums.gov.uk 01524 64998, offers 800 years of history. Visit Hadrian's Tower, the dungeons and the 'Drop Room' from where the condemned were taken to the gallows. See where prisoners were publicly hanged. Open daily, 10am-5pm. Schools **Open all year Price B.**
Maritime Museum*, Custom House, St George's Quay, www.lancsmuseums.gov.uk 01524 64637. Relish the sounds and smells of the past as you learn about the port of Lancaster's fishing industry and about Morecambe Bay and its ecology. Open daily, Easter-Oct, 11am-5pm, Nov-Easter, 12.30-4pm. Schools **Open all year Price A.**

Leyland, British Commercial Vehicle Museum, King Street, www.commercialvehiclemuseum.co.uk 01772 451011, is the largest commercial vehicle museum in Europe and is home to historic vans, trucks and buses. Open Apr-Sept, Bank Hol Mons, Sun, Tues-Thurs, 10am-5pm; Oct, Suns only. Schools **Price A.**

Nelson(near), **Pendle Heritage Centre,** Park Hill, Barrowford, 01282 661702; Is due to open in January 2004. Learn about the history of the house and follow the story of Pendle witches. Animal barn and art gallery. Open daily, 10am-5pm. Schools **Open all year** Price A.

Padiham, **Gawthorpe Hall*,** NT, www.lancsmuseums.gov.uk 01282 771004. A stately home, noted for its interior and textile collection. Follow the I-spy trail and take a riverside or woodland walk. Events programme. Gardens open daily, 10am-6pm. Hall open Apr-Oct, Tues-Thurs, Sat-Sun and Bank Hols, 1-5pm. Schools **Open all year** Price A.

Preston, **The Museum of Lancashire*,** Stanley Street, www.lancsmuseums.gov.uk 01772 264075. Discover the county's past, from Celtic times to the present day. See the Victorian schoolroom and the 1940s street. Great events programme with a range of family activities. Open Mon-Wed and Fri-Sat, 10.30am-5pm. Schools **Open all year** Price A.

Rufford, **Rufford Old Hall,** NT, 01704 821254. A 16th century building famous for its spectacular Great Hall. Rufford's meadow is a lovely place to picnic and play. Quiz sheets and toys for the very young in the sitting room. Special events programme. Open 3rd Apr-end Oct, Sat-Wed. Grounds, 11.30am-5.30pm. House, 1-5pm. Schools Price B.

Thornton-Cleveleys, **Marsh Mill Windmill,** Fleetwod Road North, 01253 860765, is a restored working flour mill with guided tours and information centre. Special events and children's activity workshops during school holidays. Open daily, Easter-Oct, 10.30am-5pm, Nov-Easter, 11am-4pm. Telephone to confirm times. Schools **Open all year** Price A.

Turton, **Turton Tower*,** Chapeltown Road, www.lancsmuseums.gov.uk 01204 852203. Explore this country home where period rooms re-create history. A 'Billy Badger' pack includes a woodland discovery trail and indoor mystery tour. Events programme with family activities. Telephone for opening times. Schools Price A.

MERSEYSIDE

Aintree, **The Grand National Experience,** Aintree Racecourse, Ormskirk Road, www.aintree.co.uk 0151 522 2921. Enjoy this world-famous race from the saddle by riding in a virtual reality machine. The visitor centre also includes a museum. Racecourse tours must be pre-booked. Open Jun-mid Oct, Tues-Fri, 10am-5pm. Schools Birthdays Price B.

Birkenhead, **Historic Warships,** East Float Dock, Dock Road, www.warships.freeserve.co.uk 0151 650 1573. An opportunity to get close to this collection of fighting ships. Visitor centre with interactive displays and models. Open Mar-Dec, daily, 10am-4pm. Schools Birthdays Price B.

Liverpool, **The Beatles Story,** Britannia Vaults, Albert Dock, www.beatlesstory.com 0151 709 1963. This popular museum charts the sensational rise to fame of the famous group from Liverpool. Children's activity pack with puzzles and games. Special events. Open daily, 10am-6pm. Schools **Open all year** Price B.

Croxteth Hall & Country Park, Muirhead Avenue East, www.croxteth.co.uk 0151 228 5311, is an Edwardian country house with a working farm and rare farm breeds collection. The country park has an adventure playground and miniature railway. Park open all year until dusk. Opening times vary for hall, farm and gardens. Schools **Open all year** Price B.

Fingerprints of Elvis, Albert Dock, www.fingerprintsofelvis.com 0151 709 1790. Accompanied by an audio guide, walk around this new exhibition dedicated to the life of Elvis Presley. See his gold Mercedes, his last Harley Davidson and his famous stage suits. Children's quizzes and competitions in school holidays. Open daily, 10am-6pm. Schools **Open all year** Price C.

Liverpool Football Club Museum and Tour Centre, Anfield Road, www.liverpoolfc.tv 0151 260 6677. Discover the club's history and take a tour of the ground. Football fans can walk down the tunnel or be the coach in the team dug-out. No stadium tours on match days. Open daily, 10am-4pm, ring first to book. Schools **Open all year** Price C.

The Slavery History Trail, 0151 726 0941. Guided walking tour departing from the Merseyside Maritime Museum. Learn about Liverpool's connection with slavery. Operates Sat-Sun, departing at 11am. Schools **Open all year** Price A.

Western Approaches, Rumford Street, 0151 227 2008, is situated below the streets of Liverpool in the original command headquarters for the Battle of the Atlantic. Relive wartime Britain. Open Mar-Oct, Mon-Thurs and Sat, 10.30am-4.30pm. Schools Price A.

Williamson Tunnels Heritage Centre, The Old Stableyard, Smithdown Lane, www.williamsontunnels.co.uk 0151 709 6868, opened in 2002. These fascinating tunnels were created by an eccentric in the early 19th century. Guided tours (telephone for times). Open Summer, daily, 10am-6pm; Winter, Thurs-Sun, 10am-5pm. Schools **Open all year** Price A.

Port Sunlight, Port Sunlight Heritage Centre, 95 Greendale Road, www.portsunlightvillage.com 0151 644 6466. Learn all about this unique village. Follow the village trail or ask in advance about guided walking or coach tours. Open Apr-Oct, daily, 10am-4pm; Nov-Mar, Mon-Fri, 10am-4pm, Sat-Sun, 11am-4pm. Schools **Open all year** Price A.

St Helens, The World of Glass, Chalon Way East, www.worldofglass.com 08707 444 777, tells the story of glass-making. Tour the tunnels wearing a hard hat and watch glass-blowers at work. Open Tues-Sun and Bank Hol Mons, 10am-5pm. Schools **Open all year** Price B.

Speke, Speke Hall, NT, The Walk, 0151 427 7231, is a half-timbered mansion with children's activity packs and costumed tours. Woodland walks and play and picnic areas. Gardens open daily, 11am-5.30pm or dusk. Opening times for Hall vary. Schools **Open all year** Price B.

Widnes, Catalyst – Science Discovery Centre, Mersey Road, www.catalyst.org.uk 0151 420 1121. Hands-on activities and touch-screen computers guide you through the world of science. Workshops during school holidays. Open Tues-Fri and Bank Hol Mons, 10am-5pm, Sat-Sun, 11am-5pm, and most Mons in school hols (please ring to confirm). Schools **Open all year** Price B.

Choose a topic from this list:

**GIRLS NAMES
BOYS NAMES
MUSICAL INSTRUMENTS
ARTICLES OF CLOTHING
ANIMALS
FRUITS OR VEGETABLES
TREES OR PLANTS
PARTS OF A CAR**

One person starts by naming one thing in the category, such as Girls Names eg RACHEL

The next person has to call out another name, not yet used, beginning with the last letter of the previous word, eg LAURA, the next person could say ANNE, and so on.

Free Places

Included here are free places of interest in the area, also museums, parks, open spaces and other places that offer free family entertainment and some ideas of activities you can participate in.

Although free admission, there may be significant car parking charges, extra charges for schools and special activities or requests for donations.

Some of your days out to free places will be the most memorable if you plan ahead; go for a family picnic and bicycle ride and discover the free pleasures around locally.

CHESHIRE

Buwardsley, Cheshire Workshops, 01829 770401. See candles made and glass artists at work. The many activities and workshops for children include model making, and tile painting (telephone to book). Play area. Open daily, 10am-5pm. Schools Birthdays **Open all year**.

Chester. The most complete walled city in Britain and famous for its magnificent half-timbered buildings and Roman connections. The city centre is a vibrant mix of shops, cafés and stunning architecture. Why not follow the Chester Millennium Trail, a city walk covering buildings from the last 2,000 years, or a walk around the city walls? Contact Tourist Information 01244 402111.
Grosvenor Museum, 27 Grosvenor Street, 01244 402008. Follow video tours with a keeper as a guide and discover the collections in the computer gallery. Find out about Deva, the military fortress. Open Mon-Sat, 10.30am-5pm, Sun, 1-4pm. Schools **Open all year.**
Grosvenor Park, Vickers Lane, close to the town centre, has a miniature railway which runs daily in Summer school holidays, and Sat-Sun at other times. Schools **Open all year**.

Chester(near), Cheshire Farm Ice Cream, Drumlan Hall Farm, Newton Lane, Tattenall, 01829 770446. A working dairy farm with a selection of animals and aviaries for rescued owls. Playbarn for under 6s and ice cream parlour. Open daily, Apr-Oct, 10am-5.30pm, Nov-Mar, 10.30am-5pm. Closed for two weeks in early Jan. Schools Birthdays.

Crewe, Queens Park, Wistaston Road, is a traditional park with a large boating lake and pets corner. Listen to music from the bandstand on Sundays in Summer. **Open all year.**

Englesea Brook, Englesea Brook Chapel and Museum, 01270 820836. Find out about 'The Ranters' and their beliefs. Pilgrim trail and Victorian Sunday school where children can use a slate to write and dress up in original clothes. Open Apr-Nov, Thurs-Sat and Bank Hol Mons, 10.30am-5.15pm, Sun, 1.30-5.15pm. Schools.

Macclesfield, Jodrell Bank Visitor Centre and Arboretum, www.jb.man.ac.uk/scicen 01477 571339, has an environmental centre and 3D theatre. New for 2004 is the observational pathway around half of the base of the famous telescope. Picnic area, playground, nature and planet trails, special events and activities. Open mid Mar-Oct, daily, 10.30am-5.30pm; Nov-mid Mar, Mon-Fri, 10.30am-3pm, Sat-Sun, 11am-4pm. Schools **Open all year.**
West Park Museum, Prestbury Road, 01625 619831. Located in one of the earliest public parks, the museum is home to a permanent Egyptian collection which includes a mummy case and afterlife displays. Activity sheets, temporary exhibits and special events. Open Tues-Sun, Easter-Oct, 1.30-4.30pm, Nov-Easter, 1-4pm. Schools **Open all year.**

Nantwich, Nantwich Museum, Pillory Street, 01270 627104, covers the history of the market town. Discover Nantwich's part in the Civil War. Children's competitions during school holidays. Open Apr-Sept, Mon-Sat, 10.30am-4.30pm; Oct-Mar, Tues-Sat. Schools **Open all year.**

Northwich, Blakemere Craft Centre, Chester Road, Sandiway, 01606 883261. Shops and galleries are built around the cobbled courtyard of Edwardian stables. Try your hand at some of the crafts. Special events and activities. Open Tues-Fri, 10am-5pm, Sat-Sun and Bank Hols, 10am-5.30pm. **Open all year.**

Northwich(near), Delamere Forest Park, Delamere, 01606 889792. Take a picnic and explore the countryside. Visitor centre and ranger-led organised activities throughout the year with extra events during school holidays. Schools **Open all year.**

Runcorn, Town Park, Palacefields, has landscaped gardens and a miniature railway taking you on a mile-long journey. Railway operates most Suns, 1.30-4.30pm. **Open all year.**

Warrington, Walton Hall Gardens, Walton Lea Road, Higher Walton, 01925 601617. A large park with small zoo, great play area, crazy golf and pitch and putt. Heritage centre and ranger service with special events and activities. Park open daily until dusk. Telephone for zoo opening times. Schools **Open all year.**
Warrington Museum and Art Gallery, Museum Street, 01925 442392. Visit the time tunnel, try on a costume and guess what's in the 'feely' boxes. Have a go at fossil rubbing or make a dinosaur flip book. Changing exhibitions. Open Mon-Fri, 10am-5.30pm, Sat, 10am-5pm. Schools **Open all year.**

CUMBRIA

Hadrian's Wall World Heritage Site, www.hadrians-wall.org 01434 322002. This famous frontier was built by order of the Roman Emperor Hadrian. Along its length are many museums, forts and temples. Follow the new National Trail – Hadrian's Wall Path, an 84-mile trail from coast to coast with links to 40 short walks.

The Lake District is the largest of England's National Parks and offers stunning scenery, a mixture of lakes and mountains. Walking is without doubt one of the most popular ways to explore, from challenging hill walking to one of the many trails along the shores of the lakes. Tourist Information Centres are a great source of information from which you can plan a family outing, learn about the wildlife and get away from the traffic.

Ambleside, The Homes of Football, Lake Road, www.homesoffootball.co.uk 015394 34440. Happiness for any football fan, this unique collection of photographs captures the spirit of the game. Open Apr-Aug, daily, 10am-5pm; Sept-Mar, Wed-Mon. Schools **Open all year.**

Barrow-in-Furness, The Dock Museum, North Road, www.dockmuseum.org.uk 01229 894444, is built over a Victorian dock and explores the history of shipbuilding and its impact on the town. Fantastic displays, re-creations and a themed adventure playground. Open Easter-Oct, Tues-Fri, 10am-5pm, Sat-Sun, 11am-5pm; Nov-Easter, Wed-Fri, 10.30am-4pm, Sat-Sun, 11am-4.30pm. Schools **Open all year.**

Braithwaite, Whinlatter Forest Park, 017687 78469. Spend a day in this mountain forest which has a badger's sett, family walks, orienteering, a visitor centre with exhibitions, playground and picnic area. Events and activities. Park open daily until dusk. Visitor centre open daily from 10am, closing times vary. Schools Birthdays **Open all year.**

Brockhole, The Lake District Visitor Centre, Windermere, 015394 46601, uses interactive exhibitions and special events to teach children about Lakeland life. Adventure playground and programme of activities. Open Mar-Oct, daily, 10am-5pm. Schools Birthdays

Carlisle(near), Eden Benchmarks, East Cumbria Countryside Project, 01228 561601, is a unique collection of ten stone sculptures placed at different locations along the length of the River Eden. **Open all year.**

Hawkshead, Grizedale Forest Park, 01229 860010. Look out for the famous forest sculptures and follow the waymarked nature trails. Picnic areas, visitor centre and Go Ape! outdoor adventure (check out 'Adventure' chapter). Visitor centre open daily from 10am, closing times vary. Schools **Open all year.**

Keswick, The Teapottery, www.teapottery.co.uk 01969 623839. An opportunity to learn about the history of tea and teapots. Watch a video of how teapots are made and see some of the wonderful and wacky designs. Due to relocate late 2003, ring for details. Open daily, Apr-Oct, 9am-5pm, Nov-Mar, 9.30am-4.30pm. **Open all year.**

Lindal in Furness, Colony Country Store, 01229 461102, stocks a big range of candles and home accessories. Visit the exhibition centre and learn all about candle making and the history of the area, or have a go and dip your own - telephone for details. Open Mon-Sat, 9am-5pm, Sun, 10.30am-4.30pm. Schools **Open all year.**

Newby Bridge, Fell Foot Park, NT, 015395 31273, is a restored Victorian Park with a children's adventure playground, rowing boat hire and picnic areas. Programme of children's activities. Open daily, 9am-7pm or dusk if earlier. Schools **Open all year.**

Penrith, Brougham Hall, This country house is undergoing restoration, but some sections are open to the public. The craft workshops remain open and Alice's Wonderland, 01768 895648, with over 1,700 dolls and 24 dolls' houses, is one of the main attractions. Open Easter-end Oct, Mon-Fri, 11am-5pm, Sun, 11.30am-5pm. Schools.
Penrith Museum, Robinson's School, Middlegate, 01768 212228, is housed in an old school building and examines the history of Penrith and the Eden Valley. Open Mon-Sat, 10am-4.45pm; also Apr-Oct, Sun, 1-4.30pm. Schools **Open all year.**
Rheged, Redhills, www.rheged.com 01768 868000. Watch a demonstration of chocolates being made. Giant cinema screen showing large format movies, the Helly Hansen National Mountaineering Exhibition and a soft play area for younger children. Admission charge for some activities. Open daily, 10am-5.30pm. Schools Birthdays **Open all year.**
Wetheriggs Pottery, Clifton Dykes, www.wetheriggs-pottery.co.uk 01768 892733, is the home of the UK's last steam-powered pottery. Try your hand at throwing your own pot or paint a pot or plate (charges apply). Children's play area and café. Open daily in school hols, 10am-5pm. Ring before visiting at other times. Schools Birthdays **Open all year.**

Penrith(near), Abbott Lodge Jersey Ice Cream, Clifton www.abbottlodgejerseyicecream.co.uk 01931 712720. A working dairy farm where you can see the Jersey cows, try the ice cream or run around in the adventure playground. Open Easter-Oct, daily, 11am-5.30pm; Nov-Easter, Sat-Sun, 11am-5pm. Schools Birthdays **Open all year.**
Aira Force Waterfall, NT, 01768 482067. A magnificent beauty spot and the starting point for many walks and nature trails. Aira Force and the surrounding countryside are home to a large variety of birds, mammals, insects, flowers and reptiles. Schools **Open all year.**

Sellafield, Sellafield Visitors Centre, Seascale, www.BNFL.com 019467 27027. A contemporary museum exploring production of nuclear energy and the issues it raises in the thought-provoking 'sparking reaction' exhibition. Excellent audiovisual displays and interactive games. Open daily, May-Oct, 10am-6pm, Nov-Apr, 10am-4pm. Schools **Open all year.**

Sizergh, Low Sizergh Barn, 015395 60426. Follow the farm trail at this organic dairy farm and watch the milking from the tearoom gallery after 4pm. Picnic area and large organic produce shop. Open daily, Easter-Christmas, 9am-5.30pm, Christmas-Easter, 9.30am-5pm. **Open all year.**

Whitehaven, Haig Colliery Mining Museum, Solway Road, Kells, www.haigpit.com 01946 599949. Learn all about life down the mines for children in Victorian times and about working in the 1950s. Hands-on activities. Open Thurs-Tues, 11am-5pm. Schools **Open all year.**

GREATER MANCHESTER

Ashton-under-Lyne, Central Art Gallery, Old Street, 0161 342 2650, has a varied and changing exhibition programme, often showing the work of local artists. Children's activities and workshops during school holidays. Open Tues-Wed and Fri, 10am-5pm, Thurs, 1-7.30pm, Sat, 9am-12.30pm, 1-4pm. Schools **Open all year.**

Museum of the Manchester Regiment, Old Town Hall, Market Place, 0161 342 3078. Displays and interactive exhibits tell this military story. Visitors can try on a soldier's headdress or experience a First World War trench. Open Mon-Sat, 10am-4pm. Schools **Open all year.**

Park Bridge Heritage Centre, The Stables, Park Bridge, 0161 330 9613. Follow the trail around the Medlock Valley and discover the area's industrial heritage and local wildlife. Exhibitions and great countryside events programme. Visitor centre open Wed-Thurs and Sat-Sun, 12noon-4pm. Schools **Open all year.**

Portland Basin Museum, Portland Place, 0161 343 2878. Family-friendly activities in a canal-side setting. Learn about clog making, how lock gates work and some playground games from years ago. Events programme. Open Tues-Sun, 10am-5pm. Schools **Open all year.**

Setantii, Town Hall Building, 0161 343 4343. A walk-through museum telling the story of the area from Celtic times through to the present. Events and activities during school holidays. Open Mon-Fri, 10am-4pm, Sat, 10am-1pm. Schools **Open all year.**

Bolton, Bolton Museum Art Gallery and Aquarium, Le Mans Crescent, 01204 332211. Find out about natural history and Egyptology or see the underwater world. Events programme with activities and workshops. Open Mon-Sat, 10am-5pm. Closed Bank Hol Mons. Schools **Open all year.**

The Elephant Walk is a trail around the town centre. Discover how many elephants you can spot - you will be surprised at how many you can see! Leaflets available from Bolton Tourist Information Centre, 01204 334400. **Open all year.**

Jumbles Country Park, off Bradshaw Road, Bradshaw, 01204 853360. Take a picnic and follow the circular trail around the reservoir looking out for the different birds, trees and plants. Ranger service with café and information centre. Park and café open daily. Schools **Open all year.**

Moses Gate Country Park, Hall Lane, Farnworth, 01204 334343, supports many forms of wildlife. Pack a picnic and follow one of the waymarked trails, or feed the ducks and swans on one of the three large lakes. Ranger service with events programme. Visitor centre open daily, 9.30am-4.30pm. Schools **Open all year.**

Moss Bank Park, Moss Bank Way, Halliwell, 01204 334050. A traditional town park with play area, miniature steam railway most Sundays and Bank Hols, Animal World and butterfly house. Events and fun days. Park open daily until dusk. Telephone for Animal World opening times. Schools **Open all year.**

Eccles, Barton Aerodrome, 07866 083334. Take a tour of the aerodrome and learn about its history as the original airport in Manchester. See helicopters, hangars and aeroplanes and visit the control tower and visitor centre with museum. All tours by arrangement and children must be accompanied, ring before visiting. Open May-Sept, Sat-Sun 10am-4pm. Schools.

Failsworth, Daisy Nook Country Park, Stannybrook Road, 0161 308 3909. Enjoy a day outdoors. Activities include orienteering, walking and bird watching. Countryside centre with exhibitions and family activities. Park open daily. Centre open Wed-Fri, 1-4pm, Sat-Sun, 10.30am-5pm. Schools **Open all year.**

Leigh, Pennington Flash Country Park, 01942 605253. The Flash, a lake formed by mining subsidence, is now a site for recreation and conservation and home to a thriving wildlife and bird community. Bird hides, trails and play and picnic areas. Ranger service. Schools **Open all year.**

Littleborough, Hollingworth Lake Country Park, Rakewood Road, 01706 373421, has a trail around the lake and a nature reserve. Use the hide to spot birds or try a boat trip in the Summer. Picnic area, events and junior helper club. Visitor centre open daily, Apr-Sept, 10.30am-6pm; Oct-Mar, Mon-Fri, 11am-4pm, Sat-Sun, 10.30am-5pm. Schools **Open all year.**

Manchester, Greater Manchester Police Museum, Newton Street, 0161 856 3287. See the original Victorian cells, uniforms and equipment. Learn about forgery and forensic science. Open Tues, 10.30am-3.30pm. Schools **Open all year.**

Imperial War Museum North, Trafford Wharf Road, Trafford Park, www.iwm.org.uk 0161 836 4000, opened in 2002 in a unique building. Relive history with the help of the three Big Picture shows, Time Stacks and Time Line. Programme of events and activities. Open daily, 10am-6pm. Schools **Open all year.**

Manchester Airport, Aviation Viewing Park (follow signs from the airport). A great trip out for any children who love aeroplanes. Hear the roar of the engines as you see planes taking off and landing. Small visitors centre and picnic area. **Open all year.**

Manchester Art Gallery, Mosley Street, 0161 235 8888, houses a fine art collection. The Clore Interactive Gallery is for 5-12 year olds with a range of hands-on activities. Open Tues-Sun and Bank Hol Mons, 10am-5pm. Closed Good Fri. Schools **Open all year.**

The Manchester Museum, The University of Manchester, Oxford Road www.museum.man.ac.uk 0161 275 2634, has a changing programme of events and exhibitions. 'Backpacks', quizzes, family art and drama workshops and drop-in sessions at weekends and school holidays. Open Mon-Sat, 10am-5pm, Sun, 11am-4pm. Schools **Open all year.**

The Museum of Science and Industry in Manchester, Liverpool Road, Castlefield, www.msim.org.uk 0161 832 2244. A great family day out with lots to see and do. Displays and demonstrations together with re-creations, interactive exhibits and special events. Open daily, 10am-5pm. Schools **Open all year.**

The Whitworth Art Gallery, Oxford Road, Manchester, 0161 275 7450. See the popular 'textile tower' with art materials available, and at weekends and in school holidays try the art cart with drawing materials and quizzes. Family events programme. Open Mon-Sat, 10am-5pm, Sun, 2-5pm. Schools **Open all year.**

Norden, Three Owls Bird Sanctuary and Reserve, Wolstenholme Fold, www.threeowls.co.uk 01706 642162, aims to take in any wild bird in distress, rehabilitate it and return it to the wild. Between 400 and 1,500 birds can be seen. Open Suns, Summer, 12noon-4.15pm, Winter, 1-3.15pm. Schools **Open all year.**

Oldham, Gallery Oldham, Greaves Street, 0161 911 4657. A mix of contemporary and traditional art together with exhibitions of local interest. Participate in hands-on events and activities during school holidays. Open Mon-Sat, 10am-5pm. Schools **Open all year.**

Prestwich, Heaton Hall and Heaton Park, Middleton Road, 0161 773 1085. Appreciate the beauty of this historic home containing the 'Peoples Park' exhibition. There are also family activities and events. Facilities in the park include a boating lake, farm centre and hatchery, pets corner and tram museum. Park open daily; times and days vary for farm and pets corner. Hall open Apr-Oct, ring for further details. Schools **Open all year.**

Reddish, Reddish Vale Country Park and Local Nature Reserve, Mill Lane, 0161 477 5637, includes a small farm and museum, butterfly conservation park and mill ponds. Follow the nature trail and look at displays in the visitor centre. Opening times vary. Schools **Open all year.**

Rochdale, Springfield Park, Bolton Road, is a large traditional park which has a miniature steam railway running most Sunday afternoons in Summer. **Open all year.**

Touchstones, The Esplanade, 01706 864986. Houses an art gallery, museum and local studies centre. Family workshops and activities at weekends and school holidays. Open Mon-Fri, 10am-5.30pm, Sat-Sun and Bank Hols, 11am-4.30pm. Schools **Open all year.**

Saddleworth, Brownhill Countryside Centre, Wool Road, Dobcross, 01457 872598, provides information about the countryside with displays and exhibits. Younger children will love the woodland 'crawly' tunnel. Open Wed-Fri, 11am-4pm, Sat-Sun, 10.30am-5pm (4pm Nov-Mar). Schools Birthdays **Open all year.**

Huddersfield Narrow Canal Sculpture Trail was designed by local artists and influenced by ideas from local schoolchildren. Walk the trail to see these unique works of art alongside the canal. Two themed play areas, both located in Diggle. **Open all year.**

Salford, Irwell Sculpture Trail, along the river Irwell, 0161 253 5892. The largest public art scheme in the UK, starting at Salford Quays and extending to the West Pennine Moors. There are presently 28 sculptures to admire and events are organised throughout the year. **Open all year.**
Ordsall Hall, Ordsall Lane, Ordsall, 0161 736 2649, has an interesting events programme during school holidays and family fun days on the first Sunday in the month with workshops and activities. Open Mon-Fri, 10am-4pm, Sun, 1-4pm. Schools **Open all year.**
Salford Museum and Art Gallery, Peel Park, The Crescent, 0161 778 0800, is an opportunity to see both old and new. A Victorian street scene is re-created and there are clothes to dress up in. Activities, computers and family events programme. Open Mon-Fri, 10am-4.45pm, Sat-Sun, 1-5pm. Schools **Open all year.**

Stockport, Stockport Art Gallery, Wellington Road South/Greek Street, 0161 474 4453. A traditional art gallery with children's Saturday club and activities for families in Summer school holidays. Open Mon-Tues and Thurs-Fri, 11am-5pm, Sat, 10am-5pm. Schools **Open all year.**
Stockport Museum, Vernon Park, Turncoft Lane, Offerton, 0161 474 4460. Learn about past and present with interactive displays and stories on the audiovisual shows. Trails and special events. Open Apr-Oct, daily, 1-5pm; Nov-Mar, Sat-Sun, 1-4pm. Schools **Open all year.**

Trafford Park, Trafford Ecology Park, Lake Road, 0161 873 7182. Located in the centre of a large industrial estate, this unique park has now gained status as a Site of Biological Importance. Bird and bat boxes, mini-beast piles, a sensory garden and habitat mounds. Open Mon-Fri, 9am-5pm. Schools **Open all year.**

Wigan, Haigh Country Park, Haigh, www.haighhall.net 01942 832895, has a narrow-gauge steam railway and children's play area. Make sure you visit the Stables Gallery/Workshop with hands-on activities and demonstrations most days and a great events programme. Open daily, 9.30am-4.30pm. Schools Birthdays **Open all year.**

Wythenshawe, Wythenshawe Hall and Park, 0161 998 2117. This historic house is furnished with original items from the Tatton family. The surrounding park contains a horticultural centre, woodland gardens and community farm. Park open daily. Hall open Apr-Sept, Thurs-Sun, 10am-4pm. Farm open daily, 11am-3.30pm. Schools **Open all year.**

LANCASHIRE

Accrington, Haworth Art Gallery, Haworth Park, Manchester Road, 01254 233782. Situated in lovely parkland, the gallery is home to a large collection of Tiffany glass. Art materials available for children to use and events, exhibitions and Summer schools. Open Wed-Fri and Bank Hols, 2-5pm, Sat-Sun, 12noon-4.30pm. Schools **Open all year.**

Blackburn, Blackburn Museum and Art Gallery, Museum Street, 01254 667130, has a changing programme of contemporary and community exhibitions with associated family and children's activities. Open Tues-Sat, 10am-4.45pm. Schools **Open all year.**
Lewis Textile Museum, Exchange Street, 01254 667130, is an addition to the Museum and Art Gallery. Learn about the history of cotton production and see the textile machinery used. Hands-on activities. Open Tues-Sat, 11am-4pm. Schools **Open all year.**
Witton Country Park and Visitor Centre, Preston Old Road, 01254 55423. Woodlands with nature trails and a collection of small mammals. Children can also enjoy the riverside walk, cycleway and orienteering courses. Park open daily. Visitor centre open Apr-Sept, Mon-Sat, 1-4.30pm, Sun, 11am-4.30pm; Oct-Mar, Thurs-Sat, 1-4.30pm, Sun, 11am-4.30pm. Schools **Open all year.**

Blackpool is always a family favourite. With a beach, donkey rides, tram system, numerous amusement arcades, adrenalin rides and three piers to choose from, you are sure to find plenty to do. Children love the Illuminations which bring the whole seafront to life with dazzling lights. In 2004 they can be seen from September to the end of October. Contact Blackpool Tourist Information Centre for more details on 01253 478222.

Stanley Park, West Park Drive, is a large family park with children's play area. Try a trip on the lake with boats for hire or a picnic in the beautiful gardens. Schools **Open all year.**

Blackpool(near), ILPH Penny Farm, Preston New Road, Peel, www.ilph.org 01253 766095. Dedicated to the rescue and rehabilitation of horses, this farm gives you a chance to see and meet the animals in their care. Information centre and guided tours available. Open Wed, Sat-Sun and Bank Hols, 11am-4pm. Schools Birthdays **Open all year.**

Burnley, Towneley Hall Art Gallery & Museum, Towneley Park, www.towneleyhall.org.uk 01282 424213. Visit this historic house, local craft museum and natural history centre with interactive activities – all located within the park. Special events. Opening times vary. Schools **Open all year.**

Weavers' Triangle Visitors Centre, Burnley Wharf, 85 Manchester Road, 01282 452403. A trip back in time to discover life in a mill town. See the Victorian classroom and working model fairground. Special events. Open Easter-Sept, Sat-Tues, 2-4pm; Oct, Sun, 2-4pm. Schools.

Lancaster, Lancaster City Museum, www.lancsmuseums.gov.uk 01524 64637, has clipboards and worksheets for children to use as learning tools. Investigate the history and archaeology of Lancaster and the surrounding area. Exhibitions and events programme. Check out Lancashire County Museums in 'History' chapter. Open Mon-Sat, 10am-5pm. Schools **Open all year.**

River Lune Millennium Park. Rich in birds and wildlife, this park has footpaths, cycleways and information stations. Take a walk and discover the works of art along the way. **Open all year.**

Leyland, Worden Park, 01772 421109. This historic park includes an arts and crafts centre with a programme of workshops and activities. Try a trip on the miniature railway or a game of crazy golf (telephone for times). Open daily until dusk. Schools **Open all year.**

Lytham St Anne's, Ribble Discovery Centre, RSPB, Fairhaven Lake, 01253 796292, is next to the Ribble estuary and promotes an understanding of the area and its wildlife. Interactive displays, mud sampling, guided walks and special events. Centre is open daily in Summer, 10am-5pm; ring first for Winter opening. Schools **Open all year.**

Morecambe, Happy Mount Park, Marine Road East, 01524 582847. Enjoy a trip on the miniature train, a paddle in the pool or crazy golf. In addition the park has an indoor play area, woodland walk, trampolines and a roundabout. Park open during daylight hours, some facilities are seasonal. Schools **Open all year.**

Oswaldtwistle, Oswaldtwistle Mills, Colliers Street, www.o-mills.co.uk 01254 871025. Mill shop with textile museum, sweet factory and wildlife reserve. Adventure play area and nature walk. Special events including fairground rides at weekends. Open Mon-Sat, 9.30am-5.30pm, Sun, 11am-5pm. Schools Birthdays **Open all year.**

Preston, Harris Museum and Art Gallery, Market Square, 01772 258248. Visit the 'Story of Preston' gallery and find out the town's history. Programme of exhibitions, contemporary art shows and lots of family activities. Open Mon-Sat, 10am-5pm. Schools **Open all year.**

The National Football Museum, Sir Tom Finney Way, Deepdale, www.nationalfootballmuseum.com 01772 908442, is based at Preston North End FC. Learn how football was developed and take part in a special edition of Match of the Day. Hands-on exhibitions and activities. Open Tues-Sat, 10am-5pm, Sun, 11am-5pm; telephone for match day opening times. Schools **Open all year.**

Preston(near), **Guys Thatched Hamlet,** Canalside, St Michael's Road, Bilsborrow, www.guysthatchedhamlet.co.uk 01995 640010. A canal-side hamlet with events, shops, and Punch and Judy show most Sunday afternoons. **Open all year.**

Rossendale, **Rossendale Museum,** Whitaker Park, Rawtenstall, www.lancsmuseums.gov.uk 01706 244682, is set in a picturesque park with aviary, playground and picnic area. A natural history section features historic taxidermy and includes a young African elephant. Major building work is being carried out with re-opening planned for early Summer 2004, ring for details. Check out Lancashire County Museums in 'History' chapter. Schools.

Rufford, **Mere Sands Wood,** Holmeswood Road, 01704 821809, is managed by the Wildlife Trust. Follow footpaths through woodland and see pondlife, birdlife and wildflowers. Bird hides are available for public use. Visitor centre open daily, 9am-5pm. Schools **Open all year.**

Stannah, **Wyre Estuary Country Park,** 01253 857890, is an important site for wildfowl and wading birds. Wild flowers, a variety of walking trails and ranger service with a dedicated dog-free picnic area. Park always open. Ecology Centre open daily, Apr-Oct, 10.30am-4.30pm, Nov-Mar, 11am-3pm. Schools **Open all year.**

MERSEYSIDE

Bidston, **Tam O'Shanter Urban Farm,** Boundary Road, www.tamoshanterfarm.org.uk 0151 653 9332, is home to traditional farm animals including some rare breeds. Ranger service and events programme. Open daily, 9.30am-4.30pm. Schools Birthdays **Open all year.**

Birkenhead, **Shore Road Pumping Station,** Hamilton Street, 0151 650 1182, is home to the 'Giant Grasshopper'. Learn about the construction of the Mersey railway tunnel. Open Sat-Sun, Summer, 1-5pm, Winter, 12noon-4pm; also school hols. Schools **Open all year.**

Formby, **Squirrel & Nature Reserve,** NT, Freshfield, 01704 878591. Feed the red squirrels, follow one of the walks or join in an event from the activity programme. The beach is part of one of the largest sand dune systems in England. Open daily from 9am. Schools **Open all year.**

Liverpool, **Albert Dock,** 0151 708 8854. Home to many of Liverpool's attractions, this restored Victorian dock is the largest group of Grade I listed buildings in Great Britain. Enjoy a lively mix of museums, galleries, shops, bars and cafés together with temporary exhibitions, events and entertainment. Open daily from 10am. **Open all year.**
Conservation Centre, Whitechapel, 0151 478 4999, gives a unique insight into museum and gallery conservation. Watch the conservators at work and go behind the scenes by taking one of the weekly tours to the workshops. Special events and activities. Open Mon-Sat, 10am-5pm, Sun, 12noon-5pm. Schools **Open all year.**
H M Customs and Excise National Museum, Merseyside Maritime Museum, Albert Dock, 0151 478 4499. Learn about the battle against smuggling over the years. Activities include identifying the smuggler! Special events all year. Open daily, 10am-5pm. Schools **Open all year.**
Liverpool Museum, William Brown Street, 0151 478 4399, is home to a variety of collections and exhibitions which include a Natural History Centre and Planetarium. Family workshops and activities programme. Some building work underway with some galleries temporarily closed, ring for details. Open Mon-Sat, 10am-5pm, Sun, 12noon-5pm. Schools **Open all year.**
Merseyside Maritime Museum, Albert Dock, www.merseysidemaritimemuseum.org.uk 0151 478 4499. Children can find out about Liverpool's connection with the slave trade. See the street scenes or take part in the family activities. Open daily, 10am-5pm. Schools **Open all year.**
Museum of Liverpool Life, Pier Head, www.museumofliverpoollife.org.uk 0151 478 4080, explores the social history of Liverpool, from the diverse cultures and communities to housing and health. Family events and activities. Open daily, 10am-5pm. Schools **Open all year.**

Sefton Park and Sefton Park Palm House. This large open park is a great place for a picnic and a chance to run around and let off steam. The recently restored Palm House has an events programmme, go to www.palmhouse.org.uk or ring 0151 726 2415 for details. Schools **Open all year.**

Tate Liverpool, Albert Dock, 0151 702 7400, displays modern and contemporary art. Drop-in activities on Sunday afternoons, 1.30-4.30pm, (for children aged 5-12, with accompanying adults) include games and trails. Events programme. Gallery open Tues-Sun, 10am-5.50pm. Schools **Open all year.**

The Walker, William Brown Street, www.thewalker.org.uk. 0151 478 4199. This renowned art gallery, displaying paintings, sculpture and decorative arts, also offers a range of children's activities and study days. Open Mon-Sat, 10am-5pm, Sun, 12noon-5pm. Schools **Open all year.**

Port Sunlight, **Lady Lever Art Gallery,** www.ladyleverartgallery.org.uk 0151 478 4136. A traditional gallery and home to a collection of paintings and sculpture. Family packs and quizzes. Open Mon-Sat, 10am-5pm, Sun, 12noon-5pm. Schools **Open all year.**

Prescot, **Prescot Museum,** 34 Church Street, 0151 430 7787. Visit the 'time' room with costumes to try on, time-related interactive exhibits and activity trail. Special events with workshops in school holidays. Open Tues-Sat, 10am-1pm and 2-5pm, Sun, 2-5pm. Schools **Open all year.**

Seacombe to New Brighton, **Millennium Trail.** Follow this walkway and discover the seven works of modern art along the route. **Open all year.**

Southport, **Atkinson Art Gallery,** Lord Street, 0151 934 2110. A traditional gallery with colouring sheets and crayons available for children to use. Family activities and workshops in school holidays. Open Mon-Tues, Wed and Fri, 10am-5pm, Thurs and Sat, 10am-1pm. Schools **Open all year.**

TRAVEL GAMES

What can you see from the car window?
If there are 2 or more of you, who can see the following things first?
Keep score!

Caravan	Zebra crossing	Traffic lights
Dog	Black and white cows	Bridge
Motorway sign	Car transporter	Milk float
Tunnel	Sheep	Stretch limousine
Level crossing	Red letter box	Telephone box

For every letter of the alphabet starting with A you need to spot an object beginning with that letter before moving on to the next letter.

You can play this individually or as a team.

46

Farms, Wildlife & Nature Parks

All children love animals and there are many species to see within the North West. Enjoy a range of farms, animal parks, zoos, aquariums and nature parks. The places listed here have admission charges, but there are many other attractions, including farms and places of natural interest, which are free to visit. Check out the 'Free Places' chapter as well, so you don't miss anything.

CHESHIRE

Chester, Chester Zoo, Upton-by-Chester, www.chesterzoo.org 01244 380280, was voted Zoo of the Year 2003 and has over 7000 animals. Allow a full day to explore and see an amazing range of wildlife. There is always something new to see and do, with 'Bears of the Cloud Forest', miniature monkeys and new aviaries opening in 2004. Explore the 'Spirit of the Jaguar' enclosure and learn about the Asian Elephant Survival Campaign. Take a trip on the Zoofari railway or the seasonal water bus boat. Daily programme of activities and events includes feeding times, and the new Fun Ark outdoor play area is a great way to let off steam. Open daily from 10am (closed 25th Dec). Please call for closing times and prices. Schools Birthdays **Open all year Check out page 50**.

Crewe(near), Lakemore Country Park Animal Kingdom, Clay Lane, Haslington, 01270 253556. Otters, lemurs, llamas, wallabies and rare breeds live at this family-friendly zoo with indoor and outdoor play areas. Open Easter-Oct, Wed-Sun, 10am-5.30pm, and daily during school hols. Schools Birthdays **Price B.**

Ellesmere Port, Blue Planet Aquarium, Cheshire Oaks, www.blueplanetaquarium.com 0151 357 8804, is the ultimate underwater adventure. Watch sharks feed and see scary piranhas! Meet the residents in the interactive rock pool. Activities and events. Open daily from 10am, closing times vary. Schools Birthdays **Open all year Price C.**

Malpas, Cholmondeley Castle Garden, 01829 720383. Enjoy a walk in the magnificent gardens then see rare breed farm animals in the paddock. Children's corner with small animals and free-flying birds in the aviary. Special events, lakeside picnic and two play areas. Open 4th Apr-26th Sept, Wed-Thurs, Sun and Bank Hols, 11.30am-5pm. Schools **Price A.**

Northwich, Cheshire Waterlife Aquatic and Falconry Centre, Blakemere Craft Centre, Chester Road, Sandiway, 01606 882223, has aviaries and flying displays. Aviaries open daily, 10am-5pm. Flying displays Mar-Sept, telephone for times. Schools Birthdays **Open all year Price A.**

Stockley Farm, Arley, www.stockleyfarm.co.uk 01565 777323. Your visit starts with a tractor ride to the organic dairy farm. Farm trail, birds of prey displays, baby animals to hold and feed, straw bounce and activity corner. Open Easter-3rd Oct, Sat-Sun and Bank Hols, 11am-5pm (Tues-Sun during school hols). Schools Birthdays **Price B.**

Stapeley, Stapeley Water Gardens, London Road, www.stapeleywatergardens.com 01270 623868. On site is the Palms Tropical Oasis with zoo room, tamarin monkeys, world of frogs and the stunning stingray pool. Children will love the tropical Tunnel of Underwater Life. Open daily, 10am-6pm (5pm mid Sept-mid Mar). Schools Birthdays **Open all year Price B.**

Tarporley, Cotebrook Shire Horse Centre and Countryside Park, Cotebrook, 01829 760506. A small friendly centre with helpful staff who introduce the animals and horses, including Charlie the prize stallion. A tractor ride is included in admission price. Nature trail and picnic area. Open Wed-Mon, 10am-5pm. Schools **Open all year Price B.**

CUMBRIA

Cockermouth, Lakeland Sheep & Wool Centre, Western Lake District Visitors Centre, Egremont Road, 01900 822673. Come face to face with sheep during one of the indoor presentations which are held four times a day. Sheep shows run Mar-Oct, Sun-Thurs. Visitor centre open all year, daily, 9.30am-5.30pm. Schools **Price B.**

Dalton-in-Furness, South Lakes Wild Animal Park, www.wildanimalpark.co.uk 01229 466086. Home to a wide range of animals, big and small. Daily events programme which includes feeding the tigers and kangaroos. Safari railway, adventure play and picnic areas. Open daily, 10am-5pm (4.30pm in Winter). Schools **Open all year Price C.**

Keswick, Trotters World of Animals, Coalbeck Farm, Bassenthwaite, www.trottersworld.com 017687 76239. From exotic farmyard breeds to snakes and from tractor rides to birds of prey flying displays, there is something for everyone. Play and picnic areas. Open daily, 11am-4.30pm. Schools Birthdays **Open all year Price B.**

Lowther, Lakeland Bird of Prey Centre, 01931 712746. A sanctuary for eagles, falcons, hawks and owls from around the world. Daily flying demonstrations and experience days. Open Apr-Oct, daily, from 11am, closing times vary. Schools **Price B.**

Maryport, Lake District Coast Aquarium, South Quay, www.lakedistrict-coastaquarium.co.uk 01900 817760. Get close to the sea life which is native to Cumbria. Daily programme of activities and talks, and an opportunity to stroke the rays. Remote-controlled boats and adventure playground. Open daily, 10am-5pm. Schools Birthdays **Open all year Price B.**

Milnthorpe, Lakeland Wildlife Oasis, www.wildlifeoasis.co.uk 015395 63027, houses a variety of animals and includes a tropical hall and butterfly house. Interactive displays and an opportunity to meet some of the residents. Open daily, Easter-Aug, 10am-5pm, Sept-Easter, 10am-4pm. Schools Birthdays **Open all year Price B.**

Newby Bridge, Aquarium of the Lakes, Lakeside, www.aquariumofthelakes.co.uk 015395 30153. Discover the wildlife above and below the lakes, walk underwater along the re-created lake bed and enjoy the talks and activities. Open daily, Easter-Oct, 9am-6pm, Nov-Easter, 9am-5pm. Schools Birthdays **Open all year Price B.**

Penrith(near), The Alpaca Centre, Snuff Mill Lane, Stainton, www.thealpacacentre.co.uk 01768 891440. A chance to see alpacas on this small farm which breeds and rears this unusual animal. Shop and tearoom. Open daily, 10am-5pm. **Open all year Price A.**

Eden Ostrich World, Langwathby Hall Farm, Langwathby, www.ostrich-world.com 01768 881771. Allow at least two hours to visit this working farm with lots of activities. See the amazing sight of ostrich chicks hatching, and children will love to stroke the baby animals in pets' corner. There are many rare breeds and you can watch the sheep at milking time. Take a riverside walk, or enjoy the large traffic-free play area. Daily programme of events during school holidays and weekends. Picnic area and indoor play area. Open daily, Mar-Oct, 10am-5pm, Nov-Feb, Weds-Mon. Schools Birthdays **Open all year Price B Check out page 50.**

Sedbergh, Holme Farm, www.holmeopenfarm.co.uk 015396 20654, has a daily programme of events, beginning with a nature trail. Then take a farm tour, enjoy demonstrations and feed baby animals. Open daily, Mar-Sept, 11am-5pm. Schools Birthdays **Price A.**

GREATER MANCHESTER

Bolton, Smithills Open Farm, Smithills Dean Road, www.smithillsopenfarm.co.uk 01204 595765. Pony and donkey rides, pets corner, fallow deer, chickens and ducks. Also a chance to see cows being milked or to help with lamb feeding. Adventure walks. Open mid Mar-Christmas, Tues-Sun, 10.30am-5pm. Schools Birthdays **Price A.**

LANCASHIRE

Arkholme, Docker Park Farm Visitor Centre, www.dockerparkfarm.co.uk 01524221331. A real working farm where children can enjoy a tractor ride, feed the rabbits and see chicks hatch. Farm trail, picnic area and indoor play barn. Open Easter-Oct, daily, 10.30-5pm; Nov-Easter, Sat-Sun, 10.30-4pm, and daily in school hols. Schools Birthdays **Open all year** Price B.

Blackpool, Blackpool Zoo, East Park Drive, only five minutes from Jn 4 on the M55, www.blackpoolzoo.org.uk 01253 830830. With over 400 animals in 32 acres of mature lakes and parkland, close to one of Europe's most popular seaside resorts, this popular zoo is full of excitement! There are lots of close encounters, animal feeding times and keeper talks throughout the day. Recently voted `Tourist Attraction of the Year', the zoo is home to some amazing animals including lions, tigers, gorillas, baby orang-utans and red pandas plus a huge family of primates. Don't miss the fabulous 'Creepy Crawly Corner' and regular animal handling sessions. Learn all about the preservation and conservation of endangered species and take an active part by getting involved in one of the many conservation schemes available. The zoo also has a miniature railway and outdoor children's play area, restaurant and free parking, together with a special bus service (seasonal) which departs from the Promenade near Blackpool Tower. Open daily from 10am, closing times vary. Schools Birthdays **Open all year** Price C **Check out page 46.**

Sea Life Centre, Golden Mile Promenade, www.sealife.co.uk 01253 622445. Discover the marine world, from shrimps to sharks and from starfish to seahorses. Venture into the amazing ocean tunnel. Daily feeding displays, demonstrations and talks. Open daily from 10am, phone for further details. Schools Birthdays **Open all year.**

Burnley(near), Rockwater Bird Centre, Foxstones Lane, Mereclough, 01282 415016. Displays include pheasants, black swans, ornamental poultry, waterfowl, foreign birds and birds of prey. See the children's pets and chipmunks. Open Easter-Sept, Sat-Sun and Bank Hols, 10.30am-6pm, and Tues-Sun during school hols. Schools Price A.

Burscough, Martin Mere Wildfowl and Wetlands Centre, 01704 895181. One of Britain's important wetland sites and home to birds and other wildlife. Events and activities programme during school holidays and a wetland adventure playground. Open daily, 9.30am-5.30pm (5pm Nov-Feb). Schools **Open all year** Price B.

Windmill Animal Farm, Red Cat Lane, www.windmillanimalfarm.co.uk 01704 892282, offers a wide variety of farm animals together with a children's pets area, indoor and outdoor play and a train ride to the lake. Open mid Feb-Easter, Sat-Sun, 10am-5pm; Easter-Sept, daily; Oct-Christmas, Sat-Sun. Schools Birthdays Price B.

Carnforth, Leighton Moss Nature Reserve, RSPB, Myers Farm, Silverdale, 01524 701601, is the largest area of reedbed in the North West and home to rare birds, common species and estuary wildlife. Nature trails, hides and visitor centre. Reserve always open. Visitor centre open daily, 9.30am-5pm (4.30pm Nov-Jan). Schools **Open all year** Price A.

Chipping, Bowland Wild Boar Park, www.wildboarpark.co.uk 01995 61554. A stunning location. See wild boar, deer, llamas, wallabies and more. Four farm trails and tractor and trailer rides. Lamb feeding from Easter to Summer. Play and picnic area. Open daily, 10.30am-5.30pm. Schools Birthdays **Open all year** Price A.

Fleetwood, Farmer Parrs Animal World, Wyrefield Farm, Rossall Lane, 01253 874389. A collection of farm and rare breed animals can be seen with the chance to touch and feed the babies or enjoy a pony or tractor ride. Play and picnic area, together with a large heritage centre. Open daily, 10am-5pm. Schools Birthdays **Open all year** Price A.

Helmshore, Cronkshaw Fold Farm & Environmental Study Centre, off Alden Road, 01706 218614, is a traditional hill farm which focuses on sustainable farming. Public open days throughout the year with seasonal themed activities for children. Schools Birthdays Price A.

Lancaster, Williamson Park, www.williamsonpark.com 01524 33318. Enjoy the tropical atmosphere of the butterfly house, the mini-beast centre and bird enclosure as well as the traditional park. Entry to the park is free; charges apply for butterfly house and mini-beast centre. Open daily, 10am-5pm (4pm Oct-Mar). Schools **Open all year** Price B.

MERSEYSIDE

Brimstage, Brimstage Hall, www.brimstagehall.co.uk 0151 342 7558. Courtyard craft centre and shopping plus a small family farm with play and picnic areas. Children's craft classes and maize maze in Summer. Telephone for opening times and prices. Schools **Open all year.**

Kirkby, Acorn Venture Farm, Depot Road, 0151 548 1524. Goat-milking demonstrations and pony rides at weekends and in school holidays allow children to get close to the animals. Woodland walk, play area and activities. Open daily, 10am-4pm. Schools Birthdays **Open all year** Price A.

Knowsley, Knowsley Safari Park, Prescot, www.knowsley.com 0151 430 9009. Take the five-mile safari drive to see a whole range of animals from lions and elephants to giraffes and rhinos at home in the safari parkland. Play, picnic and amusement area. Open daily, Mar-Oct, 10am-4pm, Nov-Feb, 11am-3pm. Schools Birthdays **Open all year** Price C.

Liverpool, National Wildflower Centre, Court Hey Park, Roby Road, www.nwc.org.uk 0151 737 1819. Enjoy delightful wildflowers grown in an environmentally friendly way and get some ideas to try at home. Play trail with wormery and tree house. Special events. Open Apr-Sept, daily, 10am-5pm. Schools Birthdays Price A.

Neston, Ness Botanic Gardens, South Wirral, 0151 353 0123. Renowned gardens with visitors centre and walking trails. Children's adventure playground and picnic area. Open daily, Mar-Oct, 9.30am-5pm, Nov-Feb, 9.30am-4pm. Schools **Open all year** Price A.

Wallasey, Seacombe Aquarium, Seacombe Ferry Terminal, Victoria Place, 0151 330 1444. Use the interactive displays to learn all about the marine life of the River Mersey at this small aquarium which is home to baby sharks, a blushing octopus and a conger eel. Open daily, 10am-6pm. Schools Birthdays **Open all year.**

Places to go outside the area

Visit some exciting places just a little further afield.

BERKSHIRE

Windsor, **LEGOLAND®** www.legoland.co.uk 08705 040404, set in 150 acres of lovely parkland, offers an exciting and imaginative day out with lots of hands-on, interactive discovery. A brand new Jungle Coaster ride for 2004 promises thrills of acceleration, speed and high drops along a wild roller-coaster track that is themed to simulate an automobile test! Exciting experiences await as you wander through the Creation Centre, discover the Imagination Centre, enter LEGO® EXPLORE Land and have a go in the Driving School. Take the younger children to the Waterworks area, watch the daring stunt shows, scale the challenging Climbing Wall, brave the Pirate Falls and explore Miniland, made from over 35 million LEGO® bricks. Open 20th Mar-31st Oct, daily (except some Tues, Wed in Spring & Autumn), from 10am, closing times vary. Schools **Price G Check out page 53.**

DERBYSHIRE

Chapel-en-le-Frith(near), **Chestnut Centre, Otter, Owl & Wildlife Park,** www.ottersandowls.co.uk 01298 814099. Situated in an attractive area of the Peak District National Park this is an acknowledged centre for breeding, care and rehabilitation of wild animals. Otters are of particular concern here and every year otter cubs are raised for release into the wild. Display boards help to interpret the countryside scene and there are various specially designed enclosures with otters, wildcats, foxes, owls, polecats and deer. Follow a one-mile nature trail through field and woodlands. A conservation club for 4-11 year olds meets regularly in the Education Centre. The club provides up to date information on all the residents. Open daily, (weekends only in Jan), 10.30am-5.30pm (dusk in Winter). Schools Birthdays **Open all year Price B Check out page 54.**

SUSSEX

Cambridge Language & Activity Courses. CLAC, www.clac.org.uk 01223 240340, organises interesting Summer courses for 8-13 year and 14-17 year olds at two separate sites in lovely countryside locations, Lavant House and Slindon College, West Sussex. The idea is to bring together British and foreign students to create natural language exchange in a motivated and fun environment. There are French, German and Spanish classes for British students and English for overseas students. Fully supervised in a safe environment, there are lots of activities such as swimming, tennis, team games and competitions, drama and music, in addition to the language tuition. Residential or not, these courses offer enjoyable multi-activity weeks with 20 hours of specific tuition in small groups. Courses run weekly during July and August. Please call for more details and a brochure. Birthdays **Check out page 54.**

YORKSHIRE

Skipton, **Skipton Castle,** www.skiptoncastle.co.uk 01756 792442. This 900 year old fortress standing at the top of Skipton's main street is considered to be one of the most complete medieval castles in England. The historical site is fully accessible for children to explore. Visit the castle kitchen and the banqueting hall and imagine life living and working in the castle. Learn about the three year siege which took place during the Civil War. Children will be fascinated by the dungeons and ancient toilet arrangements! Fun self-guiding tour sheets in a choice of languages, quiz and picnic area available. Check out website for pre-visit children's activities and make a cut-out model or face mask. Open daily, 10am-6pm, Sun from 12noon, Oct-Feb till 4pm. Schools **Open all year Price B Check out page 52.**

LEGOLAND WINDSOR

NEW FOR 2004

42-foot-drop, abrupt twists and wild 180-degree turnarounds.

LEGOLAND® Windsor's new roller coaster is the fastest ride in the Park, topping speeds of 26mph while zipping along 1,300 feet of steel track. It also has the highest drop of any other attraction in the Park, towering nearly five stories above the ground. The attraction was designed after one of the popular LEGO® toy lines and is themed to stimulate an automobile test track while riders experience accelleration, breaking and maneuverability.

NEW FOR 2004!

£5 OFF ENTRY

LEGOLAND WINDSOR

V200225

04 Opening Dates - 20th March - 31st October

ormation and booking Number 08705 040404

r more information visit www.legoland.co.uk

Index

Best wishes

Jue Bareham

SEARCH FOR A MOTHER

Tina Bareham

MINERVA PRESS
ATLANTA LONDON SYDNEY

SEARCH FOR A MOTHER
Copyright © Tina Bareham 1999

ISBN 0 75410 379 X

First Published 1999 by
MINERVA PRESS
315–317 Regent Street
London W1R 7YB

Printed in Great Britain for Minerva Press

SEARCH FOR A MOTHER

Acknowledgements

My very warm and grateful thanks are due to my friend, Jan Judson, for her generous help in correcting and improving many pages of the manuscript.

Other friends have given me assistance and encouragement in various ways, but in particular, my heartfelt thanks must be said to Nigel Cox, Joan Rosier-Jones, Marcia Roberts, Barbara Pengelly and Dr Cathie Dunsford.

To my husband, Ray, for his loving support during my search to find my mother and in the consequent writing of this book, and to my sons, Nigel and Laurence, for patiently allowing me to disrupt their lives over the past five years. I love you all.

Tina Bareham
raytina@xtra.co.nz

Foreword

Tina Bareham's book is a welcome addition to the literature on the effect of being separated from one's birth family when very young.

New Zealand is home to quite a few people who, like Tina, moved here as adults, after spending their childhood in institutions or with private foster or adoptive families in the UK. The distance of half a world makes it doubly difficult for them to find out about their birth families.

Barnardos New Zealand runs a small service which helps such people find out where to go for information, and also helps them adjust to that information when they get it. Many of its clients are 'old boys and girls' of Dr Barnardos. Our experience of working with them has taught us the same truths that Tina reveals in this book – that not knowing your origins can affect your whole life, and that, when you do find out what there is to know, it can be devastating. People often need the empathy of a counsellor to help them cope with the knowledge of opportunities lost or the realities of a bleak background.

The stories of many of our clients also bear out the truth of Tina's experiences as a child in institutional care. Until the late Sixties it was sincerely believed that children would thrive better if they didn't know too much about their origins, and little was known about how much their emotional security depends on receiving love and affection from a stable primary caregiver.

But the fact that child care organisations, including Dr Barnardos, acted as they did with the best of intentions does not change the damage they did to some of the children in their care. As Collette Bradford, the manager of Barnardo's UK's After-Care Centre wrote in a recent issue of the magazine for their old girls and boys, 'There are occasions when, no matter how hard we wish, all we can do is say sorry. We can't change the past or give back what was taken away.'

Barnardos New Zealand welcomes the contribution this book will make to keeping us mindful of what children need to grow up happy, secure and able to realise their full potential.

Mary Collie-Holmes, National Public Relations Adviser
and Robyn Henley, Counsellor
Barnardos New Zealand
November 1997

Contents

Istanbul

Did it drift across the ocean
through the waves,
a magic notion
sent to me from land afar?
Will my ears, forever burning,
never cease their restless turning
to the call of distant star?

Eastern wind from eastern beaches
calling me before it reaches
other ears on which to fall.
Constantly the voice is near,
quietly, but very clear;
who am I to heed its call?

So in answer to your pleading
I'll go where my heart is leading
to this magic, distant land.
For Istanbul my heart is bleeding
to your whisper I am heeding,
let me hold you by the hand.

Let me drift along your waters,
show to me your sons and daughters,
charm me with your ancient grace.
Wrap your welcome arms around me,
love me dearly,
hold me,
keep me,
for, at last, I've seen your face.

Tina Suleyman
1963

Prologue

Naturally, in order to have been born, a mother and a father are essential prerequisites to one's existence. I knew neither of them. In fact, so far as I knew, there was no one on this earth who was related to me in any way.

Nobody explained to any of us children living in the Dr Barnardo's home about our families, nor did they ever discuss with us why we were there instead of in an ordinary house with parents, siblings and other kin somewhere around.

I was born at the beginning of the war, thereby becoming a statistic as a war baby. During the war, as in most wars, there was a boom in illegitimate, unwanted babies like myself, and the need to house them somewhere became urgent.

Barnardo's was fashionable and respected as one of the largest children's organisations in Britain, providing a secure childhood for thousands of youngsters like myself. People who were so rich they could afford to give away mansions no doubt earned a few Brownie points for their generosity.

The country mansion where I was placed as a small baby was a Barnardo 'show home', where I spent the first thirteen years of my life. It was branded by the philosophy of people who regarded us as unfortunate objects of charity to be cared for but never truly loved.

John Bowlby, in his book *Child Care and the Growth of Love,* shows how the deprivation of mother-love in early childhood can have a far-reaching effect on the mental health and personality development of a human being. In particular, the child who is brought up in an institution often has no one person who cares for her in a personal way, and therefore suffers complete deprivation. Many children did have a nurse who specially liked them, or an outsider who took an interest in them. That didn't happen to me. I often cried myself to sleep, and dreamt of having a mum and dad of my own, or someone to cuddle me and tell me they loved me. Although I was adequately looked after in a secure environment, I never received any hugs, not even when I was ill.

According to John Bowlby's theories, I was a child who had been completely deprived. When I left Barnardo's there was a huge emptiness in my life. Very quickly I had to learn the skills of sole survival – how to live in the outside world on my own after being insulated from society for all of my childhood, with the only model for womanhood being the tyrannical matron of the home. How could I master the prescribed socially acceptable behaviours when I had no suitable role model? I was unable to sustain any close relationships even though I desperately needed them. I was afraid to accept love from others, and I avoided marriage and motherhood until I was in my thirties.

Over the years I asked the question of Barnardo's, my supposed legal guardians, 'Who am I? I must be somebody's child. Don't I have any relatives in the world? Why was I never adopted?' They told me as little as possible.

'It wouldn't be in the best interests of your mother for you to find her in case she has made a new life for herself' was the official line. Information that was deemed appropriate by the social worker at the time was filtered through to me very slowly, over many years, and I remember the short, inadequate answers I was always given to any questions I felt brave enough to ask.

I do not wish to judge the actions of those long dead by today's values, when different standards and norms prevailed. Nowadays the importance of finding out about oneself and one's origins is recognised in Barnardo's After-Care, and much work is being done to make amends for the past by piecing together the jigsaw for those who have no links with their families and for whom what is on record is all that is known.

Philosophically I accepted what life had dealt me, and fortunately I have a strong constitution and a will to match. Although depression is not in my make-up, there were times when my mild-mannered passivity erupted into anger and frustration. Deprived of any contact with my family, I grew up with a profound sense of injustice. I knew no other person who was an orphan. It marked me as someone different. I felt utterly and irrevocably alone.

A spell in hospital brought on a severe bout of self-pity, for it dawned on me that if I died absolutely no one would mourn me. But it also galvanised me into taking the first positive steps towards searching for my mother.

I would have been happy to find any blood relation, perhaps a sister or brother, an aunt or uncle, even a distant cousin. Every human being deserves the right to know their heritage, but not until I was fifty-two years old did I find out the real truth about my parents.

As I wrote this book it made me think of the needless misery I felt throughout the years when I was alone, of how I had no relatives and how I had to search for my family without assistance from anyone. Of how I was only given a strictly censored version of my personal history. Writing about everything has put my past into perspective and has helped me work through a host of negative feelings I have had all my life of being abandoned and unwanted. The mental screen behind which my feelings have been hidden has at last been taken down. Putting it all down on paper has been a powerful catharsis. Finally I can find peace within myself.

Chapter One

Farm Hill

If nothing else, my mother gave me the gift of life, and bestowed on me the Turkish name Fatma Suleyman. I was born at the prestigious St Mary Abbott's Hospital in the Royal Borough of Kensington, London, on 15th March, 1940, although the first few weeks of my life were spent in the more humble habitat of the Islington Public Assistance Institution.

Being one of a batch of orphans and illegitimate babies born during the turbulent war years, no one quite knew what should be done with us. Eventually it was decided that, as my mother was too young to look after me, the National Council for the Unmarried Mother and her Child would care for me on a temporary basis.

As bad luck would have it, a prearranged adoption fell through after I developed a severe bout of gastro-enteritis and I spent a period of time in the Great Eastern Isolation Hospital in Tottenham, North London.

At the age of seven months, I came under the care of Dr Barnardo's homes, the largest Christian children's charity in the United Kingdom. I was promptly cut off from any tenuous roots I might have had and sent to a holding centre for bewildered babies at Dr Barnardo's homes in Barkingside, Essex, until my future was decided.

Finally, on 29th January, 1941, nine months after being shunted from one place to another, a nurse was given the duty of transporting me by train from Liverpool Street Station to Kelvedon, a small town in the heart of the Essex countryside.

I was to spend the next thirteen years in a Barnardo home. It was called Farm Hill, an Edwardian mansion which presented itself to the world at the end of a long, winding driveway, neatly edged with lavender bushes and roses. It was ringed by handsomely landscaped gardens and meadows, complete with four staff cottages, two large greenhouses and three play huts. The home could be found in an isolated region of flat, fertile farmlands amidst fields of corn and sweet peas. It stood sandwiched between the important railway town of Kelvedon two miles to the south, which provides a one hour train service to London, and the historic market town of Coggeshall, three miles to the north. Coggeshall is situated on the banks of the river Blackwater, and stands on the line of the old Roman military road leading to England's oldest recorded town of Colchester, ten miles on.

Large and illustrious, Farm Hill was built around 1900, and was typical of the network of homes found in country areas all around the British Isles. The elegant front door led into a large porch, where the housemaid showed visitors through to the superior end of the house. They were ushered into the lovely, oak-panelled hallway, graced with a curved oak stairway leading up to the front bedrooms. A door from the hallway led into the elegant staff dining room, known as the White Room. The starched tablecloths were always laid out with the best silver and crockery, and the grand piano in the corner gave it the ambience of a plush restaurant. Wide bay windows overlooked a manicured lawn and a lavender-lined, red-brick path led to the meadows beyond. The chapel next door was used occasionally for services when folding doors were pushed open to reveal a ready-made altar. A few paces away stood the office, where we could be summoned to at any time.

At the western end of the five acres stood another stately home, where about fifty babies were looked after by nursery nurses who were sent to Farm Hill for a two-year training course. On reaching the age of five we were moved across to the main house in the east, where another fifty children were cared for in various nursery groups.

Whenever there was a heavy air-raid, Farm Hill received a big influx of babies and children. Some were orphaned, and many, like myself, were illegitimate or misplaced. Barnardo's, as it was later shortened to, claimed to be 'the largest family in the world' and we were constantly being reminded how lucky we were to have been 'rescued'. We didn't always see it that way; deprived of freedom and cut off from family contacts, we had to learn the skills of group survival.

Every child was put in a nursery group with about twelve others of a similar age. The tiniest baby group was Treasures, the name obviously implying that they should be handled with the utmost care.

When I was admitted to Farm Hill at nine months, I was placed in the Babies' nursery under the care of trainee nurse Muriel, a pretty, bubbly girl of eighteen. A Barnardo girl herself, I was to come across her again when I was a bit older. At the age of about two I moved up to Tweenies, with an interesting ethnic assortment of toddlers. After a couple more years in Gnomes, I was then shifted across to the main children's home where I started school as an Imp. By the time I moved on to Pixies and then Elves, I noticed that parents used to visit some children at weekends, and it started me wondering whether I had a mum and dad, or any other relatives. Who were they? Were they alive? But no one ever told me anything about myself and I remained ignorant about my origins for the best part of my childhood.

Whoever conjured up the quaint names for our nurseries must have had in mind The Little People, and I suppose we have to be grateful we weren't called something like Gremlins or Goblins. We worked our way up the mythological rungs of the ladder until entering Elves at the age of twelve. The last nursery was IPs, when we suddenly became an Important Person. Adolescence was obviously deemed to be a notable milestone in our lives, but heaven knows why one couldn't be an important person at any age. I used to think, What was so special about being older? We only had to work harder.

We lived most of the time in our own quarters at the modest end of the house, comprising dining room, airing room, large cloakrooms and a huge kitchen with a walk-in larder, which we raided with regularity when the cook went off duty.

Flying bombs might well have been falling all around the Essex countryside when I was a toddler, but precise details of incidents have faded over the years. I do recall falling victim to many of the childhood illnesses which swept through our close-knit community. I am told I made a good job of having scarlet fever, chicken pox, measles, mumps, German measles and whooping cough.

The happy memories that remain sharp in my mind are of having picnics in the meadow and riding in the pony-trap to school and to nearby farms, where we watched the cows being milked. I was about nine when Princess Margaret, the then President of Dr Barnardo's homes, visited Farm Hill. I remember we were given a day off school for the sole purpose of entertaining her.

Christmases were always a treat with lots of donated presents and plenty of parties. We had a brief encounter with the world outside when we travelled by hired buses to circuses, shows and the Royal Gala performance in London. We also went to an American Air Force Base where we played party games and sat down to eat and drink as much as we could. They certainly were times of warmth, fun and fellowship, and the matron never missed an opportunity to remind us what lucky children we all were.

All the children, as well as the nursing staff at Farm Hill West and East, were under the strict control of the matron, Miss Simcox. She was known as Simmie to her friends, but everyone had to call her 'Mother', which was a blatant misnomer; she just wasn't motherly. I don't suppose it was easy mothering so many children in not just one home but two, but I know for sure she wasn't my idea of what a real mother should be like, as she never once gave any of us a hug or a kiss. We lived in an utterly loveless, sterile environment.

In 1940, at the age of thirty-five, Mother was appointed superintendent of Farm Hill. Supposedly accountable to head office in Stepney, London, Mother's long, autocratic reign lasted for twenty-five years until she retired in 1965. The isolation of the home in deepest Essex made it easy for her to run a strict regime according to her own rules.

Whenever I think about Mother now, I can't help thinking of the Queen. I used to watch her straight, regal figure walk along the cold corridors of her palace, and it seemed to me that we were all her subjects who had to obey her commands. But when her fiery temper exploded we called her 'the Dragon', and we would scatter in all directions to get as far away from her as possible. She inspired fear in staff and children alike and I don't remember her displaying any warmth or affection towards anybody. Her brown hair was neatly kept in a bun, often secured by a brown hairnet, and she wore a tight Victorian dress, buttoned all the way down.

Mother was ruled by her own rigid self-discipline from which she rarely wavered, but she was never afraid of manual labour and often did loads of hand washing in the airing room sink, which was also used for bathing us when we were younger. With her strong hands scrubbing us in the hot, soapy water she almost turned into a normal human being, as it was her only physical contact with us, but I was so afraid of her that her very closeness always turned my tummy into a tight knot. Even now as I write I can see her stiff face rising vividly before me, producing memories of the terrors which I held inside. In the controlled, fear-ridden environment that was my home I grew into a nervous, reticent and obedient child.

There are names of people and places which are bound up with my childhood memories, those of the three villages and their surrounding hamlets – Coggeshall, Kelvedon, Pattiswick and Bradwell, no doubt remembered because we attended church services at each village. From the age of five, a large group of us walked to the Infant School at Coggeshall, a distance of nearly three miles. Although there was no official school uniform, we Barnardo kids all wore identical navy pinafore frocks to school, which we hated as it set us apart from the other children. In the summer the walk was pleasant enough. We would pick wild flowers from the roadside to give to the teachers. But it wasn't so nice in the winter, trudging through deep snow with our gloves sewn on a cord of elastic going up the sleeves of our coats so we wouldn't lose them.

I might have considered Mother to be intimidating, but far more disturbing to my peace of mind as a youngster was a fat, black jackdaw waiting to torment us as we walked to school past its nesting ground. This monstrous bird chased us across the road, pecking at our ankles, and so petrified were we to pass by that we were often late for school. We could hear the bell ringing as we scurried, breathless across the playground. The local kids would chide, 'Here come the Bananas, late as usual.' We were used to suffering the slings and arrows of name-calling from the outside children, and our prompt retort was ten times better:

If we're the bananas you're the skins
We live in houses and you live in bins.

Nurse Muriel, by now in charge of Pixies, accompanied us each day to school. She then had to return on foot to the home and repeat the process in the afternoon. She stood only five feet tall, and when I met her again as an adult I was surprised she hadn't grown since I was in her care. 'I never had a chance to grow because of all the walking we had to do at Farm Hill,' she told me with a twinkle in her eye.

Each group had its own dormitory with ten or twelve beds, but we had no bedside cupboards in which to keep our personal items. Not being able to have your own possessions was, I think, one of the worst aspects of life at Farm Hill. If you were given a toy or a game for Christmas, it would be put into a pool to be shared. I don't recall receiving any personalised presents, so the pool rule made it fairer for those of us without any relatives. Many of the children had sisters with them at the home. There were also quite a few twins and even a set of triplets, who all left the home well before they reached their teens. A hard core of about twelve of us stayed together right through adolescence.

Two of the girls in my peer group were dark-skinned Trixie Mutton, and her sister Pauline, nicknamed the 'Mutton Chops'. They had a brother, Alan, a real misfit as he was the only boy allowed to stay on beyond the usual age for boys. The 'Mutton Chops' were Mother's favourites and the rest of us were envious of the fact that their education was paid for by a wealthy 'aunty' from outside, so they could attend a private school in Colchester. Freckle-faced Geraldine, or Gerry, and myself were the only two in our group without sisters, though Gerry learned much later that she had three siblings who lived elsewhere. My two best friends throughout my childhood were the snub-nosed, raven-haired sisters, Audrey and Pauline Wilbraham. We three stuck together in times of trouble.

I especially liked being with Audrey as she was a compulsive chatterbox, whereas I didn't say much. We were always getting the giggles and were known as the two gigglers. A saucy smile habitually lit up her moon-shaped face and her thick black hair was worn in the customary fringe, unlike my own which was tied in bows. We had no choice in our hair styles. I would never have chosen to wear my fine hair pulled back tightly and tied with huge white ribbons. I wondered how nurse Joan, in charge of Elves nursery for ten years, decided which style was most suitable for each child, or indeed who made the final choice. It was typical of an institution in that era to give us arbitrary hairstyles and dress us identically. It must have made things easier to lump us all together and eliminate any individuality.

Audrey was a wonderful friend to me, not only because she was willing to eat the lumps from my semolina pudding or the skin from my cold custard, both of which I detested, but I marvelled at her daring disobedience. She was continually in trouble. When Mother started throwing one of her fits and yelling at her you could see Audrey's knees shaking and she would usually end up wetting her knickers. We would laugh about it later, but we knew it would happen when she was put on the spot. She just couldn't stop herself. Pauline and I, with our more cautious natures, generally kept out of trouble. I only sought to be approved of and was usually obedient, except when being confident of not getting caught. Then I was as much a dare-devil as the rest of them. I can see the three of us in the backyard now, bent over a huge bowl of muddy water full of potato peelings. To take our minds off the big sack of potatoes at our feet we sang a favourite round:

Rolling round the world
Looking for the sunshine which never seems to come my way.
Bye bye rainy day, bye bye snow,
Got no time to waste, I must go.

I was mad about singing and was forever pestering Audrey and Pauline to harmonise with me and pretend to be The Beverley Sisters, a popular trio at the time. Of course, we always made sure Mother wasn't around before bursting into song, but whenever we had to do hateful jobs we would daydream about leaving Farm Hill and finding our own families, so that song was a mixture of hope and despair. I was profoundly jealous when Audrey and Pauline went to stay with members of their family in the holidays. I asked the question, Why couldn't it be me? Forlornly, I hoped that one day a member of my own family would arrive at the home to claim me.

My unusual birth name troubled me more and more as I grew older. Now at this distance I can think of it and know with certainty that nothing humiliated me more than the name bestowed on me by parents whom I never knew. I was always known as Fatima, but I learned many years later that although the name Fatma was on my birth certificate an 'I' was added, changing it to the more familiar Fatima. It was pronounced Fateema, with the accent on the second syllable, but people would often say FATima, emphasising the first syllable, which I hated even more as it made me sound as though I was fat. Big and tall I was, but fat I wasn't!

I'll never forget how one day, when I was in Elves, Mother embarrassed me in front of everybody. I was helping to serve lunch for the staff and a few visitors in the White Room, and as I placed a steaming dish of runner beans on the table, freshly picked from our kitchen garden, I heard Mother shout in front of everyone, 'For goodness sake, Fatima, do pull your shoulders back, girl.'

Then in a quieter voice, but loud enough for me to hear, she declared, 'We're not sure if Fatima is Arabian, Turkish or Egyptian, but we think she might be part-Turkish.'

What a way to find out something so personal! Hanging my head in shame and hoping no one could see my red face, I couldn't get out of the room fast enough. It was so typical of Mother to speak to *other* people about you, rather than to you personally. I began to loathe my obviously foreign name which no one could pronounce.

'Oh, what a lovely name,' they would lie when being introduced to me, glancing at me queerly as though I was from another planet. I really didn't know how to cope with the inevitable questions people asked when they first heard it, and consequently grew up dreadfully self-conscious and uncertain about my real identity.

It didn't seem right that I should be considered foreign because my skin wasn't even as dark as that of the 'Mutton Chops' and some of the younger children, with thoroughly English names, were as black as the Ace of Spades. With my light brown hair and only slightly olive skin I looked as English as anyone. It seemed so unjust to me.

My feelings fluctuated from condemnation towards my anonymous mother for leaving me alone in the world, (*and* with such a ghastly name), to bewilderment about my orphaned state. It was impossible for me to try to imagine what she looked like, so I didn't even try, but in my heart of hearts I knew she would be kind and loving – total contrast to the iron-willed matron. I promised myself that when I grew up I'd look for my own family.

Little did I know then that just twelve years later I would be travelling to Turkey in the hope of being reunited with my mother.

Caught up in the busy routine of life at Farm Hill, months would pass when I didn't even give my mother a second thought. I thought even less about my father, who held no curiosity for me then.

The nurses, quite understandably, favoured certain children, though I regret to say I was never one of them. Much later, nurse Muriel told me I was probably ignored because I wasn't 'cute or cuddly' like some of the children were. Mother always made me stand at the back because I was very tall for my age, so I got used to blending into the background, unnoticed. Just the same, my obviously solemn, 'unhuggable' appearance possibly ruined my chances of receiving the physical closeness which I so yearned.

I became adept at keeping out of the way of Mother, or her assistant, Miss Hoadley. None of us had any respect for Miss 'Oadley, as we called her, because she couldn't say any words that started with an 'h'. Stout and greying, with a huge wart on the side of her face, she was under Mother's thumb, as scared of her as we were, and would creep about trying to catch us in the middle of some misdemeanour. She was a woman to be watched, to be circumnavigated, but not to be feared for she didn't carry the same clout as Mother and we rarely took any notice of her. One day she asked me to 'go and 'ang the tea-towels on the 'edge'. Audrey and I had just finished drying up all the dishes, and we couldn't resist having a bit of fun with her. I tried the edge of tables, chairs and benches, before we both collapsed in a heap of laughter with me receiving a stinging whack across the face. Of course, we both knew she meant to hang the tea-towels on the lavender hedge, where they always went, but it was our way of breaking the monotony of the never-ending chores.

There was always extra work for us when a coachload of visitors was expected. This happened all too often because we were a Show Home. We would sing and dance for them, and help to serve them afternoon tea. Often after these visits, some of my friends would disappear and I wondered whether they would come back. It was a little while later that I realised they had been chosen for adoption or fostering. With a pang of envy, I hoped it might be me one day. I believe now that my Moslem, and very un-Anglican, name was a definite handicap to my chances of being 'rescued', and as a child I thought I was never chosen because of my funny name or my bad lisp. As a consequence, I developed low self-esteem and an inferiority complex. Mother's constant nagging to 'work faster', 'stop daydreaming' or 'don't mumble' compounded my feelings of unworthiness that built up inside me as I grew older.

I read somewhere that it is the law of human relations that physical closeness between human beings should trigger an array of feelings, be they nasty or nice, but the long lasting effects of experiencing no warm affection from anyone probably turned me, around the age of eight, from a naturally reserved child into a severely introverted one. I was conditioned to be unobtrusive, to keep my feelings to myself. With no one coming to claim me as their own I thought of myself as invisible – a nonentity. I was nobody's child. How I longed to be swept up into someone's arms, to be told how much I was loved and wanted. It didn't happen to me and as a consequence I became more and more withdrawn. The only physical encounters I recall – aside from the scrubbings in the bath – were the slaps around the face or legs for a minor misdemeanour, though I did witness other more perverse punishments inflicted by

Mother and one or two of the nastier nurses on the so-called 'naughty' children.

The rules at Farm Hill decreed that your behaviour must not be naturally exuberant and you were marked down for a punishment if caught laughing or talking at the wrong times, so any spontaneous behaviour was knocked out of us.

On occasions I saw Mother whacking a child over the knuckles with a hairbrush and I was terrified it might be my turn one day.

I'll never forget the night Audrey and I were clowning around in the attic dormitory and as a punishment we had to sleep on our mattresses in the passage where Mother could keep an eye on us. Another time I spent the whole night standing behind the bathroom door, for reasons since forgotten. The most common punishments were being sent to bed without food for the rest of the day, or having to sit under the airing room table next to the dog basket.

It was a tyrannical regime but I was not consciously unhappy for, on the whole, life was secure and regulated. It must have been difficult for a large institution such as Farm Hill to acknowledge a child's individuality. Rules had to be set to maintain control. We did manage to have moments of fun even though we had to work hard most of the time. Because the house was so big and the grounds so spacious it was easy to sneak off and hide up in the attic or down in the cellar.

But the meadow was the best hiding place of all, for it covered a few acres of land and was filled with dense undergrowth and plentiful fruit trees. I would go there whenever the opportunity presented itself. One day a few of us were sent down to the meadow for a picnic, to get us out of the way of some important visitors. After a while, Audrey and I started fooling around and I climbed on to a chair to try to get a ride on the donkey. I managed to stay on it for a few seconds until he showed his displeasure by throwing me off, and I landed on the chair. Luckily I wasn't hurt but the chair was smashed to bits. To avoid getting a hiding we hid it deep in the bushes. Fortunately, no one ever found out.

Although conditions were stringent and every minute of our lives structured, there were compensations with all the training we received in learning how to keep clean and tidy. But it was the speech training and elocution which were particularly helpful for me with my bad lisp. The girls teased me mercilessly about the way I spoke. Whenever we had sausage and mash for dinner, someone would ask, 'Fatima, say "sausages" for us,' and keeping a straight face, I would oblige with my 'Thauthegeth'.

I got used to them making fun of me, for I was well-known for my own wise-cracks. Sometimes it felt good being the centre of attention even if it was for the wrong reasons. I was a chronic giggler and used to love a good laugh even though it was directed at me. 'I only talk funny,' I quipped, 'because I'm Turkish and I'm not really meant to be speaking English, so there!'

'No, you should be talking like a turkey, Gobble, Gobble,' they would gibe, as children do. Usually I took it all in my stride but if I was in the wrong sort of mood I got quite touchy about it, secretly loathing their taunts, but I would never let it show.

★

A big plaque hung on the dining room wall above the black, cast-iron coal range, and whenever I sat down at one of the tables my eyes would be drawn to it. It read, in beautiful black copperplate, 'God is the head of this House'. What a blatant lie, I used to think. Mother's name should be there. She's the real head of the house, and didn't we know it, though God did come a close second! We sang grace with our heads bowed and our eyes closed:

> Thank you for the world so sweet,
> Thank you for the food we eat.
> Thank you for the birds that sing,
> Thank you Lord for everything. Amen.

Our own version was:

> Thank you Lord for what we've had.
> A little more and we'll be glad.

Every child at Farm Hill was brought up on a strict diet of Anglican doctrine. On Sundays we were issued with Viyella smocked dresses to wear to church. The younger ones had to go twice, but as we got older we were marched off to three separate services and walked six miles to the Norman church at Bradwell. We were given a penny for the plate, but sometimes we slipped a coin from the plate into our pocket instead. It was our way of getting around the lack of pocket money. I used to find the sermons so boring that I often dropped off to sleep, but I did enjoy the hymn singing, and to this day I must know every verse of every hymn in the Ancient & Modern hymn book. A service was also held in our own chapel, which was also used for christenings. Every baby was christened and given a godmother, as is the usual custom, but I'm still piqued when I think how my godmother never did carry out her Christian duty by identifying herself to me – a shame really, as I could have used a surrogate mother.

The days of the week were run to a strict timetable. We were called at six o'clock and before breakfast we made our beds (always with hospital corners), and swept under them ready for inspection by Mother. No speck of dust eluded her and if it didn't pass we had to do it again before breakfast, which often made us late for school.

After school our time was never our own. A typical week ran thus: Monday, ballet/dancing, Tuesday, choir practice, Wednesday, piano lessons, Thursday, elocution/drama, and Friday, physical training/old-time dancing.

Our choir had become so well-drilled by Mrs Rowlands, the conductor, that we were famed throughout the local community for our spine-tingling part-singing. Sometimes I would be called on to play a nervous rendition of Beethoven's *Für Elise* in front of visitors, and I would solace myself with the thought that at least I was getting the chance to play the grand piano in the White Room, which was usually out of bounds. Music became my deep love, but I wanted it for my own private delight, not for public presentation. In retrospect, life at Farm Hill wasn't all that bad, and now I am enormously grateful for the opportunities we had to expand our cultural horizons even though it was the last thing we wanted to do at the end of a long, tiring day.

My musical aptitude was a source of curiosity to me as my willingness to spend long hours practising on any of the four pianos at our disposal set me apart from the other children, and is an indication to me that I was born with characteristics that I had surely inherited. I began to muse over how much my abilities could be attributed to exposure and training in the home and how much to heredity.

Why too was I fastidious about keeping my hands clean when other kids were happy to get gloriously grubby? And from whom had I inherited my long angular body, my double-jointed arms, shy traits and speech problems? I needed to understand something of my heritage to confirm and strengthen my image of myself but many years would pass before those questions could be answered.

★

Every June, on Founders Day, we were inundated with visitors who had to be entertained with singing and dancing. We dreaded this day because of all the extra duties we had to do to make the house spick and span. After scrubbing all the outside stone steps, my usual Saturday chore, I then had to help Audrey polish the brown linoleum floor of the chapel. To relieve the tedium we used to give each other rides on the 'bumper'. Sometimes Mother's voice could be heard calling for someone. She always knew the exact pitch required to ensure her voice was heard from every corner of the house. We feared being summoned in this way, as we knew it meant more work.

The red and blue Barnardo box was brought out every Founders Day and placed in a strategic position on a table in the hall. Entry was by donation for the general public to view, in the flesh, real, spirited orphans who had so much talent! What a shock our guests must have received when they saw how smartly dressed and well-spoken we were. From their surprised faces it was obvious they were most impressed with our accomplishments, though I'm positive we didn't fit the prescribed image of what orphanage inmates were supposed to look like. We felt like a group of trained monkeys, and if Mother was satisfied with our performance she would hand out sweets from a large glass jar. If she was unhappy she would fly into a rage and punishments were meted out to the culprits.

I was at an age when I was getting curious about my background, and it began to prey on my mind that I knew absolutely nothing about myself. We were never told anything and were too scared to ask, and I wondered why no one visited me like they did other children. I remember one balmy summer, when I was about twelve, I managed to sneak a look at my file. That day, unusually, both Mother and Miss Hoadley were out. Ann, another girl in my group, suggested we sneak into the office and take a look at our personal files. We thought they might be kept in the wooden cabinet next to the Secretary's desk. For weeks we had been looking for just such an opportunity and we couldn't believe our luck. Ann stood guard while I quickly found the files, and we skulked into the White Room where we could scrutinise them. Whenever we heard someone coming we slipped them quickly into the cutlery drawer and pretended to be laying the tables.

Eagerly I searched for details which would tell me something about myself. The date of my admission into Farm Hill at the age of nine months interested me. But where, I wondered, had I spent the first nine months of my life? With my mother perhaps? It was disappointing that there were no other facts about my origins provided, which would have given me something to latch on to. All I wanted to know was a little bit about my mother or father. But I would have to wait a few years before learning anything of my heritage.

I memorised the words in my file. It wasn't difficult as they were few and far between. Even now they are lodged in my memory: 'Fatima is affectionate, but has an inferiority complex. She is conscientious and inclined to be self-conscious. She has clean habits and her health is good, though she takes tonics for her anaemia. She is keen on school work and is improving with speech therapy.' As I read what someone, presumably Mother, had written about me, I thought, if she knows all these things about me then she must have been taking notice of me after all!

I had to look up the meanings of some of the words. The word 'anaemia' I knew all too well because of my occasional dizzy spells, but the one which really stumped me was the word 'affectionate'. I knew what it meant, of course, but for the life of me couldn't understand how anyone would know if I was affectionate or not as I had never been given the chance to show it.

Ann already had a sister, Margaret, living with her in the home, but she discovered that she had other relatives whom she had never met. As for me, I pondered over the dearth of information there seemed to be about my family. All I could do was to use my imagination to help keep alive my hopes and dreams of finding out about any kin who surely must be living somewhere on this earth.

When Mother returned an hour later, the files were safely back in their place. She caught us talking as well as loitering without intent, a mortal sin in her eyes, so a job was soon found for us. We were sent off with a pramload of old clothes and shoes to Monks farm. All the gifts-in-kind and cast-off clothes that landed on our doorstep were passed on to needier folk in the outlying farms and villages.

The sensation of being released into the open air, away from the constraints of the institution, was unbelievably sweet as we helped each other push the overloaded pram. We were happy to have the opportunity to mull over the information gleaned from our files, and we chattered away like a couple of birds set free.

Mother was always very strict about cleanliness and instilled in us such a sense of sartorial snobbery that we charity children turned up our noses at second-hand clothes. Wearing them would be quite beneath us.

We picked a bunch of hard-to-resist sweet peas and offered them to the farmer's wife. The woman seemed quite overcome with our generosity and invited us to see the new litter of piglets. As we wound our way home I remember feeling quite superior, giving some charity instead of receiving it. I held my nose in the air for a long time after.

★

As summer holidays approached with the prospect looming of being sent to an outside family, I became extremely anxious. Some children went to stay with relatives, others to favourite 'aunties', but it seemed to me that I was sent to a different family each year. On the whole I enjoyed staying with an 'outside' family, once I got used to the different environment, but I might have liked it better had there been other children for company. There was only one family that I really enjoyed going to, a dentist with his wife and six children, who were all very uninhibited and a bit eccentric.

Usually though, I went to childless couples, who had probably been persuaded to have me because Mother didn't know what else to do with me. After trying me with up to ten different families, most of which I rarely returned to, the offers from Mother's long list of volunteers were fast running out.

My temporary residence with these 'aunties' and 'uncles' never developed into any close or long-term relationships. Had that happened it might have stemmed the tide of inadequacy which was gradually washing over me. A complaint was made once about my behaviour when one 'aunty' grumbled to Mother that she 'couldn't get a word out of me'. I know I was a difficult child to talk to, for I was unpractised in the art of conversation with adults and had no idea what to talk about. But most, I felt the hurt of not being wanted by anybody on a more permanent basis.

Sometimes, especially as I grew older, I was used as an unpaid servant to help with the housework and run messages. I well remember when I was about twelve being left in the house all day and given shopping to do while one 'aunty' went to work. When she returned I said something I shouldn't have and was immediately sent back to Farm Hill in disgrace for being insubordinate. The real reason was that I was bored and missed my friends, but I was never allowed to give my side of the story. My punishment was to do piles of ironing which took all day, but I didn't mind for even though Farm Hill was still half empty at least it was my home.

The two 'aunties' whom I enjoyed staying with the most were Aunty Molly and Aunty Ivy. They lived together in Finchley, north London. Three or four of us children of varying ages would be put on the London-bound train at Kelvedon Station, and The Holly & The Ivy, as we nicknamed them, would be waiting by the barrier at Liverpool Street Station, wearing their familiar church-going hats.

The carpeted rooms and comfortable chairs in their suburban house were in stark contrast to the hard floors and wooden chairs we were used to and it always took a few days to adjust to the relatively cramped, homely environment.

Aunty Molly had enormous, elephantine legs and when she flopped with supreme effort into the groaning armchair, she spread them, showing us all her long, white bloomers. Eating was, for her, one of life's pleasures, and during our daily outings we would end up at a tea shop where it was such a treat to be able to choose our own cream cakes.

When Aunty Molly laughed her whole body vibrated in a rippling effect as she held both sides of her torso, presumably to stop them from splitting. Rocking backwards and forwards, her face turned into a beetroot while we watched and waited, fascinated, for her to catch her breath. She then dabbed her eyes and took some deep breaths, thoroughly worn out by the effort. Being more used to guarded giggles in the home it made a nice change to let yourself go and belly-laugh openly and wholeheartedly, knowing that you were expected to enjoy yourself.

The two of them together were a comedy duo as they bounced jokes off each other. Each night they gave us the dreaded slobbery kiss, which made me squirm with embarrassment. The two younger children 'topped and tailed' while I slept in my own bed in the corner of their big bedroom with a good view of the pair of them sharing a double bed. The word 'lesbian' was not commonly used then, but when I think of them now, I suppose it would be appropriate. If the Barnardo hierarchy had known about them I'm sure we would never have been allowed to stay there. It was difficult trying to sleep while Aunty Molly crunched her way through a whole packet of ginger biscuits. What a sight she was, propped up in bed, dunking her biscuits into Ovaltine, her greying hair tucked into a hairnet. With her glasses halfway down her nose, she was quite oblivious to the world as she did the newspaper crossword.

My night's sleep was again disturbed when Aunty Molly's loud snorts whistled intermittently through the night, building up to a crescendo of double forte and eventually even waking her! The next minute she heaved herself over the side of the bed, retrieved the large chamber pot from under the bed, and with an almighty effort managed to cover it. I lay quietly observing her, wondering how on earth Aunty Ivy could sleep through the cascading water streaming into what must surely by now be an overflowing chamber pot.

Every Sunday we used to trudge along to The Holly & The Ivy's church in Finchley. They believed wholly in God but never pushed their personal beliefs down our throats.

Along with boxes of chocolates in their secret cupboard, they stocked up on presents to give to the children they chose to have for Christmas, and luckily sometimes I was one of them. I often wished I could have them to myself, as my own special aunties, but they must have taken in every child from Farm Hill over a thirty year period. Even when Aunty Ivy died from cancer in 1970, well after I had left the homes, Aunty Molly continued having children for

holidays. My contact with her persisted when I left
Barnardo's and she took me in for temporary periods
whenever I needed somewhere to rest my head.

Aunty Molly died in June 1993, aged eighty-seven. She
left legacies to fifty of her friends, evidence of the way she
dispersed her affections to as many people as possible
during her lifetime. I was privileged to be one of the
beneficiaries to whom she gave half a per cent of her estate.
I owe her a deep gratitude for the support she gave me
when I was alone. She taught me the most important thing
in this world – to laugh at life, but more especially, to laugh
at myself.

★

I was doing quite well at the local Secondary Modern
School in Braintree, and after two years I made a few
friends. Many of my classmates travelled on the bus with us
during the ten mile journey, and I noticed that they always
carried money around with them. We began to resent the
fact that we did not get any pocket money ourselves. Now
and again we skipped school dinners so we could use our
dinner money to buy sweets in the village shop, but one day
Mother found out and had us lined up in the chapel to
receive the venom of her fury. We were all sent to bed for
the rest of the day as punishment, but as I tired easily I
welcomed the opportunity to have a few more hours' sleep.
Not long after, we did get about two shillings a week but it
was never on a regular basis.

Audrey bought some cigarettes one day and
unfortunately for us, someone in the village saw us both
having a puff and reported it to Mother. Poor Audrey, who
seemed to have the knack of drawing attention to herself,
had to smoke the rest of the packet until she was sick,
whereas I managed to get off with no punishment.

I must have been about thirteen years old when I was
called in to Mother's office one crisp morning. Geraldine
had also been summoned. Without giving us any
forewarning she came straight to the point.

'Now I want you to know that you two girls have been
chosen to attend a newly opened Barnardo boarding school
and you'll be leaving Farm Hill in the New Year.'

Gerry and I looked at each other in amazement, our
faces suddenly blanched. I didn't take in anything else that
was said for by now I was in a daze. We were not given the
opportunity to discuss the matter, and in any case, Gerry
and I were too afraid of Mother to argue the point. Making
a supreme effort to arrange my face in an expression of
indifference, I knew that the alarm I felt at that moment
showed only too well.

I spent the next few days in a vacuum of shock as the
news sunk in that I would lose all my friends and live in a
new environment amongst total strangers.

When Audrey got to hear the bad news she suggested I
run away with her, but I was far too scared of the
consequences to consider it seriously. After all, Farm Hill
was the only home I knew. Where else could I possibly go?

Christmas that year was memorable for my unhappy
feelings about my imminent uprooting, and tears dampened
my pillow every night. Each room was festooned with
decorations we had all put up days before, and the chapel
was filled with streamers and balloons ready for the
traditional New Year's Eve fancy-dress party.

On the night of the party Mother was unusually jovial.
She shocked us all by sauntering down the oak staircase
wearing a gym slip and long pigtails, and sucking a huge
lollipop. She let her hair down, literally, that night. I could
merely stand and watch in amazement as everyone laughed
aloud at Mother's outlandish, uncharacteristic behaviour. It
seemed as if I was the only one not amused. I've always

been a keen observer of human behaviour, and after spending the entire evening becoming gloomily critical of Mother's aberrant conduct, it suddenly dawned on me how much I loathed her for the mother-figure which she was supposed to represent but did not. I saw her then in all her human frailties and scarcely knew how to contain my bitter feelings towards her. My mind wanted to scream out: 'I hate you for what you're doing to my life,' but the words stuck to the roof of my mouth, as they did so often when I was unable to express my real feelings.

To console myself during my last remaining days at the home I had lived in for almost thirteen years, I hammered out as many melodies as I knew on the piano and found it a great release for my pent-up emotions. I tried to tell myself that going from one Barnardo institution to another should not on the surface have seemed such a great change, and my spirits were somewhat buoyed when I knew I would be returning for the Easter break.

On the eve of my departure I kept remembering that by the next day I would no longer be living at Farm Hill. The memory remains for me a surreal blur of anguish as I walked from room to room saying sad farewells to my close comrades. I realised with a rush that never in my life before had I felt so wretched. The ache I carried was partly from the thought of being wrenched away from my friends and the comfortable familiarity of my home, and partly from my fear of the future. It seemed to me that there was no one who truly cared about my welfare.

It was not in my nature to be in a permanent state of melancholy, and once I became resigned to my fate, which I knew there was no way of escaping, I tried valiantly to face the future in a positive frame of mind.

Chapter Two

Princess Margaret School

Could I ever forget that year of 1953, the year of Queen Elizabeth's coronation? I was facing the daunting prospect of living in a new home and starting a new school, all on the same day.

The occasion of that first day at Princess Margaret Boarding School imprints itself firmly in my memory as one both momentous and terrifying. At the age of thirteen I was buffeted by forces beyond my control, and continued to be helpless in playing any part in the destiny of my life. Whichever direction it would take was now more or less in the hands of a few nameless people who made up the management of Dr Barnardo's Headquarters in Stepney, London.

Geraldine and I arrived at the Garden City, Woodford Bridge, Essex, on the outskirts of north-east London, on a blustery January day. The Princess Margaret School, named after the Patron of Dr Barnardo's homes at that time, was opened two years earlier as an experiment to help girls of my age sit the General Certificate of Education, the supposed passport to better career options.

There were over twenty cottages in the thirty-acre estate of the Garden City, which was self-sufficient with its own church, hospital, swimming pool and gymnasium. The buildings at the southern end of the complex were used entirely for the eighty pupils and staff of the school. They consisted of a cluster of four large Victorian 'cottages' and an ivy-covered school house.

It is easy for me to remember, even at this distance, walking through the front door of a pale stone building called Wakefield House, which was to be my home for the next three years. I put down my blue cardboard suitcase, filled with my few worldly possessions, and closed the door. I was introduced to the housematron, Miss Dovey, a tall, slightly stooped woman with twinkling grey eyes and an encouraging smile. The soft undertone in her voice as she welcomed me to Wakefield House put me immediately at ease.

Geraldine was billeted next door in Corby House, and from then on we were cut off from each other as we were also streamed in different classes.

My first few days at PMS, as we were soon calling it, were spent getting to know the twenty other new girls who had arrived from other Barnardo homes. Some girls, it seemed, were only too happy to leave their previous situations while others, myself included, could not understand, nor sought to ask, why we were the chosen few. None of us had any choice as to whether or not we wanted to come to this experimental boarding school.

Soon we were all fitted out with grey dresses, grey blazers, grey sports knickers and grey socks. The greyness seemed to permeate everything in those first unsettling days.

The school's special character as an alternative secondary school allowed small classes, so I could no longer merge unnoticed into the background, but my school work prospered with the individual attention I was now receiving. The lopsided curriculum, with its emphasis on English, Scripture, cookery and music, with plenty of team sports, fitted in nicely with my own interests.

Without much difficulty I got into the school netball and hockey teams. I loved the strenuous activity in the keen air and looked forward to the Saturday morning games against other schools in the area, our only real contact with people from the community outside.

Although we lived a cloistered lifestyle and had little contact with the outside community, I enjoyed the familiar, ordered routine of boarding school life and revelled in the comparative freedom at Wakefield House, where little time was spent on housework. I began to look back over my years at Farm Hill and the longer I distanced myself from the regimented administration and the manipulating control of Mother, the more I appreciated my present abode. Invitations were continually flooding in from various charity organisations to take us to circuses, orchestral concerts and the Royal Command Performance in London.

The closeness of our living conditions made it easy to develop 'crushes' on each other, or on some poor unsuspecting teacher. By the middle of the term, for the first time in my life, I became strongly attached emotionally to an adult person. Miss Dovey, our housematron, was the object of my affection because she showed me extra kindnesses that no other person had ever done, and I slowly began responding to the affection she showed towards me in particular.

The other girls swiftly got over their crushes, but it took me somewhat longer. I was completely incapable of displaying any overt signs of affection. Fortunately, Miss Dovey understood my reserve, leaving little notes around bearing endearing words unheard of in my vocabulary, such as 'poppet' and 'sweetie'. It does seem odd when I think of it now, but although we tacitly understood our fondness for each other, we rarely conversed directly.

By the time summer turned into winter I had well and truly settled at PMS and made new friends. I formed another positive relationship with a staff member. She was Miss Corby, the plump, white-haired teacher of Scripture and music. Although she wore a fixed smile on her face and her mannerisms seemed to convey a sense of pious resignation, no doubt as a result of doing missionary work in Africa, I developed a good rapport with her during my piano lessons. With religious zeal she awakened my innate feelings for music and opened up a whole new world in the realms of rhythm and expression. Her enthusiasm was so infectious that my lessons with her were pure joy. With every ounce of energy I threw myself into a rigorous practice routine of scales, exercises and pieces, with the consequence that my piano playing improved dramatically.

It was through our mutual love of music that I made friends with Jean Ware, who slept beside me in the dormitory and sat next to me in class. I admired Jean's slender figure, compared to my burgeoning one, her russet, wavy hair and pearly white teeth, and her beautiful violin playing. We played duets in the common room, and even the other more hard-nosed girls seemed to enjoy listening to our 'Ave Maria'.

When we returned from our summer holidays that first year I related to Jean how unhappy mine had been as I was only at Farm Hill, one week before Mother sent me off to a new 'aunty' and 'uncle' in Norfolk. I listened incredulously to Jean's account of her marvellous holiday spent at her home, 'Hatherley' in Cheltenham, and how she adored her matron. It made me realise that the regime was far stricter at Farm Hill than it was at other homes, and from then on a mountain of resentment began to build up inside me. How I wished I could stand up to authority and announce that I didn't want to return to Farm Hill. But where could I go?

I'm certain now that having my movements restricted and living with a whole gamut of petty rules hindered my ability to stand up for myself, which I had neither the capacity nor the courage to do. But I made a private decision to call Mother 'Matron', from now on, or the more formal 'Mother Simcox'. The word 'Mother' had too many unsettling connotations for me at that point in my life.

My first year at PMS was notable for the one week in which we had the chance to be film stars. We were in a classroom scene at Pinewood Studios, with Lana Turner as our teacher. Victor Mature and Clark Gable were the two male stars, whose autographs I still have and treasure.

We had to learn the German words to Schubert's Rose Among the Heather, and as we were to be portrayed as Dutch school children in a wartime film called *Betrayed*, we also sang the Dutch national anthem. Some of us wore brightly coloured pinafores over the top of our grey uniforms, and in the middle of one scene I was asked to play a dummy piano. At the end of our exciting debuts as actors we were presented with two huge cakes and had our photos taken with Lana Turner. I don't know to this day whether or not our scenes were ever used, but I shall never forget how we rubbed shoulders with the rich and famous.

The year I turned fourteen I caught a strong dose of religious fever. Etched with minute precision in my memory is the day Miss Prior, the religious headmistress, took some of us in two coaches to the Haringey Arena to hear Billy Graham, the American Evangelist. My fervent love of choral singing, which remains with me to this day, revealed a sensitive spot in my nature, as with hundreds of others I strode to the front, carried away on the tide of emotion, and gave my life to Jesus.

Billy Graham's mesmerising message somehow convinced me that there was someone who really did care about me. It is obvious to me now that the inspirational mass singing, coupled with the magnetic power of Billy Graham's supplications, propelled me forward in the spiritual intensity of the moment. I was incapable of separating the stirring music from the religious message. The idea that someone loved me was overwhelming in its appeal. I came away from the meeting thinking that at least I could talk to God about my fears and insecurities, which I was unable to communicate to any human.

While still coping with the challenges of my recent conversion, another traumatic event was about to take place in my life. One Saturday, in pain, I hobbled up to the outpatients' department at the Garden City's hospital, where I was about to have a verruca removed from my heel. When the sister in charge discovered my name, she turned to take another look at me, and said, 'Well I'm blessed. What a coincidence that we should meet again! I was the nurse responsible for taking you by train to Farm Hill when you were a few months old. I remember because of your Turkish name.'

She couldn't take her eyes off me, and we chatted away like old friends. I asked her if she could tell me anything about myself, as I knew nothing, and although she was unable to help me, she suggested I write a letter to Barnardo headquarters asking for information.

A few days later, Jean helped me to compose a letter to Barnardo's, which I then secretly posted, as all our letters were monitored, and I was worried that it might not pass the scrutiny of Miss Prior.

All I knew about myself at the age of fourteen was what I had read in my file two years earlier. I was now at an age when I needed to know something of my own heritage. Many weeks passed before Miss Prior called me into her office and handed me a letter. When I read it, it was to have a profound and unsettling effect on me. That I still have the letter now, forty years later, is evidence of its extreme impact on my life. It read:

I should like to tell you very much about your relations but there is very little that can be told, and I am afraid there is no one with whom we can put you in touch. Your father was a British soldier who served abroad, and your mother was a refugee from Turkey. She was unable to keep you, as she lost sight of your father. We were asked if you could join our homes and then I understand your mother returned to Turkey.

You therefore have both British and Turkish blood in your veins. Turkey is a wonderful country and you can be proud of this, but as far as actual relations are concerned, you will have to let Barnardo's act as your parents and the many friends you make as your brothers and sisters. One day we hope you will have a very happy home of your own.

I was only able to absorb the words 'There is no one with whom we can put you in touch,' written so succinctly.

I read it over and over again, trying to understand the implications of its contents. At last I had received the indisputable confirmation, printed in black and white, that I did have a real mother. And, more importantly, that she might still be alive. Because my father had apparently died at Dunkirk, I put him out of my mind altogether, and focused all my attention on my mother.

The letter raised more questions than it answered. At least I now knew I hadn't been found under a gooseberry bush or in a carrier bag at a railway station. What did they mean, though, that 'my mother had lost sight of my father'? Whereabouts in Turkey was my mother living? Would I ever be able to find her? Turkey seemed so far away. Was it really possible that she had dumped and then deserted me? I refused to believe it.

I cried for days after reading that letter, and wove my own web of misery just imagining what my future must now hold. The prospect of being completely alone did not appeal, and I went around in a stupefied state of disbelief. I was always a quiet girl and I nursed my anguished emotions in such a way that no one knew how I really felt.

I remained in a state of suspended animation, feeling neither hunger nor thirst. I really found it hard keeping my mind on my school work. Miss Dovey called me into her room when she noticed I was even more quiet than usual. She gently explained that, although it appeared on the surface that I had no family to call my own, it was quite likely that my mother was alive and well somewhere in Turkey. There was a good chance that we could find each other. It was the first real conversation the two of us had had and I drew much comfort from her encouraging words.

Now that I had positive proof that I had a mother, I spent the rest of my school days conjuring up mental images of how she might look. So much did I want to see her that I lived in a dream world all of my own. Unrest was deep within me, and never for long was the thought of my mother out of my mind. I felt that I only had to see her and she would sweep me up in her arms and take me into her world.

The whole of my last term at PMS had the mechanical vagueness of a bad dream. Miss Dovey became ill with cancer, forcing her to leave the school. I was inconsolable, and lacked the motivation to study for the important end of year exams. It was inevitable that I should fail four of the School Certificate exams I sat, although I did manage to scrape through in two – English and Religious Knowledge. Additionally, I was the first girl in the school to pass the Royal School of Music Grade Five piano examination.

The authorities at the school made plans for me to attend a secretarial course at Pitman's College, and live in a Barnardo Hostel for Girls. The social worker took great pains to explain that 'shorthand typists can earn a living anywhere' so, as was my habit, I complied meekly.

At the moment of parting from Jean and all my classmates I broke down in tears. Everyone in the school seemed to be crying. We signed each other's autograph books and got our favourite teachers to scribble a verse in them.

I memorised the inspiring poem which Miss Dovey wrote in my autograph book before she left so prematurely. It comes back to me every now and then whenever I think about her ready smile and her warm, wise words. I still quote it whenever I find myself struggling with self-pity. It goes:

Now listen my friend I'll admit right away
That things aren't always all they should be.
There's much that is wrong, there's hardship and
   pain
As the simplest among us can see.
But there's kindness and courage,
There's love and there's hope.
There is humour in every long day.
There's something – believe it – for which to thank
   God
Every mile of life's shadowed highway.

★

My first week at Ellesmere, the Barnardo Hostel for Girls, was less painful than I had expected for I shared my shyness with the other girls, all of us apprehensive and anxious to learn what life was like in the 'real world'.

Ellesmere resembled a large suburban house in a leafy residential street, and was as close to living in an authentic home as I had ever experienced. What a relief it was to walk in and out of the front door just like a local, with not a Barnardo's sign up anywhere! The thought occurred to me that as I grew taller my place of abode was getting decidedly smaller.

I was not fluent in conversation and only my few close friends were privy to my occasional outbursts of humour. I was still ashamed of my Turkish name, as well as my eleven stone frame, and was incapable of engaging in any small talk with an adult. The one intimate friend that I made at Ellesmere was Doreen, an attractive, intelligent girl from another Barnardo home. The two of us attended Pitman's College, walked together to the intersection of the Woodford Road and caught the red double-decker bus to Forest Gate.

There were few better places than Pitman's College where one could learn shorthand and typing, book-keeping and other business-related subjects. The determination to work hard and pass all my Pitman's exams would, I hope, compensate for my relative failure in the School Certificate exams.

At the college, a grey, cheerless building, I learned the mysteries of short-forms and grammalogues so thoroughly that I can still think in shorthand now. In every test Doreen and I topped the class. I remember the teacher beaming at us, saying, 'You two Dr Barnardo lasses have taken to shorthand like a cat takes to milk.' We did not appreciate the accolades, and were suffused with blushes of embarrassment since everyone else in the class now knew we were from the homes. Until then we had managed to delude our classmates into thinking we were just a couple of average adolescents living in a normal family environment in Woodford. To protect myself from questions about my background, I learned to swiftly change the subject, or I fabricated a family on the spot, which was not a good idea as I usually ended up tripping over myself with more lies. I was unhappily aware that people did consider me strange because of my foreign name, and I did everything possible to prevent them learning about my Barnardo background by adopting an air of secret intrigue.

In later months I changed my name to Tina. I had often been called 'Tima', short for Fatima, and most people thought I meant 'Tina', so it was relatively easy to start calling myself that, which I've been known as ever since.

We were given five shillings allowance each week, which had to pay for our fares, clothes, shoes and lunches. It doesn't sound like very much now but at the time it was more than adequate. Doreen and I saved money at lunch time by eating only a buttered bread roll and tomato soup at Lyons Cornerhouse, as we knew we could have a good feed back at Ellesmere.

The superintendent, Mrs Weaver, was a charming woman, with the art of gentle persuasion, which she used to full effect when cajoling me to play the piano for the Sunday School services at the local Evangelical church. After years of being given commands and obeying them, I reluctantly agreed.

The three staff members at Ellesmere all had strict evangelical backgrounds and visits to the cinema were frowned on as being ungodly. We were encouraged to attend church services, though many of the girls, with more temerity than I, refused to go. Typically for me, it was the joyous Gospel singing accompanied by the gripping cadences of the church organ which held me captive every Sunday.

At the end of year prize-giving, when I was due to receive my certificates for the shorthand and typing exams, I was laid low with a severe strain of Asian 'flu, which spread over the whole of Britain in 1957. Doreen accepted the certificates on my behalf. No one was allowed to visit me in my room, where I was isolated from the rest of the girls; amazingly, I was the only one who had caught the highly infectious virus. For two weeks I could barely talk and every limb in my body ached. By the time I eventually managed to walk I had lost half a stone in weight… and my college days were over.

The day came for me to be formally 'farewelled' from Barnardo's. Mrs Weaver took a group of us up to Stepney headquarters in London, where I was presented with a Bible and a shortened birth certificate, with neither my mother's nor my father's name printed on it. After a short service in the chapel I had my photograph taken. The after-care worker deftly stalled any questions I felt brave enough to ask and no more explanations were offered other than what was written in the letter Barnardo's sent to me at The Princess Margaret School.

I left the care of Dr Barnardo's homes with a new outfit and an air of anticipation. Although I had real fears for what the future might hold, I felt a sense of freedom; of being released from a life of incarceration. There would be no more petty rules and regulations which had dictated my life from the time I got up till the time I went to bed; no more having to do as I was told, or feeling compelled to attend church services. I was like a prisoner set free, and I looked forward with high expectations to a new life on the outside.

Chapter Three
World Outside

At the end of the year the great day arrived when I began my first terrifying progression towards adulthood. After being cocooned in institutionalised care for the whole of my childhood, securely sheltered under the protective umbrella of the Barnardo's organisation, I was suddenly thrust into the big, wide world to start earning my own living. The thought of being responsible for my own actions and having to assert myself, without being ordered about by anyone both thrilled and frightened me.

A woman from Barnardo's After-Care accompanied me, a gauche and spotty seventeen year old, to the centre of the city of London. I went for my first interview as a junior typist with Ellerman Shipping Lines, and much to my surprise, got the job.

Overwhelmed as I was by my sudden propulsion into a world where I was no longer a child, it took me a long time to settle into my new job, knowing I was now in charge of my own life. My inferiority complex restricted my ability to make friends easily, and at morning and afternoon tea I sat silently, forever fearful someone might ask embarrassing personal questions. However, the company I worked for transported dried fruits from Turkey, and the longer I was there the more it fed my unabated passion for anything remotely connected with my mother. I flung myself heart and soul into the job. I inwardly resolved to learn everything I could about my mother's country, and although my everyday working knowledge was limited to the various brands of figs and apricots and the names of Turkish ports, nevertheless it kept my dreams at the forefront of my mind.

One day I stepped into a phone box, picked up the phone and asked the operator how much it would cost to telephone Turkey. She thought I meant Torquay, a coastal resort in Devon, south-west England. Of course, I knew no one in Turkey to telephone, but that innocent act demonstrates my obsession with the country. My mind was drenched with impressions of my mother and, quite simply, Turkey held a magnetic allure for me because of its links with her.

Although everyone now knew me as Tina, my first and second birth names, Fatima and Suleyman, were always leaping up at me whenever I read books on the subject of Turkey, which I got out of the local library. I discovered that my surname was the same as the famous sixteenth-century sultan, Suleyman the Magnificent, and I also found out that 'Fatima' was the daughter of the prophet Mohammed by his first wife, and was given the same high place of honour in heaven as the Virgin Mary in Roman Catholicism. Knowing this somehow made me feel important, and my continuing fantasies about my mother were now remodelled on someone of a more elevated status. I announced to myself, and to the few friends who were privy to my confidences, that I could well be the daughter of a princess, or whatever the Moslem equivalent was!

Although I did my best not to broadcast the fact that I was an orphan, people were naturally curious and sympathetic when they did manage to wheedle out of me that I knew of no relatives whatsoever. I'm convinced they thought me quite an oddity, but the last thing I wanted was their pity. Not having parents was simply one of the hazards of life which, outwardly at any rate, I accepted with cheerful equanimity, though I was never able to fully exploit my position because I was considered too big and healthy to be a *real* orphan!

Although I was agonisingly reserved, those who persisted in trying to get to know me better would see glimpses of my dry wit and sense of humour. They would also observe my relatively serious outlook on life. If any rude jokes were being tossed about, I was the only one who kept a straight face, which had more to do with not getting the joke than being prim and proper.

By now I was sharing a flat with Doreen, my friend from Ellesmere who, like me, continued going to the occasional church service, but our partnership was not a success. Instead of feeling drunk with the sense of freedom and enjoying our new-found independence, we spent our days trying to make ends meet. On a weekly wage of nine pounds, we each had to pay three pounds per week for two small rooms, and anything left over went towards food, fares and recreation.

Every Saturday morning we cleaned the small flat and did the shopping together. We bought food such as sausages and fish fingers because they were easy to cook in the frying pan, and we became dab hands with the tin opener. Neither of us liked cooking, and my own culinary skills were limited to what I had learned in cookery classes at school, such as cheese straws and stewed apples. I doubt whether anyone could inflict more harm on a simple sausage or an inoffensive lamb chop than myself. Anything that could be eaten on toast was our favourite snack; the cheaper and quicker the better. Barnardo's had not prepared us for the realities of everyday living, and we were hopelessly ill-equipped to look after ourselves properly. It would have been easy to make a career on the musical stage, with all the

music and dancing I learned during my childhood, but as
for boiling an egg…!

It didn't take long for tempers to fray with the living
conditions such as they were, and the crisis point came
when we saw a mouse. It ran across the kitchen floor
prompting me to leap onto a chair, broomstick in hand.
Quite what I expected to do with it I don't recall, but when
we saw lots of mice droppings in the fridge of all places, we
were loathe to eat anything. That incident marked the end
of our flatting days together and we made the decision to go
our separate ways. We had been together for less than six
months.

Since receiving that unforgettable letter from Barnardo's,
I knew that I would have to walk through life alone and
make my own decisions, but it was during this unsettling
period in my life that it was really put to the test. I
remember the stranded feeling of not knowing what to do
or where to go. I had no particular friend to whom I could
turn for advice or in whom I could confide. Life so far had
trained me to adopt a passive, obedient posture, allowing
others to make my decisions for me. Now the grim reality
of resolving my problems was entirely in my own hands. It
was up to me. In some ways it felt good to be in charge of
my own destiny.

The first giant step I took for myself was to make a
phone call to the Turkish Embassy. I was seized with the
crazy notion of finding some sort of office work there. I was
referred to Mr Halefoglu, the assistant to the ambassador,
and when I told him of my desire to go to Turkey he totally
floored me by offering me a job in his own house as a live-
in nanny for his two children. I knew nothing about
children but my longing for things Turkish made me
desperate enough to give it a go, especially as
accommodation was included. When he dangled the carrot

of going with the family to Turkey at the end of the year before me, I knew what my answer would be.

I said farewells to the few friends I had made during my twelve months' work at the shipping company, and although apprehensive about the future, I felt distinctly relieved as I walked away from the familiar territory of the Woodford suburb.

Within the week I found myself travelling with my faithful blue suitcase to Park Mansions, Knightsbridge – the other side of London. Arriving at the entrance hall of the block of luxurious flats on the High Street near Harrods, my mind swarmed with foreboding images of unmanageable children, as I had read stories about spoilt children of rich folk. My experience had been limited only to living with children, not looking after them.

The lift went up to the third floor and I nervously pressed the button. While waiting for the door to open I had a bad case of butterflies in my tummy, wondering what this Turkish family would be like, for I had never before set eyes on anyone who was Turkish. I was led inside by the maid and ushered to a chair in the beautifully furnished living room. I sat, listening to Mr and Mrs Halefoglu explain my duties to me, in a sort of trance. They were a strikingly good-looking couple, dignified in their speech and mannerisms, and I couldn't help feeling overawed by them. I was introduced to the children, a boy of five and a girl of seven whose names I've forgotten, and when they refused to walk towards me and shake my hand I knew things would not be easy.

In spite of my efforts, the boy stubbornly refused to have anything to do with me, and it was a constant worry to me when he would not hold my hand crossing the busy intersection leading into Hyde Park. When I tried to teach him some English words he remained persistently uncooperative. I had neither the skill nor the experience to handle such a precocious child, so I more or less gave up on him and concentrated on the more malleable girl. She was prepared to teach me a few Turkish words while I spoke to her slowly in English.

The other members of staff, the cook and the maid, could only say, 'Hello' and 'Goodbye', so my conversation with them was non-existent. When I returned to the apartment after walking the children to school, I made their beds and did some ironing. I never felt comfortable living in someone else's home. I rarely saw the parents, and my lack of communication with anyone frustrated and saddened me. In spite of living close to the busy streets and bright lights of Knightsbridge, the apartment was like a prison, enclosing me within its walls. I felt increasingly alienated and came to dread the thought of facing another day.

The turning point came one afternoon when Mr Halefoglu discovered his son all alone in the lift.

'You should be watching him,' he yelled at me, his face black with fury.

I ran to my room, flung myself on the bed and soaked my pillow with tears. Nothing was working out. My dream to visit Turkey was shattered after less than three months. I accepted that I had made the wrong decision. It was a major setback and I felt terribly let down, but it was obvious to me that I was well out of my depth. During a sleepless night I brooded over my options, and when morning came I handed in my notice. The price of a free ticket – even to Turkey – just wasn't worth it.

★

Where to next? That evening my mind was in a turmoil. I had neither a job nor accommodation. I was rudderless in a vast ocean, and knew I would have to either sink or swim.

I chose to swim, but no immediate ideas came to mind as to where I would swim, so I decided to phone Mrs Weaver and ask if she could put me up at Ellesmere Hostel until I could find somewhere to live. I needed to summon up all my courage to make the request, for officially I was no longer a Barnardo resident and was meant to be making my own way in life. I felt I was losing face in a way, but didn't know who else to turn to.

It was good to be back in Woodford, amongst friends. Mrs Weaver persuaded me to go to the Wednesday night youth club at the Evangelical church where I was re-united with Doreen. She was now happily flatting on her own.

Meanwhile, I travelled into the centre of London, registered with an employment agency, and quickly found a job in a small, friendly solicitor's office in Bedford Row, Holborn. Luckily for me, the working conditions were so conducive that I ended up working there as a shorthand typist for nearly three years.

Mrs Weaver helped me look for new lodgings, and by the end of the month I was living in a large room above a row of shops in George Lane, South Woodford, within walking distance of Ellesmere and the church. Mrs Collinson, the convivial landlady, was a thirty-five year old divorcée with a cherub-faced four year old daughter, Janet. She had decided to let out the upstairs bedroom to help pay the rent.

My room was spacious and comfortably furnished. The sweeping view from the window was the chief attraction, as I could look out over the top of busy George Lane as it wound its way down to the underground station. I sat and watched the comings and goings of people as they did their shopping. Right across the road stood the huge Odeon cinema where, over a period of two years, I saw virtually every film that was on offer.

Self-catering proved a formidable chore using the tiny stove in the corner of my room, and I usually ate improvised snacks, supplemented every now and then by the landlady's rabbit stew, or other leftovers which she offered me. I truly appreciated her acts of kindness, but unfortunately I was never able to convey my thanks in the accepted manner. I would coyly look away and mumble something incoherently, feeling immensely grateful but never knowing how to show my appreciation.

My general lack of communication was abysmal. Mrs Collinson would say, 'I wish you would call me Mary,' but I could not. In fact, I didn't give her any name at all. I just avoided having to speak to her. It was easier for me to talk to her small daughter, who used to climb the stairs to come and show me the new toys that her estranged father brought on his monthly visits. Mrs Collinson did her best to involve me in her life, and she often invited me to come downstairs for tea. At first I did everything possible not to go, my shyness forcing me to retreat to the sanctity of my room, where I could lie on my bed and listen to music or a play. Many months passed before I could get into the emotional gear of trust and confidence, when I allowed myself to be touched by Mrs Collinson's open arms of friendship.

Mrs Collinson's parents invited me for Christmas dinner, my first celebration of Christmas with a proper family. They did their best to make me welcome.

That evening, Mrs Collinson gave me a small plant for my room. It was the only present I had that Christmas from anyone. I watched with envy while Janet unwrapped her presents from countless relatives. It was good of them to try and embrace me into the folds of their family, but I kept wishing I had my own family who would want to shower presents upon me. My thoughts inevitably turned back to the riotous Christmases we had at Farm Hill, the rare fun times when we all helped to put up the decorations, sang lovely carols and played party games.

I really missed the camaraderie of my Barnardo friends, and I wondered where they all were now. I felt a strong wish to live as a member of a real family so I could have friends around me all the time to talk to and share confidences with.

A wireless was the first thing I saved up to buy for myself. It was my lifeline to humanity, and I learned a lot about life listening to it. As I sat on my bed and listened to beautiful music, I would be transported. I missed not having a piano to play because the impulse to make music remained as strong as ever. To satisfy my hunger for music, I joined a sixty-strong Youth for Christ choir, even though by now I was gradually shaking off the shackles of the Church's influence on my life. I didn't need God any more. What had He done for me anyway? But the music I did need, so it mattered not that we sang sacred anthems or uttered a prayer at the end of each rehearsal, because the singing was everything. Rain, hail or snow didn't stop me from walking the two miles to rehearsals. My disappointment knew no bounds when, one wintry evening, I trudged through thick snow to a rehearsal only to find the doors locked.

It was through the choir that I met Bernard, my first boyfriend. He offered me a lift home one night in his black Austin Seven. We started going out together then. I remember how I got a fit of the giggles in the middle of my first awkward kiss when his bristly moustache tickled me.

I was entering into uncharted territory when it came to boys, having had no experience of them, and I was suitably flattered when Bernard asked me out. Apart from anything else, it had the benefit of saving money on shoe leather. I was happy to let Bernard take me rowing on the lake or for rides into the country, but after six months of a steady friendship it was time to call it quits. Before long I found myself travelling the solo road again, but I had few regrets. I was earning enough money by now to spend most of it on nice clothes, something I'd never had before. Other interests started to take over and I went to evening classes to learn French. I bought myself a second-hand bicycle, complete with three-speed gears and dropped handlebars. It was my first major purchase; something I had always wanted. Doreen and I loved nothing better than to pedal for miles and miles every weekend through the flat country lanes of Essex.

Mrs Collinson, whom at last I was able to call 'Mary', started inviting me to join her and Janet on their regular Sunday walks through Epping Forest, to walk their dog, Rusty. After living with them for nearly two years we were becoming good friends and we went to health and beauty classes together. Mary succeeded in making me feel that I was a valuable member of the human race and I began to trust her enough to accept her offer of friendship. As a way of thanks, I started leaving bunches of flowers for her, and even managed to say, 'Thank you', for any kindnesses she showed me. Our lives became more and more interwoven and I knew I was depending on her good nature. It was an unfamiliar situation for me and I was fearful that our friendship could not last.

Sadly, my instincts proved correct, for one day Mary announced, out of the blue, that she and Janet would be moving to Eastbourne to share a house with her parents. I felt physically ill by the news, my heart plummeting to my shoes. I half hoped that she might invite me to go and live with them, but that was impossible in the circumstances, as it was important for her to take the opportunity to make a better life for herself and Janet. It was a devastating blow, and it made me realise that I had wanted too much from my relationship with Mary who had become a sort of mother-figure to me. I knew I could visit her at Eastbourne whenever I wished, but she wouldn't be around for me when I needed her.

I tried to console myself with the knowledge that I still had my own mother to find. I started to think more and more about her and whether there might be other relations I could claim. But where were they? I had no idea how to go about tracing them. All I could think of was how I could save up enough money to get myself to Turkey and go looking for them. I held the hope deep down inside me that one day it would happen and I would go there, although at this stage of my life it seemed like a remote dream.

After Mary left I felt acutely miserable. Lonely beyond description, I drifted from one bedsit to another. I couldn't settle anywhere. Within the space of a year I moved lodgings three times. I shared a flat with a girl I used to play duets with at Ellesmere, but that didn't last long. Doreen wasn't interested in sharing with me again. With her, it was a case of 'once bitten twice shy'. I found the new landladies cold and uncaring, and they only talked to me when collecting the rent at the end of the week. My innate shyness made it difficult for anyone to get to know me well, and I lacked the social skills to communicate.

At least there was some semblance of permanence in my work at the solicitor's office, where I had a good rapport with my employer and managed to make friends with another girl in the office.

During this difficult, peripatetic period in my life I started getting recurring tummy pains and the doctor suggested an exploratory examination in Wanstead Hospital as he thought it might be a rumbling appendix.

With only a vague notion of what it involved, I packed my bag and travelled to the hospital on a red double-decker bus. It was the morning of a cold, grey November day. I can see and feel the whole scene as if it happened last week. On entering the hospital, a short bus ride from my bedsit, I felt uneasy, for it was my first taste of hospitals.

While filling in the admission form, a phrase caught my eye: 'Name and address of closest relative.' After I wrote the words, 'None known', a heart-stopping thought struck me. What if I died – who would arrange my funeral? Who would miss me? For one chilling moment, I visualised the words on the headstone: 'TINA SULEYMAN PASSED AWAY IN THE YEAR 1961, AGED TWENTY-ONE. SHE BELONGED TO NOBODY.'

I didn't want to die until I had the chance to find out if I did have any relations on this earth; if I did belong to someone.

The nurse insisted I write someone's name, so I wrote 'Aunty Molly', adding 'Close friend'. It gave me the idea to ring her and invite myself over to her home for a few days after my spell in hospital.

I woke up the next day in a confused state. Where was I? My eyelids were so heavy I could hardly open them and my body felt numb and far away. When I came to, the doctor told me that my healthy appendix had been removed because no other problem was evident. Later, I learned that I had diverticulitis, a small protrusion of the intestine through the stomach wall, probably the result of a poor diet. I felt cheated that I had gone through it all for nothing.

That 'visiting day' will be forever imprinted in my memory. In post-operative pain, I lay under the blanket in the public ward and watched with growing dismay the stream of visitors arriving for the other patients. I had lost touch with my few friends because of my itinerant lifestyle. Mary lived too far away and Aunty Molly must have been busy with other children. Not one person walked towards my bed. I felt utterly and irrevocably alone. It seemed to me that no one cared if I lived or died.

I worked myself into a state of deep depression, and in a vain attempt to make myself invisible, slid further and further down the bed. It was all too much. I put the sheet over my head and bawled my eyes out. The deep hurt that had been persistently smouldering inside me all those years suddenly exploded into an involuntary spectacle of overwhelming grief which I was incapable of suppressing. I really went to pieces.

Until that moment I hadn't realised just how unhappy I had been. Something inside me broke, and I had no control over the loud sobs which echoed throughout the whole ward. All my loneliness was centred on not having a mum and dad like every other normal human being... or anyone who belonged to me.

Inevitably, the noisy weeping and wailing beneath the bedclothes brought over a nurse. The tears stopped abruptly as I heard a voice. The nurse asked if I was in pain. I nodded self-consciously, wishing fervently, but too timid to ask, that she would draw the curtains around my bed.

'I'll get you something for the pain, dear,' she said, with a smile on her face, vainly trying to cheer me up. Why couldn't she just leave me alone? I thought, as I hid my face in the pillow, wishing I could fall into a hole and vanish from this earth.

A young lady in the bed opposite naturally couldn't help but notice my distress, as everyone else must have too, and during the next visiting hours, she sent her mother over to talk to me. It didn't help. I had no interest in a borrowed relative, or anyone trying to masquerade as a mother. I wanted my own mother. I was plagued with the notion that I was not real and didn't exist at all. I howled my grief under the bedclothes again and the woman turned away.

If ever there was a time when I needed friendly, expert counselling, it was then, for those few days in hospital crystallised for me, with stunning clarity, the reality of my situation. It brought home the painful truth that I had cried for help and there was no one there to listen. It was the lowest ebb in my life and I sank into the darkest depths of despair. I just wanted to die. Who were they, my lost kindred? Where were they, and why did they leave me so alone?

Possibly, it was the realisation that I might have died during the operation without ever knowing a single member of my family that provided the stimulus I needed to start a search. I had always known it would be my destiny to make my own way in life, and it was now made perfectly clear to me that, like the archetypal orphan, Annie (minus the red curls), I was entirely on my own in the world.

When I left hospital I stayed with Aunty Molly in her home in Finchley, north London. There she told me the sad news that Aunty Ivy had died of cancer. To my huge relief, she agreed to let me stay with her while recuperating from my operation. How I wished I could have stayed on a more permanent basis, but it was just not possible. I needed to learn, just as I had with Mary, that I could not expect any more from people than they were willing or able to give.

After my emotional and physical ordeal it was a delight to be fussed over by Aunty Molly. Over the next three weeks she cooked huge meals, supplemented each night with cakes, biscuits and chocolates, and although the food was not exactly healthy, at least I regained the weight I had lost.

I was delighted when Aunty Molly invited Pauline, Audrey's sister, for dinner. She told me she had lost touch with Audrey, but that she had been happily reunited with her mother and another sister. How happy I was for her. We promised to keep in touch with each other.

I decided to take the first positive step towards looking for my own mother, and I paid Barnardo's another visit. I wanted to find out if they might now be less obstructive in their attitude since my 'farewell' four years earlier. Their policy then was to tell ex-residents only the bare minimum about themselves, and it seemed to me that they were more concerned with the feelings of the parents. The children had no rights of their own, and from then on I knew my fight would be a lonely one. I talked to Miss Dyson, the after-care woman who had written me the letter about my lack of a family while I was at Princess Margaret School. I told her of my plans to go to Turkey at the end of the year to make a real effort to search for my mother, knowing that if I found her I might also find other family members, for I was convinced that she had married and had more children.

It was fortunate for me that Miss Dyson was sympathetic to my urgent need to find out about my origins. She explained how my mother had been a young Turkish refugee, living in Romania, and was brought up as a member of the family of the Turkish Consul General. Then, much to my surprise, she told me their name was Akcer (pronounced 'Akcher'). Amazingly, she then revealed that my mother's name was Ayshe. At last, I had something palpable to go on. I thought the name extremely pretty and romantic. I wished it were mine instead of the one she gave me; however I would have loved any name that belonged to my mother, and I kept repeating it over and over in my head, with the faint notion that it might somehow bring me closer to her. Now I knew my mother's name she almost became a real person for me. It was my first real link with her.

Miss Dyson went on to say that my mother came with the Akcer family to live in London just before war broke out. I felt enormously grateful to her for taking the very caring, but daring, step of giving me those few crumbs of information about my background, and especially for disclosing that all-important surname, which would prove to be a vital clue once I arrived in Istanbul. I felt gratified that she obviously felt I could be trusted to use the name with discretion. She warned me about the possibility that my mother might well have made a new life for herself and might not wish to see me, but I was prepared to take that risk, for in my heart of hearts I knew she would want to see the grown-up version of her first-born.

Miss Dyson's kindness lifted my spirits as no one else had ever done. Suddenly, my goal of going to Turkey seemed well within my grasp, and I felt wonderfully light-hearted when I bid farewell to 'Jolly Aunty Molly', and the safe haven of her home.

I soon found a comfortably furnished room in a swanky part of Snaresbrook, a suburb nearer London than Woodford. The rent was higher and the gas meter refused to give out any heat unless it was fed with a daily diet of my hard-earned coins, but I felt happy with my choice. I had to share the kitchen with Mrs Radford, a grey-haired, tubby widow of unbounded curiosity, who asked me endless questions when she interviewed me, and managed to coerce me into telling her that I had no family and that I was an ex-Barnardo girl. Her reaction was one of shock.

'I've never met a Barnardo girl before. You don't even look like an orphan.'

What in heaven's name, I thought, was an orphan supposed to look like? A grubby uneducated urchin, I suppose. My big frame, robust appearance and Farm Hill-trained voice certainly did not fit the prescribed image of an orphan. I tried to tell myself that I wasn't really an orphan anyway, because I knew I had a mother somewhere. One day I hoped to find her.

Having met people who asked me probing questions about myself and making me feel that I was 'different', I gradually developed the art of evading questions and, when necessary, I fabricated a family on the spot. I remember on one occasion when I had just joined the Young

Conservatives in an attempt to make friends and to 'improve' myself, I was caught in the middle of a group of young people who were all firing personal questions at me. Without a blink of an eyelid, I found myself nonchalantly lying that both my parents had died in the war. That soon shut them up, and they all looked at me with unabashed pity in their eyes. It was only half a lie anyway because Barnardo's had stated that my father was 'unheard of after Dunkirk', so I assumed him to be dead.

By building a protective wall around myself, and learning to tell stand-up fibs, I adopted a defensive posture whenever I was cornered, and was inevitably misunderstood because of it.

At my new job in the typing pool of the Shell Chemical Company, near Regent Street in central London, the other girls knew only as much about me as I was willing to share, and few people knew I was an orphan – except Vera. She was an only child, looking for a friend, and I was flattered when she invited me home to have tea with her mum and dad. I envied her having parents and the freedom of living in a proper family home. I loved the experience of being in a normal family unit. Increasingly, I angled for invitations, looking for any excuse not to return to my lonely bedsit in Snaresbrook.

Vera became my best friend. She was pretty and vivacious, and she introduced me to the London theatres and art galleries. We went on holidays together, and I remember our first trip away was to Torquay in Devon. If only it had been Turkey! Although I longed to visit Turkey, I didn't want to go there just for a holiday. I was mindful of the time it would take to search for my mother, and I wanted to have a good look at the country. My plans were to buy a one-way ticket to Turkey and try to get a job in Istanbul. But I was still not ready for such a journey.

As Vera had a bevy of boyfriends, I often went alone to the Saturday night dances at the Chelsea Town Hall, and that is where I met my second steady boyfriend, tall, fair-haired and handsome Geoffrey. It became his usual routine to call for me each Saturday, and together we roared off on his motorbike to explore different parts of the countryside. Travelling as a pillion passenger was a new and exciting adventure for me, and that summer we drove all the way up the motorway, ending up in Scotland, where we stayed in youth hostels.

One particularly cold night, after downing a few drinks at the Chiswick Pub, Geoff persuaded me to let him come to my room for a nightcap. Usually, we would kiss each other goodbye outside the front door, because Mrs Radford made it known that boys were not allowed inside.

After coffee, things started getting a little steamy. I tried to fight off Geoff's advances while we were entwined on the settee, and I was worried that Mrs Radford might hear us. My biggest fear, though, was of getting pregnant, and I did everything possible to fob off Geoff's amorous advances without making too much noise. It was way past midnight before he could be persuaded to leave.

The next morning I walked into Mrs Radford's bedroom to take in her customary cup of tea. Her unsmiling face should have warned me of what was to come, but her shock announcement, 'Tina, I have to ask you to leave,' caused me to drop the cup of hot tea all over her fancy bedclothes, which didn't really help my cause. Her anger spilled over then.

'What will people think?' she spluttered. 'I'm not having you bringing your boyfriends into my home. You can find yourself another place.'

I had no answer as I turned and walked out of the room. Shock had silenced me. I wanted to cry out, 'YOU CAN'T DO THIS TO ME!' But my lips did not voice the shouting in my head. Life was rolling along so nicely, when, in one foolish moment, I had taken the wrong option. It all seemed so unfair. If only she knew the real me, how I wasn't the sort of girl who let a boy take advantage of me. Quite the opposite in fact. A kiss and a cuddle was all I usually allowed, and even that was under sufferance. I was in a no-win situation. How could I get to know boys better if I wasn't allowed to invite them into my place of abode?

I baulked at the idea of asking Aunty Molly for assistance again, so when Pauline offered me a room in the flat she shared in Acton, west London, I jumped at the chance of again sharing a flat – this time with three outgoing nurses.

The unfortunate incident with Geoffrey became a distant memory and after a while we stopped seeing each other. But I had another love – a brand new automatic scooter. It was called the Tina Triumph, whose very name begged me to buy it, and I rode it every day to work, revelling in my new-found independence.

By the time spring moved into summer, Pauline was married, the lease of the flat expired and we were all given notice to leave.

As I slowly came to grips with being on my own again, I decided to get away from London's bedsit brigade. I found myself a seasonal job as a waitress at Pontins Holiday Camp in Bracklesham Bay, Sussex. I had never done waitressing before, and the idea of doing something different to mundane office work appealed. With free food and board, my aim was to save up enough money to go to Turkey when the summer season finished. I rode my scooter down to the Sussex coast, with all my worldly belongings strapped on the back. At the camp I shared a chalet that overlooked the swimming pool, with two other waitresses, Jean and Kath.

There was hardly time to take a quick dip in the pool before I found myself serving at tables. When I glanced at my image in the mirror, dressed in a green smock, with a white apron and a starched white cap, I laughed out loud, for it bore no resemblance to the real me. I felt an actor playing a role in a farcical comedy, and I spent those first few days rehearsing my part.

I was given three tables to wait upon and soon learned the kitchen routine – how to set tables and how to carry four plates of piping hot meals in each hand. I learned also to sense the excitement when guests were leaving in the hope that a decent-sized tip would be left.

There was one moment of anxiety when, in my haste to put down a hot plate full of food, the steak jumped off the plate and fell onto a guest's lap. Luckily for me he saw the funny side of it.

The holiday camp was a congenial, fun place to work. I enjoyed the company, the plenteous food and the free entertainment. By the time the summer season ended I had saved enough to buy a ticket to Istanbul, and also enough money for a few days' accommodation. Jean and Kath had become good friends, and they talked about coming with me once they had discussed it with their parents, but I didn't honestly expect anything to come from it.

At the beginning of September, my waitressing days were over and I rode on my scooter to Eastbourne to say my farewells to Mary and Janet, and where I planned to sell my scooter and organise the trip of a lifetime.

Chapter Four

Istanbul

October 4th, 1963 was a threshold day for me. It was the day I left England, left my job and said goodbye to my friends. Finally, after months and months of fantasising about going there, I was at last bound for Turkey.

Sitting on their suitcases waiting for me at Victoria Station, were Jean and Kath, their eyes reflecting my own anxiety about our imminent journey. My own suitcase, crammed full of all my worldly goods, was a lead weight. I lugged it slowly along the platform towards the train bound for Paris. I felt extraordinarily tense, and tried not to think too much about what would happen once we reached Istanbul.

All my life Turkey and my mother had been part of the same recurring dream. She was over there somewhere and now I was about to travel into the dream and find them both. My future was in the hands of kismet. It was too late to turn back. Back to where? I had no home to go to. The friends who knew of my plans to go to Turkey were convinced I was destined for a life of slavery in a sultan's harem and wondered if they would ever see me again!

We made a quick checklist of our official documents: British passport, transit visas for Yugoslavia and Bulgaria, a three-month residence visa for Turkey, and lastly, a one-way ticket for the Orient Express, London to Istanbul. Later we were to deeply regret that we could not afford to pay extra for a sleeping berth as we had no proper sleep throughout the three-day journey.

Although the three of us, at the age of twenty-three, were mature enough to make major decisions, I felt some responsibility for my friends. We didn't know each other that well, and I remember thinking they were only coming along because I had dropped a hint that they could join me if they wished. Frankly, I was surprised when they took my offer seriously, but all the same delighted to have the company of two girlfriends, even though our motives were entirely different. Jean and Kath were hoping for a fun-filled holiday while my own crystal-clear intentions were to see Istanbul, where I also hoped my mother was living.

Over and over in my mind's eye I visualised the scene which had been central to my thoughts ever since I knew I had a Turkish mother, of bumping into her in a crowded street. I could see us falling into each other's arms in a tearful and dramatic embrace.

The lurching train soon brought me back to my senses as it careered through the English countryside towards Dover. We crossed the Channel and on arrival at Paris boarded the famous Orient Express. The huge locomotive and its nine carriages awaited us at the Gare de l'Est Station. The legendary train blew its whistle, ejected a blast of steam, and we began our journey to Istanbul. I watched the scenery change from magnificent mountains in Switzerland to red-roofed hamlets in Yugoslavia, on to the grey grimness of Communist Bulgaria.

When the train pulled up at Sofia two days later, crowds of peasants fought their way in, squeezing into every available space in our cramped carriage. Tempers became short for by now our food had run out, the toilets were unusable and we were dirty and tired.

Why not fly like sensible people? I thought as the train sped east across the flat landscape of European Turkey, pausing briefly at Edirne Station to allow yet more people on board. Despite the uncomfortable conditions, I managed to sleep in a sitting position, lulled by the repeated clanking of the train's wheels and soothed by the satisfaction of having made it this far on our long journey.

Hour after hour, the train roared relentlessly through the night until at last, to our tremendous relief, daylight revealed a sunny morning with bright blue skies. I forced my tired eyes to focus on the passing scene of colourful gypsy caravans making camp by the railway track. We decided to celebrate our first sighting of Turkey by eating breakfast in the dining car. As we pushed our way through the crowded corridors, we did our best to ignore the fetid body odours, and found seats in the half-empty dining car. We sipped deliciously potent hot Turkish coffee, served in tiny cups, and ate crusty white bread with rose-petal jam, black olives and feta cheese. It was my first Turkish meal.

On our third day we approached the outskirts of Istanbul. I felt a throb of pleasure when I saw the vague hills of Istanbul through the purple haze of a still autumn morning. How wonderful it was to feast my gritty eyes on the jagged skyline of the city of my mother. With satisfaction, I spied the gleaming spires of the many mosques which I had only seen in pictures, and I felt a natural surge of joy that we had at last reached journey's end.

There was pandemonium amongst the passengers as the train jerked to a standstill, emitting a burst of steam and venting its relief that it had reached Sirkeci Station, its final destination. As we struggled with our packs down the carriage steps and on to the platform, I felt limp and spent and exchanged a flustered glance at my friends before we were swept along by the surging herds and nearly lost sight of each other.

Soon our ears were assailed by strange jabberings, none of which I understood. It didn't take me long to acknowledge that the few Turkish words I learned in my *Teach Yourself Turkish* book were not going to be much help. 'Stick with me girls,' I said with false bravado. We reached the barrier. I surrendered my ticket with a flourish. It was my last link with England.

A taxi drove us to a pension near Taksim Square, a busy intersection in the centre of the city, where we booked in for two weeks. We planned to do a bit of sightseeing and then look for work.

The call to prayer, floating up to our window from the nearest mosque, woke us up every morning. Istanbul was like a fairy-tale, so unlike anything I had previously known that it might have belonged to another planet. Yet, as soon as I walked amongst the mass of people down the main thoroughfare of Istiklal Caddesi, I was aware of fitting in. The urge was very strong to immediately start scouring the streets for a face that mirrored my own, and now and again I fancied I saw an image which resembled mine.

I was intoxicated with the promise of what each new day in Istanbul would bring, and had to pinch myself when I realised I was actually standing on Turkish soil. Meanwhile, I could not communicate my enthusiasm to Jean and Kath, who complained constantly about the primitive loos and the wildlife emerging from the taps and the dirty streets, but I hardly noticed such minor inconveniences. I drank in the sounds and smells which made Istanbul such a unique and exciting place to be. The streets were packed with people even though it was autumn and the tourist season was nearly over. Istanbul caught me in its grip and held me in its heart. For a long time I had imagined what Turkey would be like. Now the fantasy was scaled down, my dream dissolved by the cold reality of being in the city of my dreams.

After two weeks of sightseeing we learned our way about, but however cheap our living was, the money did not stretch indefinitely. Through sheer necessity we placed an advertisement in the 'work wanted' column of the *Cumhurriyet* daily newspaper, and within days Jean had left to take up a position as a nanny for a business couple with three children, and Kath soon followed, having found similar work with a doctor's family.

I was left alone to start work as an English-speaking secretary in a small international electronics firm. My boss was called Hilkat Bolulu, but to everyone he was known as Hilkat Bey. He organised the necessary documentation so I could work for him for at least three months. During my interview over a cup of muddy Turkish coffee, he lit up one Camel cigarette after another, listening intently while I explained the need for a job. He appeared to be intrigued by my story, and promised he would help me in any way he could.

Hilkat Bey turned out to be no ordinary boss. Burly and balding, his aquiline nose dominated his face. He exuded charm and good-will, and I was entranced by his strong, charismatic personality and his booming baritone voice. He found me a room in an apartment near Taksim Square, the equivalent of Piccadilly Circus.

I could have caught the bus to the office each morning, but I preferred the twenty minute walk which took me past the busy waters of the Golden Horn. Heads turned at the sight of a lone English woman walking through the streets – an alien sight in a country where women were hidden from public life. I expect I was regarded as 'a loose woman', but I had no choice but to go about my business on my own. Gradually I learned to ignore their curious stares, and to cope with any unwanted attention, and one day when I had my bottom pinched in a crowded street I was so incensed that I made sure that if it happened again I would be prepared. I learned a very rude Turkish phrase, which Hasan, the office boy, taught me. With blazing eyes I would shout, 'Haydi git, ensoldesek!' ('Go Away You Son-of-a-Donkey'). There were plenty of times when I was able to put it to good use, and it worked wonders. I always got a lot of pleasure from watching the stunned looks on the faces of the offenders.

Some mornings Hilkat Bey picked me up in his sparkling green Chevrolet, and we travelled to work through the cobbled backstreets, picking up the mail at the post office en route to the office.

Hilkat Bey introduced me to his wife and two-year-old daughter, and every now and then I was invited to join them for Sunday drives along the shores of the Bosphorus, where we often stopped at a shore-side café and sampled delicious thick yoghurt, topped with icing sugar. He took me under his wing, and now and again invited me to stay with them in their weekend retreat in Büyükada, one of the nine beautiful islands which make up the group called the Princes Islands in the Sea of Marmara, fifteen kilometres south-east of Istanbul.

The ramshackled, four-storey building where I worked stood in the old part of Karaköy, close to the cone-topped Galata Tower, the most prominent building in the district. I walked up three flights of worn stone steps to the small office, never daring to take the old iron lift in case it broke down.

Once the new filing system was in place and the backlog of letters were typed, there was very little work for me to do, and to fill in time I wrote letters to Aunty Molly, Vera and Mary. To keep my mind occupied, I started drawing doodles on the old manual typewriter. The myriad of mosques I could see from the tiny window of my office captivated my imagination, and it took me quite a few days to draw one of them on my typewriter. There was also time

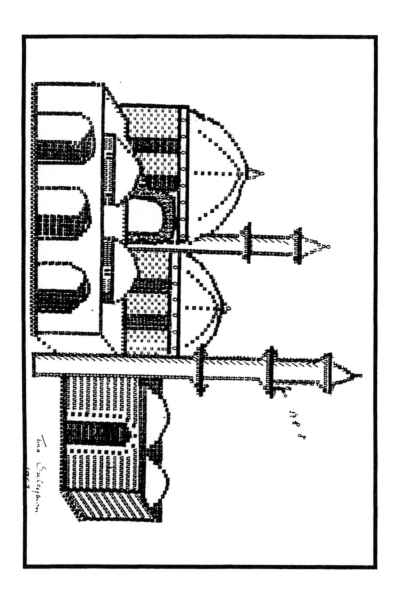

to write some poetry, and I still remember the poem that I wrote about Istanbul. Hilkat Bey was so enchanted with it he framed it and put it on the wall as a memento. As the poem depicted, I really had fallen in love with Istanbul, and in spite of occasional bouts of homesickness for England, Turkey was a country which held me in its grip.

Apart from my boss speaking fractured English with an American twang, there was no one else I could talk to. Jean and Kath now lived on the other side of the city and we had few opportunities to meet, instead keeping in touch by phone. My conversations with the two other members of staff, the Turkish secretary and Hasan, the office boy, were limited to smiles and my few words of Turkish. I started teaching both of them some English, and later I discovered there was extra money to be made from teaching English to one or two students.

With Hilkat Bey being frequently absent from the office, there was little work for me to do, and I grabbed every opportunity to get out and explore the vast city. I came to specially love the Bosphorus, the narrow waterway which separates Europe from Asia. It was not only a place of relaxation but an integral part of my life in Istanbul. After a day in the claustrophobic office I would return to the apartment, have a quick shower and a bite to eat and hurry on down the main thoroughfare against the flood of dolmuşes (shared taxis) and pedestrians. As I approached the Galata waterfront a breeze would come from the Golden Horn and I would sit and watch the passing ferries criss-crossing the narrow waterway.

Hilkat Bey made regular business trips to Ankara, and whenever he was away for days on end I got into the habit of exploring the city by foot. It was during one of these promenades that I met my first Turkish boyfriend, a tall, incredibly good-looking naval officer. As we walked past our eyes locked. In the same instant, we turned our heads, both of us craving a second look. The next moment he was by my side, hesitantly inviting me in excruciatingly broken English to go with him to a café for a cup of coffee. My sightseeing can wait, I thought to myself. I much preferred the sight I was seeing right now. I would never have acted so brazenly while walking down Oxford Street, and felt quite ashamed of myself for being such a hussy.

Although I enjoyed the freedom and the flexibility of travelling alone, after a while the unwanted attention of men became tiresome as I couldn't sit down at an outdoor café to enjoy a drink without being pestered, so a chaperone, and a handsome one into the bargain, would be extremely useful. I needed to use no rude retorts for Ismail, my newly-found, blue-eyed naval officer. For him, I turned on as much charm as I could muster. His flaxen hair and fair skin had a Nordic freshness, which belied his Turkish ancestry. He told me his parents came from the Black Sea area in the north, where people are fairer skinned. You would have sworn he was Swedish by looking at him. After swallowing several cups of thick sweet coffee, he escorted me back to my apartment and we made a date for the following week.

When Hilkat Bey returned from his business trip, I suspected he was rather put out when I told him about Ismail, and I quickly realised I would have to keep my boss at arm's length. I was pleased to have Ismail as my regular date, as I knew that my charming boss did leave me rather weak at the knees, but at the age of forty-four he was almost double my age, and I didn't want to get involved with a married man. However, so keen was he to keep me on as his secretary that he arranged for my visa to be extended for another three months. Our working relationship was excellent though, and he turned out to be more of a 'sugar daddy' for me than a serious suitor.

My Turkish was still very limited, but it improved no end when Hilkat Bey paid for me to have Turkish lessons at the Istanbul Technical Institute. He also paid for my return fare in the dolmuş, and I welcomed the chance to practise my newly-learned phrases on the taxi driver and other unsuspecting people whom I met. My stuttering attempts were usually greeted with much hilarity by everyone, but at least they seemed to understand what I was saying.

'Çok güzel,' ('Very good') they would respond encouragingly. Then they would string together a few incomprehensible phrases which totally floored me.

'Lütfen, yavaş yavaş,' ('Please speak slowly'), I always pleaded.

The days were getting colder and wetter as we entered December, and I wasn't so keen to go out. With more time on my hands, I thought it was about time I started looking for the Akcer family, as I had now been in Turkey for nearly three months. In fact, kismet itself intervened. I received a phone call from Jean. She was bursting to tell me the news that the doctor she worked for told her that he remembered going to school with a Faruk Akcer, the son of the consul general, and furthermore, he worked in the office of the city council.

The words tumbled out in a torrent of excitement and I hardly took in the news that Jean's visa had expired, and that she and Kath would have to return to Britain very soon. It meant I would be on my own. But in recent weeks I had seen very little of my travelling companions and their departure affected my life hardly at all. Jean's news was the best parting gift I could have had. Was this to be the link that would lead me to my mother? I felt an overwhelming urge to go and visit Faruk Akcer immediately. It didn't take long. The next day, in typically generous fashion, Hilkat Bey offered to pay for a taxi to take me to the city council offices, but first he made a telephone call to check that

Faruk Akcer was in the building. We both agreed it would be better to confront the man face to face rather than try to explain things over the phone.

At precisely eleven o'clock on a rainy day in December the taxi driver was instructed by Hilkat Bey to put me down at the entrance to the city council building. I then began my unnerving drive into the unknown. I felt a moment of panic when the driver aggressively steered his taxi through teeming traffic, honking his horn and shouting abuse to anyone who got in his way. It was as though he too felt the urgency of my need, and I began to wonder whether I would ever get to meet Mr Akcer after all. At last we arrived at the other end of Galata Bridge, passing through the poorer quarters of the Old City.

I tried to assemble my jumbled thoughts into some order as over and over in my mind I prepared my list of questions. The taxi suddenly lurched to a standstill outside a large, modern building. 'Teşekkür ederim,' ('Thank you') I mumbled as I stepped out and handed him a few folded notes, adding some coins for the expected tip.

Slowly, inexorably, I walked towards the swing doors. I experienced a strange tightness at the top of my head, and felt quite faint. Time stood still as my weak legs made their way in the direction of the receptionist in the foyer. 'I've come to see Mr Faruk Akcer,' I said in a shaking voice.

'He is at a meeting,' she replied in clear English. 'Do you have an appointment?'

'No, but I have come from England recently, and I have something urgent to discuss with him.'

She shook her head, an uncertain expression clouding her face.

Before she could say anything else, I spoke impulsively. 'Please tell him I want to see him on personal business which is extremely important.' I couldn't bear to think that I had come all this way for nothing.

'Tamam, ('All right') I will go and tell him you are here.'
Her voice was edged with doubt.

I felt both relieved and terrified when moments later a
tall, bespectacled man, aged about forty-five, strode
purposefully towards me, his steps echoing down the long
corridor. As he came closer, I noticed his furrowed brow,
his reddish face. His whole demeanour appeared angry.

'Yes, what is it, what do you want?' he scowled.

'I'm terribly sorry to interrupt your meeting,' I said,
fixing him with a steady gaze and trying to look apologetic,
'I'll come straight to the point. Do you remember a young
girl who lived with your family in London during the war?
She was called Ayshe Suleyman.'

He looked up at me, surprised. 'Yes, I do. What about
her?'

I gave silent thanks on two counts. He could understand
English, and he remembered my mother. Although he
continued to frown and tut impatiently, he was now
showing more interest. I paused momentarily for full effect.

'Do you remember she was expecting a baby in 1940?'
Without waiting for his reply, I heard myself blurting out,
'Well, I'm that baby!'

His facial expression promptly changed from being
annoyed to being wide-eyed. His mouth gaped as he bent
forward to scrutinise my face, at the same time unleashing a
tirade of what I presumed to be Turkish expletives
expressing absolute astonishment. Before I had time to ask
him any more questions, he turned the tables on me and
started firing some questions. What did I call myself? What
was my surname? How long had I been in the country?
How did I find him? Had I been adopted?

I felt my heart pulsating wildly as I waited anxiously for
him to tell me where my mother was. I began to feel quite
queer all over, with an inward sinking feeling of foreboding.

Then he delivered the body blow which sent me mentally reeling.

'Ayshe does not live in Turkey. She stayed behind in England after you were born, and we have lost touch with her ever since.'

My heart sank at the news. I felt an unaccountable rush of pain and despair, and I could have wept right there and then. I felt betrayed. To think I had come all the way to Turkey for nothing. Although burning with indignation, I made a real effort to force my eyes to look into his and establish strict control over my emotions. I mumbled something like, 'Oh what a shame. I always understood that she had returned to Turkey with your family.'

Numbly, I heard him say in a conciliatory tone, 'You must visit my mother in Ankara. She will be able to tell you much more. I must get back to my meeting. I'm truly sorry that your mother is not here.'

He scribbled his mother's name and address on a scrap of paper and shook my hand. As he turned away, he said, 'If you are staying for a while in Turkey, I expect I shall have the chance to see you again.'

Tears blurred my vision as I left the building, trying to absorb the meaning of his disappointing words. I was in no hurry to get back to the office, and I sat on the wall in the car park, trying to replay the scene in my mind. It was a certainty that I would not meet my mother here in Turkey, and the only thing I could look forward to now was meeting Mrs Akcer. At least I could draw some comfort from the expectation of travelling to Ankara in the near future. For now, I would have to make do with the titbit of information given to me by someone who knew her.

It had been a strange, extraordinary day and my head was giddy from it. Chasing the ghost of my mother was emotionally exhausting, but I wasn't about to give up. I decided to ask Hilkat Bey if I could travel with him on his next business trip to Ankara.

Chapter Five

Ankara

I set off with Hilkat Bey to Ankara, the capital of Turkey, on a cold January morning. It was almost a day's journey by car from Istanbul, beyond the mountains, and deep into the heart of central Anatolia. Hilkat Bey had only just renewed my working visa for another three months, and I jumped at the chance when he kindly offered to take me with him as his secretary.

The mingled excitement and apprehension of that day still lives with me as I write. I looked forward to meeting the people who could tell me about my mother, but I couldn't help feeling intimidated by coming into contact with such 'well-to-do' people, as I presumed the consul general's family to be. At the same time, I was wary about taking such a lengthy expedition with my married boss into unknown territories, as it was the first time we had travelled away together in such close proximity. A nervous passenger at the best of times, it also took me a while to adjust my thinking to the right-hand driving rules which operated in Turkey.

The long journey allowed me plenty of time to mull over the events of the past few weeks. Since my disheartening meeting with Faruk Akcer, and the devastating news that my mother had not even lived in Turkey since well before my birth, I had many times wanted to jump on the first plane back to England and delve into the Births and Marriage records at Somerset House. I felt sure she must have married in the twenty-four years since I was born, and no doubt had more children. There was a good chance that I could have half-brothers and sisters. And yet I knew that now I was in Turkey I had to take every opportunity to learn as much as I could from anyone who might have known my mother – however long ago.

Knowing that she wasn't in Turkey and that there was no hope of finding her there left me with a nagging sense of isolation. I did my best to reason with myself that the news wasn't that bad. I told myself that the people I would soon meet would be able to bring my mother out of the shadows and tell me all the things I wanted to know about her. But the other half of me refused to listen. To think that throughout the years I had assumed my mother to be in Turkey, yet she never was. She hadn't been here for many years. I had pinned my hopes and dreams on finding her. I felt abandoned, helpless. Where did I belong now? I felt only hopelessness, a citizen of nowhere.

I felt angry with Barnardo's for their policy of drip-feeding me only vague facts about my mother. I had implicitly believed them when they said my mother had 'probably returned to Turkey'. It hadn't occurred to me to make my own enquiries while I was still living in England. As my guardians, Barnardo's were my sole source of information about my background, and I had encountered nothing but resistance to my right to know. I felt I had no option but to believe what they told me. From now on I was determined to see my search through and use all my energies to do my own research rather than having to rely on other people.

Our route to the capital city took us through the dry, desolate plains of rural Turkey, where herds of angora goats roamed the craggy hills. We crossed the bare Hittite plateau passing through small villages with earth-roofed adobe houses. It was then that I felt I had arrived well and truly in Asia. Hilkat Bey was a fast but careful driver, and he constantly reassured me that he knew these roads backwards. He had taken the precaution of carrying chains which might be needed over the snow-covered mountain pass close to Ankara.

We arrived at the small town of Bolu, from where Hilkat Bey's ancestors originated. His surname of 'Bolulu' means son of Bolu, though I never heard anyone calling him 'Mr Bolulu'. He was universally known as 'Hilkat Bey', the 'Bey' being the more commonly used form of 'Mister'.

We lunched in a warm, homely Lokanta cafe and sampled the national drink of ayran, yoghurt mixed with water. Four moustachioed men stopped in their game of backgammon and stared curiously at me, no doubt because I was a foreigner.

Light snow started to fall as we passed through the massive range of mountains. This was by far the most treacherous part of the journey, and as soon as we found a garage, we had the chains put on the wheels. Outside a cold dry wind blew, swirling clouds of brown dust everywhere. Temperatures were well below freezing. Carefully, we began the descent through the mountain gorge. Even with chains on, the car skidded dangerously on the icy road.

Suddenly we were out of the valley on to the main thoroughfare leading to Ankara. It was well after dark when we reached this modern, thriving metropolis. Hilkat Bey booked me into the Palas Oteli near the city centre. Cold and exhausted, I threw myself on the bed and promptly fell asleep.

The next morning the city was obscured by thick fog and the temperatures were freezing when my good-natured employer arrived in his car to take me to the home of Mrs Akcer. He left me standing, shivering, in front of a large contemporary apartment building. This was the moment I had been waiting for. Slowly, I climbed the steps to the front door, took a deep breath, and knocked. Try as I might, I could not control my shaking body. My heart hammered against my chest when the maid opened the door. She smiled as if expecting me, and ushered me into an expensively furnished living room.

A white-haired, grave-faced woman sat in the corner on a beautifully upholstered chair. It was Mrs Akcer, the woman who had taken pity on my mother and had given her a home. Now she was holding out her arms in a welcoming gesture. I felt sorry to see that her hands shook constantly and how she appeared to have little control over her floppy head. It was obvious she had the debilitating Parkinson's Disease. I had already learned that the Turkish word for 'Mrs' was Bayan, and I also knew that in Turkey it is etiquette to kiss an older woman on both cheeks, as a mark of respect. I walked across the carpeted room, leaned over towards her and dutifully kissed her lightly on both cheeks. Another woman, who introduced herself to me as an aunt, ushered me towards a chair. I sat on the edge stiffly, self-consciously, while they both inspected me. I don't know what was expressed on my face while I sat staring, uncertain what to say, my stomach riddled with knots, but the two women were nodding and smiling at me in an understanding way.

The maid was summoned to bring in some tea and cakes. I was introduced to her. I have forgotten her name, but I remember thinking it might have been my mother serving tea in the same way.

The language barrier proved to be a difficulty. I barely understood Mrs Akcer when she whispered, 'Welcome to our home, Tina. Faruk told us you would come and see us one day. You look very much like Ayshe.'

It all seemed like a dream. I felt immensely cheered that my mother was being spoken of as an actual living person by these women who once knew her intimately. I was thrilled to hear that I looked like my mother, though somehow not surprised. In my daydreams I had always imagined we would be alike.

Mrs Akcer tried to explain in a thin, shaking voice that she had forgotten most of her English and was sorry she could not be a better hostess. The aunt, in stilted English, explained, 'Bayan Akcer is very ill.' Then she telephoned Mrs Akcer's daughter and asked her to come over and help translate.

When the daughter, Vahide, arrived, we were introduced. She was a tall, striking woman, aged about forty. At first she was shy about speaking in English. She explained carefully that she had once been conversant in the language but had let it lapse. I felt shy and embarrassed myself, but to try and break the ice a little I tried out a few of my well-practised phrases in Turkish. The three women were delighted with my efforts, and laughed politely. It must have been very difficult for them. I wondered what they were thinking about my untimely intrusion in their lives.

'Where were you brought up?' came the first question through Vahide from her mother.

'How long have you been in Turkey?'

'How old are you?'

Question and answer sessions rolled around the room, each woman asking questions through Vahide.

'My mother wants me to tell you that you look very much like your mother. You are taller than her, but your hair is the same light brown colour, and very fine like hers. You have her deep-set eyes; and your hands too are like Ayshe's.'

I gave a nervous laugh, at which point Vahide interjected. 'My mother said that you laugh like Ayshe too.'

My memories of that visit are blurred into one another as they circle round and round in my head. But one thing I do remember is the utter astonishment of my hosts once they learned I had been in Barnardo's until the age of seventeen. They were dismayed to hear that I had never been adopted, for they had assumed that my stay with Barnardo's would be only a temporary one.

Mrs Akcer's subsequent statement is one I shall never forget. She must have been forming the words in her mind because in almost perfect English, she said, with a great deal of effort, and with all sincerity, 'Tina, you are now one of the family, just like Ayshe was, and you are welcome in our home any time.'

All I could do was to look across at her and smile. Words could not convey how I felt at that moment. In a choking voice, all I could manage to say was, 'Thank you. You are very kind.'

That simple, moving gesture touched me deeply, even though, in all reality, I knew I could never take up their offer. How could I ever hope to be part of their circle? Although welcoming and unpretentious, they were strangers to me, and a vast ocean stood between our two cultures.

I waited impatiently for the chance to ask my own burning questions. As soon as there was an opening in the conversation I asked, 'Why didn't my mother return to Turkey with you?'

'Because she wanted her independence.' Vahide's grasp of English improved the more she spoke. 'Ayshe was a good-hearted girl and very quiet, but she was also strong-willed and rather stubborn.'

'Your mother was still a child when you were born, only fifteen, I think. It was impossible for her to keep you. Her pregnancy was embarrassing for us. Because she was underage, the police should have been involved, but my father didn't want that to happen and he approached Dr Barnardo's homes to take you into their care.'

She went on to explain the turmoil that existed in London during the war, at the time when I was born. 'You didn't know what would happen from one day to the next.'

With occasional prompting from her mother, Vahide related the circumstances which brought my mother to their home. Mr Akcer, Vahide's father, who had died many years previously, was the consul general in Constanza, Romania, before the war. One day, a tall peasant, aged about eighty, named Mustafa Suleyman, came to the consul's office and pleaded with him to take his eight year old daughter, Ayshe. He said her mother had died giving birth to her, and he was now too old to look after her. Apparently, it was the custom for a peasant family to ask a wealthy one to bring up a child they could not afford to feed and clothe.

Vahide continued: Romania, in 1932, was a monarchy after the fall of the Ottoman Empire, and many of the Turkish people were exiled, but many also stayed on and lived as best as they could. All were left poor and without homes.

The consul general, and Mrs Akcer, had agreed to take Ayshe as a member of their family, and train her in housekeeping with a view to her getting married, when they would give her a dowry. Vahide stressed to me that Ayshe was never officially adopted by them, and was only taken in by verbal agreement.

It came as a rude shock to hear the details coming to light regarding my mother, not only that she was so young when I was born but also that her background was one of such abject poverty. My soul cried out in sympathy for her, overriding for an instant my own pain. I tried to solace myself with the thought that, even if she had wanted to, she could not possibly have kept me, for in those days abortion was unheard of, and having a child out of wedlock was considered to be an unpardonable sin.

I told myself that all right, yes, my mother had given me the gift of life and I was thankful for that, but surely she could have made an effort to look for me, once she was a bit more mature. After all, she knew where to find me, didn't she?

I was crying inside when I asked Vahide, 'Why do you think my mother didn't come and fetch me from the homes when she was a bit older?' I tried not to sound too bitter as I asked the question which had been haunting me for so many years.

'I honestly wish I could answer that Tina,' Vahide said of her own volition, 'but I presume Ayshe has made a life for herself somewhere in England. Unfortunately, we lost touch with her when she left us and we never heard one word from her again.'

There arose in me an ominous sense of finality when I heard those words, as if that was the end of the matter, and I guess it was as far as Turkey was concerned. But I couldn't help wondering what the reason was behind the apparent rift between my mother and her benefactors. Perhaps I was the reason. The untimely arrival of an illegitimate baby to a young girl in their care might have been the catalyst.

I tried to focus on the present and asked other pertinent questions that had been gnawing away at me all my life.

'Tina, you must believe me when I say that we were all fond of Ayshe. She was a quiet, intelligent girl, and as she went about her daily tasks she had the ability to pick up phrases she heard being spoken in French and English.'

'Of course,' Vahide added, 'your mother spoke Turkish and Romanian. She was introverted and had a sweet nature.

But she also had a determined side to her which led her to choose her own way of life.'

The aunt left the room for a few minutes and returned with three small black and white photos of my mother. I looked down at the first photo, scrutinising the face of this adolescent girl who brought me into the world. What sort of person had she grown up to be, I wondered. Did she have a family of her own? Where was she living? Although she was only a young girl in the photo, I could see my resemblance to her at the same age: the straight wispy hair, the high cheekbones, the deep-set eyes.

I looked at the second photo, a close-up portrait. I was transfixed by the intensity of her gaze, her large, sad, almost pleading, eyes, staring out at me. For the first time in my life I was able to look at the face of my mother. Goose bumps pricked the back of my neck, and I shivered involuntarily.

I felt an immediate compassion for her. She had been orphaned, abandoned by her family, and only seven years later I was born and she had given away a baby of her own. It was almost more than I could comprehend – yet in my mind I knew instantly that I loved her.

The second photo was of a small girl, long arms dangling by her side, standing next to a man who looked old enough to be her great-grandfather. My heart missed a beat. Surely he could not be her father? Yes, Vahide confirmed, he definitely was her father. The photo had been taken the same day he entrusted Ayshe to their care. For him to take such drastic action must have been a desperate, brave step.

He looked extremely tall and ancient, with cropped white hair and a beard to match, and he wore the Turkish garb common in those times. I was totally bewitched at seeing my mother as a little girl, standing next to this huge grandfatherly figure.

He looked as if he was in his nineties, and it defied my imagination to believe he was her father – he looked more like her great-grandfather. But he was my grandfather. I now stand at five feet, seven inches, an above average height, and as a child I was head and shoulders above my peers. If nothing else, here was some proof that I had inherited my height from him.

My thoughts, at that moment, turned to my father. Perhaps he had been tall too? He had never featured as strongly in my childlike imaginings as my mother had. Perhaps the Akcers could tell me more. I already knew from Barnardo's that his name was Harold Kirton, a thirty year old Englishman who worked as a porter at the Turkish Embassy, which was where my mother met him.

Hoping that my persistent questions were not becoming too tiresome, I asked Vahide what she knew of my father. I told them that Barnardo's assumed my father had lost his life at Dunkirk, so there didn't seem any point in following his trail. In any case, it had always been my mother who had been the focus of my thoughts, rarely my father.

She told me their family were acquainted with his family, but they had lost track of him after the embarrassing 'affair'. She went on to describe him as a tall man with fair hair and glasses. But that was all she could remember about him after such a long time.

Three hours had now passed since I had first knocked on the door. Three hours in which I had learned more about my mother than in all my previous twenty-four years. I felt immensely grateful to Vahide and her mother for all the trouble they had taken to welcome me and tell me all they could, in spite of the language difficulties. But now it was time to go. As I stood up, Vahide said, 'You must come and visit us in our summer house in Istanbul.' She gave me their address. I kissed her mother on both cheeks and said goodbye to them all.

Outside, I took a sharp intake of cold air. I scarcely noticed the late hour. Thoughts crowded my mind as I walked down the front steps. I had been embraced into the folds of a Turkish family whose lives had intimately touched my mother's, and I knew that my life would never be quite the same again.

★

I had believed Turkey to be my destiny, the place where I would find my roots, and as soon as I had set foot in the country I was in a state of sensitivity to everything around me – the strangeness, the sounds, the climate. Once I had got over the initial culture shock, I grew to love Turkey the more I saw of it, and I became its willing prisoner. It had lured me into its web and held me captive. But now I knew that my mother was not living there, I wanted to go back to England to start again. My mother was not in Turkey. Where was she? I had to find out.

Not knowing of my resolve, Hilkat Bey had renewed my visa for another three months and I felt obligated to continue working for him. He did his best to keep me occupied with work during the day and my last few months in Turkey sped by in a haze of sophisticated nightclubs and plush restaurants, usually with clients from overseas.

That summer I saw other parts of Turkey, when Hilkat Bey took me with him on one of his extended business trips to some of the telecommunication bases in Mersin and Adana in the south. I was glad that an engineer was on the journey with us, as the opportunity could easily have arisen for a more intimate relationship to develop between myself and my boss, and I knew that was not what I wanted.

When we reached Antalya, on the southern coast, Hilkat Bey and the engineer flew back to Istanbul and I was left to spend a few days on my own to enjoy the beautiful beaches and see one or two local ruins.

There was a frightening incident on my first day on the beach when I was surrounded by a group of males, who then followed me back to my hotel. Someone must have noticed my predicament, as a policeman was called in and he strongly advised me to stay indoors. I would have none of it as I was determined to see the sights, and the next day, when I was inevitably followed around the streets again, I 'picked up' the best-looking boy around and asked him to escort me to Aspendos, a nearby Roman amphitheatre. He couldn't believe his good luck, but it was the best course of action as being a young European woman on my own made me easy prey, and my well-versed rude phrase, even accompanied by my wild eyes, was no match for their persistence.

By the time I flew back to Istanbul at the end of the week, I'd had enough of Turkey, with its constraints on my freedom and it was an easy decision for me to return to England. I felt relieved to be leaving the country, as I was isolated from people other than Hilkat Bey's immediate family circle. Normal friendships were just not possible because of the language barrier and the social differences. My friendship with Ismail had fizzled out because without an in-depth knowledge of the other's language it was almost impossible to talk to each other.

Hilkat Bey had shown me nothing but kindness and support while I worked for his company, and I was sorry to be leaving him. But Istanbul had lost its lustre. And I needed to continue my search for my mother.

My year's stay in Istanbul had a double effect. It satisfied my hunger for anything Turkish, and it helped to give my mother some form and to fill the void I had always felt about my heritage. It was a beginning, as I knew there was much more to find out. But now she was not in Turkey, I had a crisis of identity. Where did I really belong? My lineage was half Turkish and half English. I felt an inner conflict between the pull to the country of my mother who had given me a Turkish name and the call back to the country I thought of as home.

I made one last visit to Mrs Akcer, but she was now unable to speak at all and it was obvious her health was sadly deteriorating. Unfortunately I didn't see Vahide again, though I did have the opportunity to speak with her many years later.

As for Faruk, Vahide's older brother, whom I met at the city council, I talked to him again only briefly during a visit to his family home in Istanbul. He has since died of a heart attack. There was another brother, Muammer, who was at that time the Turkish Ambassador to Tunisia. I was to meet up with him too, many years later.

I said an emotional farewell to my boss, my friend and father-figure, Hilkat Bey. 'Goodbye my dear,' he said, while throwing farewell gifts into my hands, 'Inşallah (God willing) I shall see you again.'

I teamed up with Jenny, a Dutch girl I met at the British Consulate, and we travelled by coach through Europe. The journey took three days, with two overnight stays in Yugoslavia and Austria, and it was a far more comfortable means of travel than it had been by train. Jenny invited me to stay for a few days at her parent's home by a canal in Amersfoort. After rest and recuperation I then took the boat to Harwich and home.

Fatima, aged 2 or 3.

Fatima, aged 2 or 3, second on right.

Fatima, aged 5.

Fatima, at the end of the table, on Founders' Day at Farm Hill.

Fatima, (second on the left) aged 7.

Fatima, fifth from front, at Farm Hill in 1947.

Fatima, at back with 'Mother'.

Tina Sulyman, 1963.

Married Bliss!

Revisiting the old Home.

Nurse Muriel, Mother, me and Jill, 1995.

Ray, Tina, Nigel (18), Laurence (17).

Chapter Six

Back to London

It had been over a year since I'd last set foot in England, and I was relieved to be back. My long journey in Turkey had broadened my horizons, even though it had not produced my mother for me. But it had provided the key so that I knew what my next plan of action must be. I had reached the end of a fascinating period in Turkey, but it was actually the beginning of a much longer and more trying journey that would test my tenacity in ways I could never have imagined.

When I was abroad I thought of England as my home and although I had no actual home to go to, it was where my friends were and I settled back with a sense of relief.

I phoned some of my old Barnardo friends to cadge a bed for a few nights until I found somewhere to live in London. By now we all thought of each other as 'sisters', as we had grown up together as a big family in our first home. A few of the girls had now married and settled in the Essex region not far from Farm Hill. Many of them spoke with a broad Essex dialect, and they made the comment that I had no regional accent myself, no doubt due to my nomadic lifestyle. But I still had an inflection, a problem with my tongue getting in the way of my speech.

Nurse Joan, who was the senior nurse at Farm Hill, in charge of Elves, now lived in Colchester with her husband, Mick, and two sons. I stayed with them for a few days, and through her I met many of my Farm Hill 'sisters'. They regarded Nurse Joan as their 'mum', and I could see why. The whole family were so warm and welcoming. Joan and Mick drove me to the familiar landmarks around the village of Coggeshall, and whilst in the area we felt obliged to make a dutiful call on Mother Simcox's retirement cottage nearby. Mother was still supercilious in her manner, her speech still stern, but she had mellowed considerably since I last knew her. Maybe it was I who had changed! I felt good to be able to talk to her confidently on her level, and she seemed genuinely interested in hearing about my travels to Turkey. We didn't stay long, because I also wanted to have another look at my childhood home of Farm Hill, just two miles down the road. It was now a home for delinquent boys, and I felt sad to see our handsome mansion in such a run-down condition, with broken windows and unkempt gardens.

Back in London I was reunited with Vera, who now had a steady boyfriend. We both caught a bus down to Eastbourne to stay the weekend with Mary, my ex-landlady who was now a very good friend. She had faithfully corresponded with me throughout my year in Turkey, and still continues to do so. Mary and her parents made me feel very much at home, and as usual I was reluctant to leave the warmth of her family.

I needed to find work before my money completely ran out, and soon I was walking the familiar streets of London. I found a cheap room on the second floor of an old tenement block in Nottingham Place, opposite Regents Park. I relished the freedom of pacing the streets of London unrestrainedly, and it felt good to be able to come and go as I wished.

I registered with a temping agency and before long I was back into the old routine of temping in offices around the inner city.

Whenever I was working in an office that was reasonably close to Somerset House in the Strand, the longing to find my mother became active in me and I would rush over in my lunch hour and start delving into the records. Finding my mother. It sounded easy. A trip to Somerset House to see if she had married, find her address and go along and introduce myself. But it wasn't that simple.

One thing I soon realised was that nothing would happen without my effort. As each year slipped by, the chances of tracing my mother grew slimmer. But I had to keep trying. I used up many of my lunch hours frantically searching through the large, cumbersome tomes that recorded marriages from 1940 up to the present year, 1964. In an attempt to cram as much searching time as possible into about forty-five minutes, I would hurry into the rooms, eagerly turning the pages of book after book, getting sore arms and eye strain, and wondering what little hidden gem might be unearthed that day. But day after day the search was fruitless and I often returned to work frustrated and downhearted. In the meantime, when my patience was wearing thin, I resisted the urge to look through the death records.

What a relief it was when at last I saw my mother's name, 'Ayshe Suleyman' in print! My heart gave an enormous, joyful leap. I had to wait a few days for the certificate to arrive in the mail. It was recorded that she had married a Michael Anthony O'Connor in 1944 and that the wedding took place in a registry office in Kilburn, four years after I was born. Now I had another fact about my life – my mother's marriage, and the knowledge made me feel strengthened in my resolve to find her. She was nineteen and he was twenty-five. Under the heading 'Profession' it was recorded that he was a sapper in the army and she was an assembler in a munitions factory.

For a breathless second I allowed myself to fantasise that we would at last meet and I could become part of their family. Questions bombarded my mind – questions that had been kept locked up inside me all these years. But in my heart of hearts I knew there was only the slimmest chance of finding Ayshe and Michael as the trail was by now twenty years old.

Now that I knew of the marriage, I turned to the record of Births. I already possessed my own full birth certificate, which gave my name as FATMA SULEYMAN, and where my father's name should have been printed there was just a blank space. It gave my mother's name as AYSHE SULEYMAN and her occupation as a domestic servant of 10 Lower Sloane Street, Chelsea – an address I had already visited on a previous occasion, and where I could see for myself what an illustrious neighbourhood she used to live in. Now I wanted to find out if my mother had had any children, for if she had it would give me a more recent address, and possibly half-brothers or sisters.

It was a backbreaking task lifting the heavy volumes and delving through every three-monthly period for each year from 1940 up to 1964. I decided to include in my search the four year period before my mother married, in case she might have had another baby between my birth and her marriage. But nothing.

After spending weeks looking through twenty-four years of records without any trace of a birth under my mother's name, I gave up. It seemed strange that my mother hadn't had any more children, because they are the natural progression of any marriage. It didn't take long for me to work out that as she was about fifteen years older than me, it meant she had now reached the age of thirty-nine, when her reproductive years were close to finishing. I assumed that if she was going to have any children she would have had them by now. The prognostications did not look good with regard to finding her.

I wondered whether the reason that there were no birth records might have been that she and her husband had left England to live overseas, perhaps in a Commonwealth country like Canada or Australia. I doubted that they would be living in Turkey. But possibly Ireland? The name O'Connor is Irish, and the names of the two witnesses, A. Hannon and M. Casey sounded Irish. If I could find them it would give me a clue as to my mother's whereabouts, but where did one start looking?

I decided to go to the address given on my mother's marriage certificate. On a drizzly Saturday morning, I caught two buses to Kilburn and eventually found the cul-de-sac called Brondesbury Villas. It was not the sort of day I would have chosen to go door-knocking and already half the day had gone. I walked on the left-hand side of the flat, deserted street, passing a bus stop outside one of the old terraced buildings. I had visions of my mother walking to the bus stop on her way to the munitions factory where she worked during the war. My pace slowed considerably as I looked at the numbers of each house, drinking in the ambience of the street where my mother lived. Then I stopped outside No. 31 and gazed longingly at the front door, willing it to be opened by someone who knew my mother, not for one moment expecting my mother herself to still be living there. An elderly woman answered my knock.

'I'm looking for a Turkish lady called Ayshe, who used to live here twenty years ago with her husband, Michael O'Connor. I don't suppose you know where they are now, do you?'

She stared at me for a moment or two. My heart stopped as I waited for her reply. 'No, I've been living here for ten years, and I don't know that name. You could try the neighbour across the road at No. 37. She's been living here longer than me.'

After she closed the door I stood where I was, staring after her, unable to move for a while. In time I came to my senses and sauntered across the road. No. 37 looked unlived in. There was no response to my knocking. There would be no answer there for me.

As I dragged myself back to my room in Nottingham Place, I sat on my bed, feeling nothing but weariness. The trail to find my mother had gone cold. I had no idea what to do next. That evening I pored intensely over the list of names in the London telephone directory, but the name O'Connor was so common that the task was impossible. I had to try to overcome the letdowns. My search might take for ever, but in the meantime, life had to go on.

To stop myself sliding into a depression, and to keep occupied, I took on an evening job and became an usherette at the Classic cinema in Baker Street, where I worked every Thursday, Friday and Saturday evening, finishing about eleven-thirty at night. I only ever saw the one movie in the three months I worked there. I remember it in graphic detail, James Stewart starring in the black and white version of the life story of Glenn Miller.

During the intervals I had to walk up the front with a tray strapped around my shoulders filled with ice-creams, confectionery and cold drinks, and I dreaded the moment when the spotlight shone on my face, blinding me. It was the cue for the stampede to start. In the half-dark, wrestling with loose change, I was unsure how much everything cost and even less confident that I gave the correct change. Mathematics has never been my forte.

I found the work tiring, in addition to my secretarial temping job during the day, and it lasted three months. Management offered to taxi me home, but my room in Nottingham Place was only two blocks away and I preferred to get some fresh air after the dark, smoky atmosphere of the cinema. I found myself looking over my shoulder all the way home.

I might have been afraid of being assaulted in the middle of the night during my short walk home from the cinema, but an incident happened in the sanctity of my own bedroom, which I found so unnerving that I needed to think again of moving. The Polish landlord physically attacked me in the middle of the night while I lay in my bed. I suppose, looking back, that it was a pathetic attempt at a sexual assault, and I was grateful he was so drunk that he was rendered incapable of doing much at all. Luckily, when I first felt his smelly breath near my face, my defence mechanisms went into overdrive. I immediately woke up, and in a frenzy of strength I didn't know I possessed, I leapt up from my bed and frantically fought him off, searching at the same time for the light switch. As soon as I managed to turn on the light it revealed his familiar face. He slunk drunkenly out of my room, muttering something in Polish. Although he apologised profusely the next day, I knew I could not spend another night under that roof once my security had been violated.

I stayed for a few weeks with Pauline Mutton Chops, another 'sister' from Farm Hill, who was now living with her husband and daughter in south London. I was in such a state of flux, with no permanent abode, no permanent work and no steady boyfriend, that I found myself being drawn back again to Turkey, for although I knew my mother was not there, the country still held a magnetic allure for me.

Vera and I had planned a two-week holiday to the Greek island of Rhodes, and as I knew Turkey was so close by I couldn't resist the temptation to go back there, just for a month or two, while Vera flew back home. I found some work as a governess with a Greek/Turkish family who lived on the small island of Büyükada in the Sea of Marmara. My job was to chaperone the seventeen year old daughter, while conversing all the time with her in English, and also to teach English to her father.

The short time I spent on the island was idyllic, quite different from the noise and bustle of Istanbul. I whiled away the days by swimming in the warm sea, catching rides on the horse and buggy around the island, and having long siestas in the afternoon. The pace was too slow for me, and I soon grew bored with the restrictions imposed on my movements and flew back to London.

Back in England I slid into the all-too-familiar pattern of temping and bedsits. They say London can be a lonely place and I guess it was for me, for I had nobody. I felt restless and rootless. The 15th of March marked my twenty-eighth birthday. I was motherless, alone and unconnected. There was no direction in my life. The Turkish dream had died along with my hopes of finding my mother. I needed a fresh challenge, a new goal. I made a decision which would change my life irrevocably.

Chapter Seven

Australia and New Zealand

It was June 1968. From the deck of the P & O liner *Oriana*, I caught my first glimpse of Australia. I had made many friends in the six weeks that the journey took, via South Africa, but I felt relieved to see the land I had deliberately chosen to be my home for the next two years. Banners and streamers garnished the Fremantle harbour and crowds of people lined the dock waiting to welcome friends and relatives. I peered with nonchalant detachment at the expectant faces, knowing that none would be looking for me.

The decision to go on a working holiday to Australia was made easy for me when I worked as a temporary secretary at the New South Wales state government offices in London. My job there was to do secretarial work for a team of friendly, outgoing Aussies who were recruiting skilled migrants to go to Australia. Everyone who was accepted for sponsorship would have their fares paid for by the Australian Government. Compared with English bosses, where I had to use the formal title of 'Mister', here I was able to call each team member by his first name which made it much easier to fit in to the team situation.

Over the next six months I was subjected to so much propaganda that I gradually developed a taste for things antipodean, and wanted to become a migrant myself. Two of the staff members wrote me an excellent reference and agreed to sponsor me. Australia, with its open spaces, warm climate and outdoor pursuits sounded appealing.

It seemed to me that I had nothing to lose by having a two-year working holiday in Australia, as I had no permanent home to call my own, and had left no loved ones behind. Another draw-card was that the fare was a mere £ 10 for the assisted passage, although I would need a bit more spending money to start me off in my new life. At that time Australia, with only eight million people, couldn't get enough skilled migrants, and I was happy to help them out by becoming another Ten Pound Pom.

Earlier in that year of 1968 I had hit a low spot in my life. The courtship with my latest boyfriend was short-lived and we parted on mutual terms. Vera, my best friend, was engaged to be married to a journalist, so I was seeing less and less of her. I had reached an impasse in my fruitless search for a mother which left me with a feeling of pervasive loneliness. I had never had any permanent abode, with no ties or responsibilities. I was as free as a bird so, just like a bird, I decided the time was right to migrate to another land, to seek new pastures, a fresh beginning. I might as well be lonely in Sydney as in London.

Now, here I was, on the other side of the earth, bound for Sydney, my ultimate destination. As the ship rounded the southern coastline of Australia I looked back at the vast ocean which now stood between me and England. I didn't know it then, but I was never to live in England again.

From my starting point in Sydney, I took twelve months to work my way round Australia, moving on through Canberra and Melbourne in temporary office positions, and somehow managed to end up in the remote outback of north-west Australia. I signed a contract to do secretarial work for six months for the Mount Newman Mining Company in Port Hedland, seventeen hundred kilometres north of Perth. Port Hedland is a major port for the gigantic

Pilbara iron ore industry, and because it was situated north of the Tropic of Capricorn there were special tax concessions for working there. My social life improved dramatically there as women were greatly outnumbered by men, but the macho beer-swilling, down-to-earth men whom I met at the rowdy Hedland Pub were not really my type.

For the latter part of my contract I was seconded to the base camp at Newman, five hundred kilometres inland, where I was flown by helicopter. For eight weeks I lived in the red, dusty satellite township of Newman, bang in the centre of the rich Mount Whaleback mining belt.

I loved it there. At weekends I explored the wonderland of the outback with other itinerant workers, and in a cavalcade of jeeps we would drive for miles along red dirt roads. The whole area was a stunning haven of flame-coloured ranges, deep gorges and enormous mining operations. I will never forget my first sight of thousands of blue and green budgerigars and other species of parrots flying freely in the remote hinterland.

In typical Aussie fashion we ended the day under the shade of a gum tree, by a rock pool, and ate barbecued steak swilled down with a few stubbies of ice-cold beer from the chilly bin. On the way back to the base we saw kangaroos jumping around all over the place in the half-dark.

When it was time to fly back again to Port Hedland, I was almost sorry to leave behind the wild, lonely beauty of the back country. The florid cliffs and gorges were a beauty all of their own, and one day I would love to return there as a tourist.

That year of 1969 was an historic year for the world and it was a landmark year for me. It was the year man walked on the moon for the first time. I recall the high excitement we all felt when, in our office in Port Hedland, we stopped working and listened to the live radio broadcast. If nothing

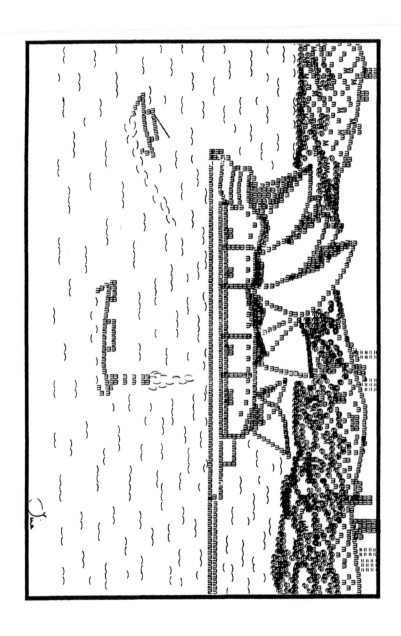

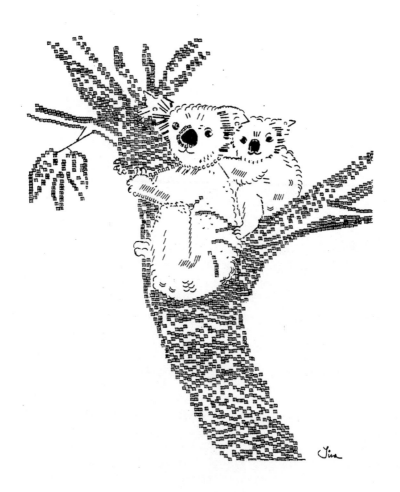

else, it helped to ease the tedium of the long working hours. Again, to keep my mind occupied, I resorted to typing letters to my friends and drawing pictures on my electric typewriter, just as I had done in Turkey and in offices in Sydney and Melbourne. This time, the pictures were Australian subjects, such as a parrot, koala bears and the Sydney Opera House, and I had quite a good little business going by selling them to shops as greetings cards. When the other office workers saw my pictures they thought they should be published, and I was persuaded to send them to the Australian *Women's Weekly*. A few weeks later a two-page article, that I had written myself, was published. In it I said that my parents had died during the war, a story I had been using ever since I had arrived in Australia, as it was a source of shame to me that I knew nothing about my family history, and I found it was the easiest solution to my problem. It saved me from bumbling, painful explanations. In any case, they might as well be dead so far as I was concerned. My little white lies were part of the protective shield I used whenever I was confronted by my piteous lack of knowledge of my own background.

Unbelievably, my article was read by a Barnardo friend, Brenda Gibbs, who also attended the Princess Margaret School in England.

She had settled with her husband and two children in Auckland, New Zealand, and she found out my address from the magazine and then wrote and invited me to be a guest in their home. Within the month I was flying across the Tasman, excited by the prospect of meeting Brenda and her family, and looking forward to a real holiday in New Zealand. I was well short of the mandatory two years' residence in Australia, and my intention was to have a short holiday in New Zealand, before returning to Australia and then heading back to England.

When the Qantas jet landed at Auckland International Terminal, little did I know that within the month I was to meet the man who was to become my husband, and that Auckland would be my home for the next thirty years.

★

After the harsh tropical climate of the Australian outback, Auckland was soft and gentle – and utterly green. It was early spring, and everywhere was filled with the fragrant aromas of jasmine and freesias. When waking on my first morning and walking in the crisp air around Brenda's garden, I felt very much at home. It was fourteen years since we had seen each other, and we spent many hours reminiscing about our schooldays. Although we had been in different classes and houses, we had usually met up on the sports field, where we both represented the school in athletics.

Brenda and Jerry introduced me to their circle of mainly English friends, and it was at one of those parties that I met Ray, who was originally from Clacton-on-Sea, in Essex, only twenty kilometres from Farm Hill. I didn't take too much notice of him at the time and spent most of the evening chatting to the other partygoers. Later I learned that his eight-year marriage had recently broken up. Without my knowledge, Brenda and her friends had banded together to plan some matchmaking with the idea of bringing Ray and me – 'two lost souls' – together. They encouraged Ray to phone me and ask me out, which he finally plucked up the courage to do, and before long we were going out regularly. Ray was emotionally vulnerable and needed a lot of support at that time. It was never my intention to fall in love. It happened when circumstances threw us together. It was the height of summer by now, and we spent most weekends walking along the waterfront or going to Auckland's many wonderful beaches, all the time talking and listening to each other's stories.

I felt that fate intervened kindly on my behalf when I made the foray across the Tasman, as Ray's loving nature captured my heart and soon I was aware that I wanted to spend the rest of my life with him, even though I knew his divorce would take two years and we would not be free to marry until then.

By now I was flatting near the university, where I had found work as secretary to the HOD, English. I'll never forget the night I invited Ray to dinner. I shared the flat with two other girls, who discreetly 'disappeared' for the evening. Ray stood at the front door, nervously smoking a cigarette, and suddenly thrust this huge bunch of flowers under my nose. 'That's to let you know that I love you,' he said sheepishly.

I was dumbfounded, too choked up to utter any words, apart from a mumbled, 'Thank you.'

After an unmemorable dinner, Ray held me in his arms while we sat on the settee and talked. Ray had to deal with all I was going through as I relived my childhood, the stigma of my illegitimacy and the emptiness inside of me. He encouraged me to unveil my darkest secrets, and without realising it, all my fears and anxieties poured out while he just sat and listened. Never before in my life had I cried so many tears in front of anyone, as I have never liked to show my emotions, but in the security of Ray's arms I felt comfortable, because he was so compassionate and caring. I suppose, because we had both experienced pain and rejection, there was a strong chemistry between us, which also grew into a physical attraction. Whenever I introduced him to my friends, every one of them remarked how handsome he was. 'Make sure you hang on to him,' they would say. I have to admit with his tanned complexion, brown eyes and raven hair he was extremely good-looking, but his initial appeal was his affectionate, cheerful nature. The physical attraction came later, though not too much later!

In the next few months I moved into a house on the Great South Road, with two other girls I had befriended. Ray and I spent as much time together as possible, and spoke a great deal about spending the rest of our lives with each other.

To get away from the trauma of his separation, I suggested that we go to Australia to find work. He agreed to come with me, though reluctantly, because he couldn't bear the thought of being apart from his two children. I had met them both and liked them instantly. Mark was an articulate and intelligent eight-year old, and Janette was a cute blonde six year old. Ray was a man of few words and he never divulged his real feelings about his broken marriage, but I could tell he was torn apart that he had 'lost' his children to another man and that he could never live with them again. But it wasn't until many years later, when Mark and Janette grew up and had their own families, that I learned to understand the pain they too felt at being parted from their father.

Ray and I found work for a few months in Sydney, and then moved on to Mount Isa Mines, North Queensland. This was Australia's largest underground mine, extending to a depth of eleven hundred metres, and was the world's biggest single producer of silver and lead. Ray worked above ground in the lead concentrator, sometimes doing double shifts, while I worked as secretary to the mine manager. We each bought a second-hand bike, as there was no public transport, and I'll never forget cycling in temperatures of one hundred and twenty degrees to the mining offices for a job interview, only to be greeted with the comment, 'Do you usually come to an interview without wearing stockings?' In spite of my 'inappropriate dress' I managed to get the job, but I hated every moment of it, mainly because of my overbearing boss and the heavy workload he gave me. No time to draw doodles here!

Ray made a quick trip back to Auckland to visit his children, as he was sorely missing them, and when our contract expired after nine months we were both relieved to return to New Zealand where we wanted to make our home.

Chapter Eight

Marriage and Children

How hard it is to find the words to describe my feelings during the simple but beautiful wedding ceremony in St Aidan's Church, Remuera. I was thirty-two and Ray was thirty-one when we married on 26th October, 1972. The thirty guests in the church, including Mark and Janette, were the sum total of our mutual friends, mainly, in fact, Ray's, because I hadn't been in New Zealand long enough to make any of my own. The NZ Barnardo representative, Jim Wilson, was there to represent Barnardo's, my first family. Brenda's husband, Jerry, gave me away. I wore a simple, white, ankle-length, two-piece dress which I brought over with me from Sydney. I carried a bouquet of beautifully perfumed yellow freesias.

As we stood at the altar I looked into Ray's eyes. My heart turned over with the tremendous importance of the occasion. He knew how nervous I was and held my hands tightly, in the hope that I would draw strength from him. So choked up was I with emotion, my eyes blinded with sharp tears, that Ray's face became a distant blur. When the time came to say our wedding vows, the words, 'I do' refused to come out.

Having shed a bucketful of tears on the way to the reception rooms at The Kiosk in the Auckland Domain, Brenda gave me a hug when I tried to explain why I couldn't say my vows. 'Weddings are never dry affairs,' she said, 'we're all delighted for you both.'

What a relief when it was all over! As we drove up to the Bay of Islands for a five-day honeymoon, I rubbed my shiny new wedding ring, a manifestation of the fact that I belonged to someone. And not just anyone. Had I really had the good luck to catch such a good, caring man – who carried an English surname into the bargain? Tina (Fatima) Suleyman was dead. Long live Tina Bareham. No longer need I be ashamed of my foreign surname, a name that no one ever knew how to pronounce – a name which had held cryptic connotations.

Until I met and married Ray I also realised just how lonely I had been. It was wonderful to be married, connected, to have for the first time in my life a relative whom I could truly call my own. Now I felt that I had joined the rest of humankind. Finally I was a normal person. Ray had what I needed: affection, a sunny disposition – and above all, a sense of humour. I had what he needed – a philosophical, down-to-earth view on life. I had found deep happiness and security with a man who was my best friend and husband. In fact he was to become everything to me – mother, father, brother. He *was* my family. Every single day I woke with Ray beside me I was comforted by his mere bodily presence. I had all the companionship I could ever want, secure in the knowledge that I was chosen. Loving and being loved helped to make me a stronger and more trusting person. It seemed almost too good to be true.

We settled down to our life together in our newly built house in Ranui, West Auckland, and set about choosing our furnishings and landscaping the garden. We did everything together, the cooking, the housework and the gardening, and when Ray added a carport and a deck, I discovered what a great handyman he was too.

He had a new job as a showroom assistant with a large textile company, and I found work as a receptionist/typist in the local council offices. Mark and Janette came over for weekends and holidays, and as they grew up they each brought a friend along. Bethells Beach on the west coast was a favourite outing for a day's picnic, or we would go for bush walks in the Waitakere ranges. Mark and Janette were intelligent, well-adjusted children, which made it easier to accept them as part of our family. I could see for myself how much they loved their dad. Ray had a mischievous streak in him and was always playing little tricks, which would bring peals of laughter from them. I had known right from the start how important it was for Ray that I accept his children. At first it was difficult for me acknowledging that Ray always wanted to be there for them, that they were part of him, but over the years we have all grown to love each other, and our boys think of them as their older brother and sister.

Our married life rolled on comfortably. I felt lighter now. I could connect with Ray's friends, who had since become my friends, and we had them over for dinner regularly. Ray could turn his hand to cooking, and at weekends he made it his responsibility to prepare the meals, which I didn't mind because cooking was not my strong point.

When I broached the subject of starting our own family, Ray wasn't so keen on the idea as he already had Mark and Janette. But I desperately wanted to have children – to have my own offspring, so I could make my own dynasty. By the time he came round to the idea, two years had already passed, and try as we might, I could not get pregnant.

Month after month passed by with no signs of pregnancy, and I became paranoid about my inability to conceive. Ray suggested we take a break from the stress of trying and go to the UK so we could introduce each other to his family and my friends in England. It was six years since I had visited the UK, and I was keen to go to Barnardo's headquarters and also to meet Ray's father and brother. Ray's mother had died when he was just sixteen, and his father was now living with Mike, Ray's older brother, and his family.

I was still in regular contact with Hilkat Bey, and he invited us to stay with him for a few days in Istanbul, en route to England. He generously paid for our hotel accommodation in Istanbul as well as putting us up for a few nights in the Princes Island. It was wonderful to see him again and to be back in the city that ten years ago had stolen my heart, and I excitedly showed it off to the man who had only recently stolen my heart and whom I now wanted to show off to Hilkat Bey and Vahide.

Vahide and her husband invited us to tea in their apartment in Bebek, north of Istanbul. I had hoped to talk about my mother, but with our husbands present, the opportunity did not present itself. The conversation was formally cordial and diplomatic, and when I tried to bring up the subject of my mother, other discussions took precedence, mainly domestic issues, and we left without having found out anything new about my mother. Because of Ray's importance in my life at that time, it didn't worry me unduly. I didn't know it then, but it would be twenty-one years before I visited Vahide again.

In England I met Ray's father and brother, Mike. Although Ray didn't have many other relatives that he knew of, it felt good to have some more familial connections, and to be part of Ray's family. When Ray's dad found out I was a Barnardo girl, he took the wind out of Ray's sails by announcing that his wife, Margaret, had also been illegitimate and in the care of Barnardo's when she was a girl. Neither his dad, nor his mum, had ever mentioned to Ray or Mike the matter of her being in Barnardo's. Taboo subjects like illegitimacy were kept quiet in those days. We all agreed what an amazing coincidence it was.

Ray and I decided to go and visit the after-care officer at Barnardo's headquarters in Barkingside to see if we could find out any more information about my time in their care, and to see if they had any records of Ray's mother. The records confirmed that in 1920 Ray's mum had been boarded out first, and had gone to live in Rose Cottage, at Barkingside Village, until 1925. Her first job was as a between-maid, but after that there was no more information. How pleased Ray was to be able to visit The Village at Barkingside, to see for himself where his mother had lived, even though many of the cottages were demolished.

Then it was my turn. I was given photocopies of a few of my personal records, such as school reports, and details of childhood illnesses, but there was no more information forthcoming about my family, and no offer made to look for my mother. I was now more or less resigned to Barnardo's continuing policy of stonewalling.

Besides, at least I had a little more knowledge about my own past, and I wasn't so concerned about finding my family now that I had the love and security of a husband, and the prospect of having children – always at the forefront of my mind.

I dragged poor Ray around to show him off to Vera, Mary and Janet, and to as many of my Barnardo friends as we could fit in. When we were summoned to have tea with Mother Simcox, Ray wasn't so keen to meet her after hearing torrid tales about her everywhere we went. I was keen to introduce Ray to her though, and as it turned out, she presented such a warm, human face to us that Ray thought we must all be telling lies.

After six weeks away we were more than pleased to be back in our own home in Auckland. We knew we must get down to the serious business of starting a family.

My first priority was to make an appointment with a gynaecologist to find out why I had not become pregnant. I was getting anxious because I was in my mid-thirties and well past the most suitable age to have children. After weeks of numerous tests, in which Ray also had a sperm count test, it was discovered that I wasn't ovulating, so the gynaecologist whose care I was now under put me on a moderate dose of Clomid, a fertility pill. Within three months, I found I had conceived. I was elated – overwhelmed with excitement at the news. We couldn't wait to tell all our friends and my workmates at the council. Everyone was thrilled for us.

It was around this time that Janet, Mary's daughter, came to live in New Zealand with her husband, Roy. They bought a house in Massey, a new suburb near Ranui. Although they were ten years younger than us, Roy and Ray hit it off immediately, and we all became very good friends, and spent a lot of time together. We were delighted when it was discovered that Janet too was pregnant.

To celebrate our fourth wedding anniversary, Ray and I hired a camp-o-matic and drove down to Pauanui Beach on the Coromandel Peninsular, some two hundred kilometres from Auckland. I was seven weeks pregnant, married to a man I loved more than I could have believed possible. Everything in my world was perfect. Early that evening we settled in, made a cup of tea, then strolled arm in arm along the white, sandy beach. In the middle of the night however, I started getting an overpowering pain, and before dawn broke I had miscarried. It was the end of a life that had hardly begun. A doctor was found and he advised Ray to drive me as quickly as possible to the National Women's Hospital in Auckland, in case the baby could be saved. But I knew I had lost it. Ray and I were terribly upset. He knew how desperately I wanted that baby, but I had to wait another six months before taking another course of fertility pills.

Once again, I found myself the subject of numerous medical tests, and for the first time in my life I had to have a full blood test. This revealed that I had a genetic blood disorder called Thalassaemia Minor, a severe anaemia usually found amongst Mediterranean people. It is indicated by abnormal haemoglobins in the blood, which do not carry enough oxygen around the bloodstream. I had always known I was anaemic, suffering as I did with occasional dizzy spells and feelings of tiredness, but the exotic sounding name fascinated me. This was something I had inherited from my unknown mother. The thought enthralled me, even if it was a blood disease!

I went on another three-month course of Clomid, with the doses being carefully monitored so I wouldn't end up with a multiple birth, and this time when I fell pregnant we were cautious about celebrating too soon. The specialist gave me 'holding' hormone injections so I wouldn't lose the baby. As my pregnancy advanced, I happily relinquished my job and discovered a new dimension to my life. I was full of wonder at the idea of a tiny life growing inside me and I took every care to make sure this baby would go to full term. My friends commented how radiant I looked. I so looked forward to the birth of my first baby, and I was determined to shower my child with the love and security that had been lacking in my own childhood. So determined was I to be as well prepared as possible for the birth, that I went to antenatal classes and read every book there was on the subject. It was fortunate for me that Janet, by now a close friend and a trained nurse, had recently given birth to a baby boy, and she gave me helpful tips about the birth process and what to expect, and handed down all the clothes that her baby quickly grew out of.

When our son was born in the year 1977, I was thirty-seven, a relative latecomer to first-time motherhood. We had already decided if the baby was a boy we would call him Nigel, for no other reason than that we both liked the name. If it had been a girl I wanted to call her Ayshe, in the romantic notion that somehow by using the name of my mother it would bring her closer to me.

Nigel came into the world unexpectedly. The drama unfolded when my waters broke in the dentist's chair while I was having a broken tooth repaired. Ray rushed me over in his car to the gynaecologist, who examined me and told Ray to drive as quickly as possible to the hospital. He confirmed that my waters had broken and, as I was having contractions every ten minutes we should get moving and he would be over later to deliver the baby. We went back to Ray's car – and, unbelievably, it wouldn't start. Over and over he turned the key in the ignition and still nothing happened. By now he was panicking. We went back inside and the specialist offered us his car if all else failed. Fortunately, we thought of our friends, Bill and Kath, who lived in nearby Royal Oak, so we rang them and miraculously they had returned home that morning from an overseas holiday. Within ten minutes, all of us trundled through the busy city streets to the hospital. By now my contractions were getting much stronger and it was difficult for any of us to remain calm.

We made record time to the hospital, but even there the crisis continued. Although my contractions were by now very strong, my cervix refused to dilate, and the baby began to show signs of distress. The specialist arrived just in time to order an emergency Caesarean section. I was shaking all over when they wheeled me away from Ray to the operating room. My teeth were chattering as well, and I just wanted the anaesthetist to stick the needle in to put me to sleep. Not wanting to affect my unborn baby with anaesthetic, I was given only a very light dose, so light that I felt the excruciating pain of the surgeon's knife as it sliced through my stomach.

I wanted this baby with all my heart and soul, but nature seemed to be working against me, first by denying me the ability to conceive, and then precluding me from giving birth in the natural way. I thought, thank heavens I live in the twentieth century, where I have the benefit of drugs to help me get pregnant, and all the modern medical facilities for a Caesarean delivery.

My ordeal ended when a healthy and beautiful baby was handed to me to have my first cuddle. What absolute relief I felt to see that my first precious baby had all five fingers and toes, and as I looked down at him I thought he was the most perfect specimen that any mother could hold in her arms.

For those few, extraordinary minutes, as I looked down into his tiny, red face, I knew what unequivocal love I had for my very first offspring, my own life-blood. I was convinced the nurse must have got him mixed up with another baby, for he was fair-haired and blue-eyed, and because we were both dark-haired and brown-eyed, we expected him to be too. Mix-ups of babies, I told myself, only happen in movies, and this was real life.

As Nigel grew up into a sturdy, curly-headed blond boy, I wondered whom he took after. Certainly, he bore no obvious likeness to either Ray or me. After rummaging through my diaries which went back over twenty years, I found the entry that I made during the year I lived in Istanbul. Written in pencil were these words: 'Vahide told me she remembers my father was tall with fair hair. She thinks he might also have worn glasses.' So now we knew. He must have taken after my father, at least in appearance. Nigel was found to be short-sighted and to have astigmatism, and he has had to wear glasses since the age of nine.

By the time Nigel started crawling I had conceived again, no doubt as a result of the still-active fertility pills. Ray and I were relieved in many ways because it took out of our hands the dilemma of whether or not to try for another child.

In the meantime, house prices were increasing and we made the decision to sell up and buy a bigger home. We found an ideal, two-storey house on a ROW section in the bush suburb of Birkenhead on Auckland's North Shore.

We were well and truly settled in to our new home when Laurence was born on the 21st July, 1978. He was two weeks overdue, and he was also delivered by emergency Caesarean section. A perfectly-formed, peaceful bundle weighing 8 lb 8 ozs, his head was covered with thick dark hair.

Just fifteen months separated our two boys, and the change to our lives with having two babies close together was immense. Our lives completely revolved around them. It was almost like having twins, with two lots of nappies and two baths. Everything was doubled up.

Ray's job as a sales representative meant that he had to travel around New Zealand, and there were many days when I was on my own. I missed his help, especially in the middle of the night as he was always the first to jump out of bed and go to the crying baby.

I was probably suffering from post-natal depression, because for two or three months after Laurence was born I felt quite low. I think having the two babies so close together took a lot out of me and at times I fell on the settee, utterly exhausted. I was having a particularly trying time one winter evening when Laurence had the croup and Nigel wouldn't sleep because his eczema rash was irritating him. My neighbour popped over to borrow a cup of sugar. I invited her to have a cup of tea with me and we chatted about our respective families. She said to me, 'I'm lucky that my mum comes over to help me with my two. Don't you have any relatives who can help?'

At that time it was not in my make-up to reveal to anybody my lack of family. I thought about my mother a lot but I rarely talked about her. How can you talk about someone who doesn't exist for you? I used to dread Mother's Day, as it was a reminder every year of my motherless state – like someone twisting a knife into me. Now, though, I felt blessed that I knew what it was like to be a mother.

No one was allowed to come too close. I staved off inquisitors with a quiet determination which probably puzzled them, and no doubt contributed to making me even more of an enigma. Of course, there were many other migrants in New Zealand who didn't have parents living close by. But that night I wasn't coping very well with being a mother. I felt so out of sorts that I overcame my reserve and shared the sketchy outline of my secret life with her. I told her that I was an orphan, brought up in a children's home and that I had no idea whether my parents were alive or dead. She gave me a look of such obvious pity that I became embarrassed and wished I hadn't confided in her. But it was too late.

She continued her probing with the question, 'How can you know how to be a mother when you've never had a mother yourself?'

It was something I had never thought about until then, and it took me a while to think of a reply. 'I guess it must be my maternal instinct?' I stabbed. As my babies grew into children, so I grew into the role of mother. I suppose I learned to be a mother intuitively. When the need arose I did what I thought best. The will to survive is instinctive, so is the role of motherhood. My intuition had only occasionally let me down in the past when I had needed to build on my resources to see me through various crises. Naturally, I devoured all the books I could lay my hands on relating to motherhood and babies, and I leaned heavily on Janet with her practical nursing experience and friendly counselling.

Whenever compliments were given about our two boys I would glow with pride. I worked hard at being a good mother and the proof that I brought them up in the best way possible is there now when I look at them and see what fine boys they have grown up to be.

Chapter Nine

My Family in New Zealand

To have a husband and my own family was the absolute fulfilment of my dreams. Never in my life had I been happier than I was now. My family continued to be an endless delight. There was now a real purpose to my life as I surrendered to motherhood and willingly spent my days washing, cooking, cleaning and ironing. Ray and I had a mutual understanding with regard to domestic arrangements. When he came home from work he helped to bath and feed the boys and tell them wonderfully inventive bedtime stories. Both of us immersed ourselves wholeheartedly into raising our family. At weekends we did the shopping and the housework together. Whenever it was one of the boy's birthdays, the house would be filled with lots of little playmates and Ray would organise some party games, which he was very good at, while I played the piano for musical chairs. The treasure hunt was undoubtedly the favourite party game, and our house and garden would be left in complete disarray while everything that could be was excitedly turned over for any hidden presents.

The children were the centre of my universe, and as I watched them grow and develop, no one was a prouder mum than I. Everyone remarked what good-looking lads we had but how different they were.

It was true. They were different in both looks and temperament, with Laurence resembling the dark features of Ray, and Nigel, with his pale blue eyes and curly fair hair, unlike either of us.

Nigel, the more extroverted of the two, often interceded for his younger brother, who with his quiet, placid nature, was content to let Nigel speak on his behalf, and the rare times he did try to speak we could not understand him. So, after consulting a specialist, Laurence, at the age of three, had his tonsils and adenoids removed and grommets placed in his ears. Even after the operation, he seemed disinclined to speak, and when he did he had a bad lisp. When I took him to a speech therapist, her first question was, 'Did either you or Ray have speech problems as a child?' Of course, I remembered having regular speech therapy throughout my own childhood. Over the next five years I took Laurence for therapy so he could learn how to talk properly. It was a source of fascination to me that I should have passed on a speech impediment to one of my sons. What else, I wondered, had I passed on to them both? And what in turn had my parents passed on to me?

Between us Ray and I had few relatives. It was unfortunate that Ray's father, now living in a rest home in Clacton-on-Sea, never expressed much interest in his family across the sea. Ray and his father had never been very close even though Ray did his best to keep in touch by phoning him on birthdays and Christmas. Ray's only other close relative is his brother, Mike, who had emigrated to New Zealand with his family the year Nigel was born, and they have lived on the North Shore ever since. We were glad to have a few more relatives close at hand.

I regretted that the boys' only grandparent lived so far away because grandparents, or other close relatives, are important in any family. When there was a 'Grandparents' Day' at kindy I agonised over the problem of who to ask to be surrogate grandparents for the day. Naturally, I felt protective of my children and didn't want them to feel that they were different from others. Eventually, our childless friends Bill and Kath who had come to our rescue with transport to the National Women's Hospital, again came to our aid. We encouraged them to be surrogate grandparents, but it didn't happen very often. They were now living in West Auckland, quite a distance from us, and apart from that, together the boys were a bit of a handful, especially for a couple whose experience with children was limited.

Much as I loved my family, now and again I needed a break from them, to have some space for myself. Ray's job took him away a lot, and I had little energy for much else in life, but there was a certain loneliness in spending almost all of my time with young children. Without the luxury of a mother, or even an aunt, to relieve me for a few hours a week, I did the next best thing and hired a nanny, even though we couldn't really afford her. She came over two afternoons a week while I went out and did some shopping or visited a neighbour. I hoped that she might become a temporary surrogate grandma, but whenever I was out of sight the boys became too boisterous for her, so she didn't stay long.

Watching the boys develop, I became increasingly aware of my own deep longings to find – to know – my own mother. The longings had never left me – only gone into abeyance in the early years of my marriage. Now, as my children were growing up, I couldn't deny the importance of my inheritance and theirs. There were still huge gaps in my life, and until I found my roots – which I felt it was my birthright to know – it seemed to me that I was not a complete person, despite being a wife and mother. I had established my own hereditary link by having children of my own, and I often thought about my heritage. I had passed a speech difficulty on to Laurence. Nigel possibly resembled his unknown grandfather. What else was there? I found myself thinking more and more about the mother I had never known. I felt bonded now, and my two boys carried my genes, but I wanted to share them with the person who brought me into the world, whose genes I had inherited. I yearned to be able to trace my mother so she could meet my husband and see her beautiful grandsons; and they too could know her. In my bones I felt that she would reciprocate the love I felt for her – that she would make our family complete.

These feelings of longing ebbed and flowed over the years depending on my state of mind. Since I had married they didn't occur so often, but when they did they were triggered by any situation which involved a mother – always someone else's, of course. Such was my subconscious longing for my own mother that whenever I witnessed a mother and daughter embracing in a public place, such as an airport or a bus station, I would stand transfixed, drinking in the sight of the two of them hugging each other, not really wanting to watch but unable to tear myself away. A lump would come to my throat and tears would fill my eyes. I was continually surprised at my emotional response to such a scene, and it made me realise the depth of my own needs.

I responded in the same way when my friends were with their own mothers. It would cut through me like a knife. I have a good friend at the tennis club who used to give me a lift each week. On the way back she would invariably call in on her gem of a mother. At times my heart ached to see the two of them together, engaging in mother and daughter small talk, and unknowingly rubbing salt into my wounds. During our journey back she would talk about what the two of them planned to do together for the rest of the week. I couldn't bear to watch them together. If only my friend knew how much I coveted her lovely mother, and the intimate relationship the two of them had. How could I possibly explain my true feelings to her?

These feelings of being jealous of my friends' mothers have gnawed at me constantly over the years. Their intensity diminished somewhat once Ray came into my life, but at the deepest level the longing was still there.

As soon as the boys were established into a routine at kindergarten, I decided to resume my search. I drove across the harbour bridge to the Auckland Public Library to look through their microfiche records. Nothing is going to happen, I told myself, unless you make it happen.

To start with, I looked up my father's name in the death records, but I couldn't find his name on the list. I had always assumed that he died at Dunkirk, but the Army Records Centre in England was unable to trace any service record of a Harold Kirton, and his name did not appear on their Rolls of Honour in the Second World War. On another visit I discovered there were four Harold Kirtons who had all married around the time that I was born. Might one of these men be my father?

I thought of writing to each of them, but it was such a long time ago, and with no real proof of his paternity, I decided to put him on hold and concentrate all my energies on tracing my mother.

But I had no more success with my mother because her birthplace was probably Romania, a previously Communist country. I pored over telephone books, checked the New Zealand electoral roll, joined international search organisations and made forays to the Church of the Latter Day Saints, all with spectacularly unfavourable results.

Many people have found searching for their ancestors to be a wonderfully relaxing, rewarding pastime, but for me it was exacting and depressing. I had to be careful that it didn't become an obsession, as I began to use all my spare time to look for the smallest crumb of information that might lead me to my mother. I was aware that I had to juggle my time sensibly so that I could still give my family all my love and attention, and yet the dark shadows from my past continued falling across my path and every now and again shrouded the blue skies that had been shining on me of late.

In 1980, when our boys were three and four, I started corresponding with two professional researchers, one in London, the other in Dublin, as I thought there was a good chance my mother and her husband might have made their home in Ireland. Alas, no records could be found of any children from the marriage of Michael and Ayshe O'Connor, in England or Ireland. Neither could the Dublin agent find any record of Michael Anthony having been born between 1916 and 1922. As a last resort, he suggested I place an advertisement in a Dublin newspaper, preferably a fairly large one, to read something like: 'Does anyone know the whereabouts of a Michael Anthony O'Connor and Ayshe O'Connor?' The name 'O'Connor' was so common in Ireland that I assumed the chances of someone recognising them would be remote indeed. I suspected that my Turkish mother probably didn't read newspapers, because, after all, English was not her first language. The odds were doubtful that they might have settled in Dublin. The dilemma now facing me was, in which of the main cities in Ireland should I place a newspaper advertisement? The possibilities were endless, the cost prohibitive and therefore another brilliant idea had to go on the scrap heap due to lack of funds.

Looking back now at what I considered to be a rational, balanced decision at the time, I can't help questioning whether it was the right one. I think to myself, if only we had had more money to spare, or I had had more tenacity, I might have placed a 'wanted' advertisement in an Irish newspaper. Had we not been living so far away communications would most definitely have been easier. This might have happened, or perhaps that might have happened. Perhaps kismet itself was playing its part.

I struggled on relentlessly search for my mother, following any faint gleam of hope through the foggy road ahead. In my hunger to piece together what little I knew of my ancestry, I continued corresponding with anyone I could think of who might be useful and my 'search' file was getting fatter and fatter. The International Red Cross eventually responded to my request for information: 'We are very strict about searching for birth parents' was their curt reply. 'The law is designed to protect those involved from being hurt.' But what about me? How could these bureaucrats presume to think that I was not being hurt? Barnardo's rock solid policy of not wanting to help people find their birth parents left me with a sense of frustration and anger. It was the same for all illegitimate children like me, and for any children under their care who had been adopted. Every one of the large children's agencies, including Barnardo's, had strict privacy laws and would not consider budging from them under any circumstances. How could I, living at the other end of the earth, battle against the international powers of bureaucracy on my own?

It was obvious I was banging my head against a brick wall and succeeding only in giving myself a lifelong headache. Since visiting the Akcers in Turkey and procuring my mother's marriage certificate in London, I had learned nothing more about my mother. Yet I still persisted in my efforts to find her, not only for my sake now, but for the sake of my children. Sometimes I felt a tremendous need to see and talk to her. The deep longing to know her was always there.

The Salvation Army had my case on their files for two years, both in New Zealand and England. In April 1984 I received the following letter from the missing person secretary: 'We are sorry to inform you that despite all our efforts we have been unable to find your mother and there is now no hope of us ever doing so. We have no option but to close our file.' They added, 'God bless you.' He might well bless me, I thought, but no one, it seemed, was willing or able to help me fit together the pieces that were missing in the jigsaw of my life.

In the meantime, our boys were growing up. We told them about our respective backgrounds, and they accepted that they had far fewer relatives than their friends had. There were just the four of us, a closely-knit family unit. Mark and Janette, Ray's first children, were the boys' half-brother and sister, but by now we weren't seeing much of them as they had grown up and formed relationships of their own.

I involved myself in the boys' school activities, and helped accompany at the school choir rehearsals. Both Ray and I assisted in fund-raising projects for the local school, having fun and making friends in the process.

I started giving piano lessons to my boys, and in order to become better qualified I put myself through a rigorous practice routine with the help of a local piano teacher, managing to pass grades six and seven. Before long I was giving lessons to other children.

Nigel thoroughly enjoyed his music, and from an early age displayed a real aptitude for it. He liked listening to Richard Clayderman piano tapes before drifting off to sleep. One night, when he was about ten, I tucked him up in his bed, and he said to me, 'Mummy, why is it that I feel like crying sometimes when I listen to music?' I knew then that beautiful music stirred the depths of his soul, just as it did with me. Not long afterwards, he began trumpet lessons. Laurence, who had always been a head-banger as a baby, not surprisingly preferred beating the drums, so we arranged for him to have lessons too, and the following year both of the boys were in the North Shore brass band.

In order to have some adult company and keep my life in balance I joined Tecorians, a speaking club, where you are encouraged to think on your feet and speak in front of a group of people. The day comes back to me with clarity when I stood up to give my first icebreaker speech, for I was shaking like a leaf. Five years later I was a more self-assured person and joined the committee as club secretary. Among other things, Tecorians gave me the confidence to be able to speak about myself to neighbours, friends and even strangers.

I had always found it hard to speak to people about myself. Over the years I had built a strong protecting shell against other people's persistent questioning into my life, and I would shy away, succeeding only in becoming even more of an enigma to them. I have to admit, my heart would turn over if I knew someone was about to ask me a personal question about my kith or kin. My reaction was to either walk away, change the subject, or, if totally trapped, tell outright lies. I became adept at telling lies.

Since living in New Zealand, I had found it easier to pretend I had relations back in England, because many of my English friends were in the same position, but often I would trip myself up, especially if the questioner became too persistent. The trouble was, I never knew what people's reaction would be if I blurted out the truth and admitted to being an orphan, even though I didn't really think of myself as being a proper one. Well, I had a mother somewhere didn't I?

My reluctance to admit to people my background stemmed from the fact that I remained abysmally ignorant about it.

When I did have the courage to declare the few facts that I knew about myself – that I had been brought up in a Barnardo home and didn't know who, or where, my relatives were – it brought mixed reactions from people. Some showed acute embarrassment, others have even cried in genuine pity. Some, unbelievably, have said, 'You're better off without parents. They're not always what they're cracked up to be.'

Over the years I have developed my own defence mechanisms by telling fibs. 'My parents died in the war,' I would parry quickly, hoping no one would probe deeper. It's not so much that I was embarrassed about telling anyone that I was illegitimate or an orphan, as half the time I didn't quite know what to label myself. And I didn't want to embarrass the questioner, as I knew so little about my forbears. I remained confused about my origins and hid beneath a veil of secrecy because I had no idea how to cope with it.

Ever since I met Ray, I have had occasional nightmares that I might lose the one person in my life whom I have cared for and loved. Many years passed before I could allow myself the luxury of believing that our relationship would last. After our sons were born the nightmares redoubled and now they included my precious boys. I understood the rationale behind them, but when they ran riot I was unable to prevent them. It was as though, in spite of my present love and security, the fears and isolation of my past could not rest. They found instead a focus in these soul-rending dreams and in my preoccupation with my mother.

Rationally or irrationally, my need to find her was becoming a burning compulsion. I remember watching a TV show called *Missing*. Its aim was to bring together people who were missing from each other's lives. I knew immediately that I wanted to be part of the programme, and applied to TVNZ, but as it was geared primarily to New Zealanders, my case was considered 'unsuitable'. In spite of not being allowed to participate, I forced myself to watch each episode as families or friends were 'found' and reunited with each other. My tears dripped copiously into a large box of tissues resting on my lap. I know my family thought I was crazy for putting myself through such unnecessary agonies by watching it. They were right. It did me no good at all. But, such was the driving force within me that it was compulsory viewing, as such programmes kept alight for me the idea that one day it would be my turn.

A little while later, on the spur of the moment, I made an appointment to visit a clairvoyant who was advertising her services in the local paper. I had no idea of her identity or even if she was any good. I dare not mention it to Ray. I don't think even he would have understood the reasons for my impulsive urge. Before leaving I grabbed two small black and white photos of my mother, which I carefully placed in my handbag.

The homely looking woman who sat before me looked as if she was in her eighties, much older than she sounded on the phone. I gave her minimal details of my life, not wanting to give her too many clues with which she might try to fabricate some tall story. She held one of the photos in her wrinkled hand and for a minute or two her eyes glazed over. When she came out of her trance, she looked me straight in the eye and told me that she was sure my mother was alive and happily married in Canada.

Now that was a new one. Canada. I groaned inwardly. Where did one start to look for someone in such a vast country miles away from New Zealand? Was she saying my mother was alive because that is what she thought I wanted to hear? I wasn't so gullible as to wholly believe that what she was telling me was fact. Should I try out another one? But how could one tell a good clairvoyant from a bad one? I had absolutely no idea.

I toyed with the thought of pursuing Canada as the next possible country to explore, but just thinking about it made me feel exhausted. Besides, I couldn't take any more rebuffs, as the pile of correspondence in my 'search' folder had produced nothing of substance to give me the one vital clue that would unlock the door to my mother. Once more, I was forced to put my search on hold.

Nothing was more important to me than my small, tight-knit family. We were now established in Birkenhead, a North Shore suburb just over the harbour bridge, and I was loving every minute of being a suburban housewife. All my past feelings of loneliness had melted away and it felt good to be alive and to know that I could pour all my love and energy into my growing family. Both the boys were tall for their age. Aged nine, Laurence was the tallest boy in his class at Birkenhead Primary School. He no longer needed help with his speech and he took the main role of the prince in the school play at the end of the year. Nigel was in his last year of primary school, and keen on sport so he started having tennis coaching for the summer. At the age of ten he began Saturday morning music classes for the trumpet. Ray's brother introduced Ray to trout fishing, and he and Ray would drive down to fly-fish in the Tongariro river, over four hours south of Auckland, at every possible opportunity.

My own circle of friends was increasing each year. Every time I walked up the hill from our house in the kauri bush estate to the Highbury Shopping Centre, I would bump into someone I knew.

Singing still remained one of my intense pleasures, and I helped to form a women's vocal quartet called 'The Silk'n Sounds'. We practised once a week, and sang to groups of older people like 'The 60's Up' clubs all over the North Shore. I felt that people liked to be with me; I liked to be with people. Life couldn't have been happier. Then I got breast cancer.

I diagnosed my own condition when I flopped on the bed one day after a hard game of tennis and discovered a small lump under my right breast. A TV programme on cancer the night before had induced me to do a self-examination, and when I felt the hard lump my whole being froze with shocked disbelief. But that action saved my life.

The surgeon recommended a mastectomy with a simultaneous reconstruction, which meant my breast would be rebuilt, using a muscle from my back and a silicone gel-filled implant. It was some consolation that after losing my breast it would be rebuilt. Hopefully no one would be able to tell the difference and I would look quite normal. For the three weeks after I discovered the lump I went about in a haze – tears when I was alone or with my beloved Ray, smiles and bravery when I was with my friends.

That year of 1987 sticks firmly in my mind, for on the afternoon of 1st December, straight after giving a concert with our quartet, I drove myself to the Mercy Hospital in Epsom.

The operation was a success. The cancer had been detected in time; the radical surgery had succeeded in removing all trace of the disease from my body. Although I knew I'd never wear a bikini again, the reconstructed breast gave the appearance of normality. I was deeply thankful.

It took me three months to completely recover from the operation and about three years to adjust to my new breast. My own resilience and the help of my family and friends pulled me through. With one in twelve women in New Zealand dying of breast cancer each year, I felt I was one of the lucky survivors. I have since had the implant removed because of the unknown lasting effects of silicone inside my body, and I'm managing perfectly well without it.

It is well known that breast cancer is a familial disease that can be passed on through generations of women. Was this something else, I wondered, that my mother had passed on to me?

Our 25th Wedding Anniversary, October 1997.

Ayshe, aged 8, and her father, aged 75.

Ayshe, aged 9.

Michael and Ayshe on their wedding day, 1944.

Ayshe, aged 25.

My mother's house in Listowel, bottom of the street far right.

Ayshe, aged 30.

Ayshe, aged 30.

Chapter Ten

The Letter

I remember very distinctly the day I flew out of New Zealand and waved goodbye to my family. It was June 1992. I felt sick with apprehension for, not only was I travelling alone, but it was the first time I'd been in a plane for eighteen years. With Ray's encouragement, I had agreed to go to England alone after receiving a tape from Mary, who pleaded with me to visit her before she got too much older. Her daughter, Janet, had returned to England many years previously to be closer to her mother, and I was looking forward to catching up with her husband and son. I also wanted to see Vera and her family, and to visit as many of my Barnardo 'sisters' as possible.

After so many years of sheltered domesticity I felt a little fearful at leaving my three 'boys', the three people in the world I really cared about. Ray was happy to stay at home and look after Nigel and Laurence, who were now fourteen and thirteen years respectively. Ray's new position as textile sales manager required him to continue working, and as the boys were studying for end of term exams it made sense for me to leave them all behind. Besides, we could only afford one fare, so my friends, who had been urging me for many years to bring my family over, would have to make do with me on my own.

London, from above, looked like a compact version of Toytown. By the time I arrived at Gatwick Airport I felt a mixture of excitement, disorientation and independence.

At the airport, Janet and Mary were there to meet me. Mary was overwhelmed with emotion to see me again. I used Janet's home as a base, and later I stayed with Mary and her husband for a few days in their cottage near Eastbourne. As we drove along the leafy lanes to have a pub lunch, it felt good to be in the summer sunshine, relaxing with my old friends in the 'mother country'.

I stayed a couple of nights in the Colchester home of Joan, who had been the nurse in charge of the Children's House at Farm Hill. While there, her husband drove me to the Barnardo headquarters in Barkingside. I was aware that the Adult Adoption Information Act had been passed in 1985, which allowed children and their mothers to contact each other, but since then I had taken scant notice of it, thinking that it would not really affect me as I had never been adopted. In any case, I had learned from past experience not to expect too much from the authorities, and that way I would not be too disappointed.

I walked into Barnardo headquarters on a mild, muggy day in the middle of June, and met Ann, an after-care social worker. I had phoned her when I first arrived in England, asking if she could give me any further background information about myself when I was in Barnardo's care. She handed me a typed, two-page letter, which summarised my history with Barnardo's from 1940 until I left their care in 1957. It told me a little bit more about my life at Farm Hill, but not much else.

After inviting me to have lunch with her in the canteen, Ann suddenly took the wind out of my sails by making an offer to trace my mother, with the help of the Salvation Army. I had to ask her to repeat the sentence, because I couldn't believe that what she was saying was true, for in the thirty-five years since I had left Barnardo's, no such proposition had ever been made to me.

In spite of my passionate desire to meet my mother, my immediate reaction was one of pessimism. 'I'm sure I'll go to my grave without ever knowing who I am,' I responded, with more than a hint of sarcasm, 'but by all means try if you like. I guess it won't hurt.'

Refusing to allow my hopes to build up to the point where I would only be disappointed, I pushed the subject to the back of my mind as I flew back to my home in Auckland. When I saw my two strapping lads waiting to greet me at the airport, dwarfing their smiling, and now greying father, I looked at them lovingly in a moment of wonder that I had brought them into the world and that this happy trio of men was my family. They looked as though they had been doing perfectly all right without me. I hoped I hadn't become surplus to their requirements while I'd been away. I needn't have worried as very soon they were asking, 'Mum, where did you put my socks?' or 'Mumsky (their endearing name for me when they wanted something), can you iron this shirt for me?' It didn't take too long to fit into the role of a mum again. In particular, I was glad to be back in my own bed.

Six weeks after settling back into my usual routine in our Auckland home, Nigel eagerly handed me a letter with an airmail stamp on it, the ones which he knows I always like to receive. We were all sitting in our courtyard having lunch and lapping up the early spring sunshine. I ripped open the envelope, unfolded the letter and started reading. It was from Ann, the after-care worker with Barnardo's.

My heart raced as I took in her first sentence... 'the Salvation Army contacted me this week to say they had traced your mother's family;' and then I saw the words I feared most. 'The sad part is that she... died eleven years ago of cancer.' The words hit me like a bullet from a gun. I felt all the blood draining from my body. For me she died that day. Momentarily my heart froze and my head spun round. The letter fluttered to the ground. I could read no more as tears blurred my vision. All I could take in was that my mother was no longer alive, and my broken links with my past would never be mended. Overtaken with grief, I succumbed to an outpouring of anguish from the very depths of my soul, and broke down and sobbed my heart out. The letter unexpectedly brought emotions to the surface that I had buried deeply within me throughout my life. While I had continued to control them, especially after Nigel and Laurence were born, they kept bubbling away inside. Now that vital bubble of hope had burst. I had lost the battle to find her. She had been found and lost in the same instant.

My life had been a series of lonely fights when my spirit was fortified by the small hope that some day it would happen – my mother and I would at last see each other.

Between gut-wrenching sobs, I asked Nigel to read the rest of the letter out to me, as Ray, who had taken upon him the maternal mantle throughout our marriage, put his arms around me and held me. For the first time in their lives my boys saw my emotional barrier slip as tears of pain streamed from my eyes, showing them the full face of my distress. I could no longer hide it from them. I just fell apart.

Naturally, being teenage boys, they were embarrassed by my overt display of emotion, and their faces showed that they couldn't understand why I should be so distraught. I realised then that I hadn't told them the news. 'My mother's dead,' I blurted, unable to say any more. I required all my inner strength, the strength of spirit that had helped me through all the years of being utterly and hopelessly alone, to pull myself together in front of my boys.

Laurence brought me a box of tissues, and after a while Nigel read aloud the rest of the letter… 'Ayshe's husband,

Michael O'Connor, died two years later. She never had any more children after you, but she did unofficially "adopt" a little girl, Kelly, who was the daughter of her husband's niece. Kelly is now aged twenty-five and married with a young daughter. She regards your mother as hers and you as her sister, though she had not been aware of you until The Salvation Army contact. She has written a letter which I have enclosed. It's disappointing for you that she came on the scene just after you left England. She will obviously be a good source of information for you about Ayshe and may help to fill the void you've always felt...'

Nigel read the last sentence that Ann had written: 'I do hope you have someone with whom you can share your sense of loss that your mother was not "found" sooner.' Her solicitous words helped to bring me back to my senses. I did have someone to share my loss – my family who were sitting in the garden with me at that very moment. How could I have borne the pain without them?

Whenever I think of the weeks that followed the news of my mother's death, a series of pictures unroll themselves through my mind.

A cold cup of tea stands before me on the table; I try to drink it, but cannot.

Traumatised, I sit alone in the kitchen. Outside in our courtyard, the branches of our native Rimu blow in a fierce gale, and the pot of red geraniums has pitched over. I stare at it listlessly, unable to move. It is late morning and I gaze up at the large tapestry of cloud. My mind wanders over to Ireland, to a town called Listowel. I think of the lovely, carefully-measured words that Kelly has written in her heart-warming letter, about how she loved 'her mam' and how she now regards me as her sister. I cannot take in her words. The concept of someone else loving my mother is too difficult to fathom.

I walk alone in a slow-motion haze through the streets of our lovely bush estate. I notice none of its beauty. Two rosellas are squawking as they fly above me. I do not hear them. I stare with swimming eyes at my feet as I walk robotically up the hill. I see nothing, nobody.

Half-consciously, my mind goes through the words of the two letters and what they mean for me now. If I didn't have Ray or the boys, would I want to continue walking through life alone, with all hope lost now that I know she is dead?

It is as if I didn't exist for her. The thought persists that she went to her grave indifferent to the fact that she had a daughter, but hardest of all to bear is the realisation that she died without leaving behind any progeny – except me, and that I still have no brothers or sisters. Even her husband has died so I cannot meet him and learn about her.

Feeling wretched and confused, I ask myself thousands of questions which I cannot answer.

The chance of her being alive had kept my hopes high and my dreams viable. Her image is constantly with me in my subconscious; she is, and always has been, in my thoughts. I know it is futile, but I continually berate myself for not being more aggressive, more diligent in my efforts. If only I had gone to Kilburn again, if only I had asked more questions of the Akcers. If only Barnardo's had been more helpful, if only… if only…

I go about in a listless daze, my mind filled with dizzying thoughts. I try to keep busy. I burst into uncontrollable tears. Ray comes home and finds me crying over the vacuum cleaner. He consoles me and makes me another cup of tea. He cannot stay long; he has to go back to work.

Every day I am filled with self-absorption of my own suffering. Over and over in my mind I hear the dead, distressing words. I am shocked at my own vulnerability and cannot fathom why I should grieve over the loss of a mother I didn't have the opportunity to know or come to love. She has left me with no meaningful memories. I cannot stop the flood of despair at the thought that we never met. How could she have the temerity to go to her grave at such an early age, before giving me the chance to find her? For days I cry deep, silent, shuddering tears. I exist as if in a void – a state of nothingness.

Gradually, over the next few weeks the numbness wears off. Slowly, painfully, emotions start to filter through. The ramifications of her death begin to gain some coherence in my mind. I type a five-page letter to Kelly, giving her a summary of my life up to the present time. I write superficially, taking care not to show her my real feelings. I tell her that she was wrong in thinking that I was adopted.

Ray sees my daily grief and it hurts him. He insists that I go to Ireland to find out all about my mother.

Chapter Eleven

Listowel

Ray and I swallowed several cups of coffee in the departure lounge of Auckland International Airport. Unbelievably, I was about to depart on an Air New Zealand Boeing 747, this time bound for Ireland. Again, I was leaving behind my forbearing family to look after themselves, and the task of finding the bulk of the fare fell, once more, to Ray. I felt guilty at deserting my boys. 'Don't you worry about us, darling,' Ray had said. 'Just go. Go to Ireland. Find out all you can. About your mother, Ireland, everything. And ring collect whenever you need to.'

Surprisingly, I felt calm and collected when the plane roared up the runway to start its long journey, and although I did not look forward to the arduous flight, at least I knew now what to expect. This time I felt more confident about flying, though the unknown days ahead in Ireland pervaded my thoughts throughout the whole trip. It all seemed like a fairy tale. Unreal. For me there would be no tearful reunion at the airport, just a brief, painful journey of discovery after the facts.

During the twelve-hour leg to Los Angeles, I struck up a conversation with a woman passenger, who asked me where I was going.

'I'm travelling to Ireland to find out all about my mother, because I never knew her.'

Uncharacteristically, I confided in this stranger about my long-lost mother, almost as if to convince myself that it really was happening and I would indeed be touching down in my mother's adopted country in a matter of days...

Tears streaked down my face when the Aer Lingus plane flew over the Emerald Isle on a drizzly Sunday in October, 1992. I was tormented by the realisation that this was the country, so like New Zealand from the air with its green-velvet pastures, that had claimed my mother for thirty years. Being a foreigner, surely she must also have felt strange when she entered an unknown land with her Irish husband many years earlier, no doubt by ship rather than by air. I empathised strongly with her in that freeze-framed instant.

Kelly had arranged to meet me at Shannon Airport, one hundred and fifty kilometres north of Listowel. There was a big crowd in the arrivals hall. My fellow passengers pressed forward to greet loved ones. Would Kelly be there to greet me? For a long ten minutes I stood self-consciously by the exit door in the passenger lounge searching the blank faces of the few people left. Did one of them belong to Kelly? I dreaded the prospect of meeting her and wished fervently she would hurry up and make herself known to me. She did have some idea what I looked like because I had sent her a photo of myself with my family and mentioned in the letter that I was tall with brown, newly-permed hair, and wearing a red jacket. I had no idea how she would look. Because she took so long to reveal herself, I suspected she might be sizing me up from a distance before plucking up enough courage to face me.

Suddenly, a short, plump figure appeared out of nowhere, protectively clutching her four-month old baby. She seemed flustered. 'I'm sorry I took so long,' she said in a soft voice, 'but I couldn't be sure if it was you.' Her pale round face could not disguise her apprehension as we kissed each other awkwardly.

'Now you're close up I can see you're so much like me mam,' Kelly continued. I was taken aback somewhat at her referral to my mother as her 'mam', and from then on whenever I heard her say 'me mam' in that familiar Irish way, I inwardly winced. I didn't like hearing it at all. Jan, a good friend back in New Zealand, had warned me that I might feel some jealousy when confronted by the reality of someone who considered my mother to be hers. It hurt more than I could have believed possible. I felt as though a tidal wave of impressions and emotions was about to engulf me. It was not a good start. I knew I had to keep my emotions under firm control if I was to last the distance.

The cold air hit me as we walked towards the car park where Kelly's brother-in-law, Peter, waited. He would drive us back to Listowel, one and a half hours away. Instinct told me it would be emotionally draining for both Kelly and myself during the next few days.

My mother's grand-niece on her husband's side, Kelly was never officially adopted, but it was obvious from her letter that she regarded my mother as hers. Putting myself in her shoes, I knew she would have received an enormous shock at my sudden appearance on the scene and was no doubt curious to meet me. And yet, how apprehensive she must also have been at the meeting.

Kelly lit a cigarette and juggled the baby from one knee to the other. We sat in the back seat of the old car, unobtrusively inspecting each other. I felt uncomfortably self-conscious whenever our eyes met as I wondered what she was thinking about me. My eyes were gritty and I felt dirty and tired. Kelly too seemed washed out. Her honey-blond hair was swept back untidily from her face as if she hadn't the time to comb it. I began to wonder how we would get on together. We seemed to be so very different – our lifestyles, our age, our life's experience. Two strangers from opposite ends of the earth, linked by a common thread – a mother whom neither wished to share.

We crossed the river Shannon, quickly passing through the sprawling, grey town of Limerick, and headed for the open country of south-west Ireland. Peter drove the car at full throttle along straight, empty roads towards Listowel in County Kerry, where I would stay for ten days as Kelly's guest. I barely noticed the flat green landscape, concentrating instead on filling the silent gaps with small talk. I learned that Kelly was twenty-five, married, with two children. Her husband, Jeff, was an unemployed postman who spent most of his time at home as a house husband while she helped out with some cooking at a local convent.

I earnestly hoped the light lunch I forced myself to eat on the plane would not reappear, as I was beginning to feel quite queasy due to the reckless speed of Peter's driving. It was wearing away the edges of my already frayed nerves. He hardly spoke a word throughout the journey, as we tore through sleepy villages and towns. Hanging on for dear life, I strained to hear Kelly's soft Irish tones against the loud drone of the engine. Conversation was stilted, sporadic, as we both strived vainly to find common ground. A heavy atmosphere filled the car, broken only occasionally by the crying of the baby. The journey became an exercise in diplomacy as Kelly opened the window so her cigarette smoke could escape. Which is worse I thought, the smoke or the blast of cold air? Perhaps sensing my disapproval, she smiled and said, 'I'm trying to give up but I'll wait till your visit is over.'

I knew then how nervous she was about meeting her mam's only blood relation. Trying to keep an open mind about everything, I too felt anxious about the girl who innocently displaced me as my mother's daughter.

As we approached the township of Listowel, I breathed a sigh of relief. The car slowed down to a comfortable speed as we entered rain-swept O'Connell Avenue, the council estate where Kelly had lived as a child, and where she and Jeff returned to live as a married couple. Already at six o'clock, Listowel was drawing down the blinds for the evening.

Kelly pointed out No. 41, my mother's small, terraced house at the end of the cul-de-sac further down the road, amazingly in sight of Kelly's house at No. 64 on the same estate. In the fading light the bare streets appeared desolate, deserted. A grotto of the Virgin Mary stuck out incongruously, bang in the centre of the crossroads. The stone cottages, in blocks of four, stood grimly in the gloom, my mother's house at the far end looking sadly forlorn. Mesmerised for a moment, I couldn't tear my eyes away. So this was where she lived all these years. Bricks and mortar are a poor substitute for finding my mother, but at least they provided something tangible for me to look at. For years I had dreamt about her living in a house, with her own family, and here it was. I could hardly believe that I was looking at it with my own eyes. Kelly promised to ask the present occupiers if we could see through it one day, and there arose in me a wave of anticipation at the prospect of actually walking through the house where my mother once lived.

Jeff, Kelly's husband, emerged from the front door. He was dark and swarthy, uncannily like a typical Turk. His face was impassive, with no welcoming smile. I began to feel more uneasy about staying with them instead of in a local hotel, which had been my original plan. I had relented only in response to Kelly's insistent invitation but now began to question the wisdom of my decision. Jeff carried my suitcase up the narrow flight of stairs to the front bedroom. He and Kelly had shifted into the back bedroom with their three year old daughter, Aysa and the baby, Jack. Grateful as I was to them for giving up their double bed for me, I felt guilty and embarrassed about disrupting their lives in such a way.

To take my mind off the freezing temperature, I hurriedly walked across the bare floor to close the window and draw the flimsy curtains, and hung up my clothes in the wardrobe. It was much too cold to stay up there for long so I went downstairs into the warm kitchen.

Facing me at the bottom of the stairs was a solitary toilet. I looked around for any signs of a bathroom, but couldn't see one. After my arduous journey I longed for a hot shower, but I was quickly to learn that here they washed down at the kitchen sink. The thought appalled me. The toilet, kitchen and tiny lounge off it were the only rooms downstairs. Upstairs there were just the two bedrooms. Theirs was a typical 'two-up, two-down' council house, with tiny rooms by New Zealand standards.

I had yet to meet the menagerie of animals that were kept in the back yard. The big shaggy dog called Jack, which amazingly shared the same name as the baby, had already made itself known to me with a big lick when I first arrived, and was smartly sent outside. I could hear the bleating of the pet goat. No doubt I would meet him soon, along with the three cats and the hamster.

The roast dinner smelt good but I knew my churned up stomach could not take in much food at that moment. Jeff put another chunk of peat in the Aga, which gave off a strange, earthy odour. Kelly explained that everyone in Listowel had free access to the local bogs which were divided up into lots for distribution to members of the community.

I gave Aysa the buzzy-bee that I brought for her from New Zealand. She was blond with a gorgeous smile and gaps in her teeth. She drove us all crazy pulling the toy up and down the bare kitchen floor.

'I loved me mam so much,' Kelly explained, 'that I named Aysa after her.' It was an innocent comment but it cut me to the quick. Even though the name was spelt with an 'a', different from my mother's, I wish I had been given the chance to do the same. I looked at Kelly with envious longing that she had been the recipient of my mother's love. If only she knew how I would have given the earth to change places with her. But social ethics and sensitivity to each other's feelings meant that neither of us could say what we really wanted to. Outwardly we both laughed when I said, 'I wanted to give any daughter of mine my mother's name, but I had two sons instead.'

Over an Irish coffee after dinner, I gingerly brought up the subject of a bathroom, or lack of it. Kelly, realising my discomfort, suggested that she could ask a friend who lived a couple of miles away if I could use her bath occasionally. We would, she assured me, meet the friend in the pub later that night.

I had been travelling for more than twenty-four hours. I was dirty, disorientated and emotionally drained. All I wanted was some space to try to order my thoughts and feelings – and some sleep.

However, to the pub we were to go. I could hardly believe my ears. A noisy, smoky pub was the last place I wished to enter.

That, however, was to be later. In the meantime, Kelly and I sat at the kitchen table attempting to talk. Jeff had gone out so it was our first opportunity to be on our own. We each wanted to get to know each other. There was so much I wanted to ask. She showed me the letter the Salvation Army had written to my mother at her old address in O'Connell Avenue, which Peter, Kelly's brother-in-law and postman, handed to her personally. When she saw the name Tina Bareham, née Suleyman, as the person wanting to trace Ayshe O'Connor, Kelly realised I must be the baby she vaguely recalled hearing about when she was a child. 'When that letter arrived,' she said, 'bits of conversation I remember hearing between me mam and dad suddenly started to make sense. I wasn't altogether surprised to learn about you.'

So, my mother had told her husband about me. Although the information was sketchy and second-hand, it was pleasing to know that she had openly admitted to someone that I existed, and I felt a real sense of validation.

As we talked, Kelly made an effort to avoid using the words 'me mam', although it still slipped out spontaneously, and we both instinctively tried to revert to neutral ground by using the name Ayshe. Knowing that she regarded my mother as hers, I felt awkward saying 'my mother' in front of her. It was probably easier for me not to say it, because it had never been a phrase that fell easily from my lips, no doubt due to successfully schooling myself over the years never to use it.

Sensing her discomfort, I told Kelly not to be embarrassed about saying 'me mam'. 'Neither of us can change the past,' I said. 'That's the way it was. You knew her. I didn't.'

'It's ironic that she was your mother and you never got to know her. I feel bad about that,' Kelly said with a quiver in her voice.

We were both trying not to hurt each other's feelings, both disguising our real feelings and fighting back the tears.

As I was old enough to be Kelly's mother, I felt obliged to play the part of senior counsellor, a role I slipped into fairly easily because of the philosophical approach I have always tried to adopt with regard to my own situation. Yet assuming the senior role meant that there was a conflict of interest, and my own imperative needs were unable to be met. I also had to deal with Kelly's needs and the difficulties she was experiencing.

The cigarette between her fingers was shaking as Kelly took a deep breath in an attempt to keep control of her emotions. She began to talk about her relations with her mother, Rhona.

Bitter invective poured from her mouth as she told me her story. It went something like this. When Rhona was just eighteen, unable to look after her illegitimate baby in Dublin, she went down to Listowel to stay with her Aunty Ayshe, who looked after Kelly while Rhona went to work. Ayshe became very fond of the baby, and pleaded with Rhona to let her and Michael bring up the child as their own. It was obvious to everyone that Ayshe yearned for a baby of her own. Rhona returned to Dublin, where she soon married and found herself again pregnant. She then gave Ayshe permission to rear the baby, but not to adopt her. Whenever Rhona could, she and her husband and subsequent daughters visited Kelly so that she would always know that Rhona was her real mother.

Kelly was just thirteen when 'her mam' – Ayshe, died. Then Michael died fifteen months later. Kelly then had to go to Dublin and live with her five step-sisters and learn to adjust to a new life with the mother who had given her away. She did not fit in and became rebellious.

As I sat at the kitchen table and listened to the unpalatable tales that were unfolding, I could almost feel the bitter resentment that existed between Kelly and her mother. Caught right in the middle of a vitriolic family feud, which had nothing to do with me, I could do nothing more than to listen helplessly and mutter sympathetic noises. There came to me a deep, dark dismay as I realised the incongruity of the situation.

The parallels in the stories of three generations amazed me. Perhaps my mother recognised herself in Rhona – a teenager in trouble – and had wanted to help her out. Perhaps she recognised her own baby in Kelly, and took her in as a substitute for the baby she was forced to give away. Perhaps she saw herself too in the child who had to be given away, as she herself was, to the Turkish Consul.

I reflected on my circumstances and concluded that staying in such close quarters with Kelly could be emotionally tortuous. It didn't matter that the living conditions were not ideal, or that Kelly and her husband were going through hard times. I could tell immediately that we were totally different personalities, a generation apart, and the next few days were not going to be easy.

I felt like an interloper, and I knew that while I stayed in Kelly's house as her guest there could be no relief for me from the years of pain and confusion. That there was no empathy between us, and that we were obviously incompatible, saddened me more than I can express. In her warm, welcoming letter, Kelly had come across as a sensitive, understanding person. The reality did not measure up to my high expectations of the sort of person I thought she would be. Already I was all too aware that I would receive neither the comfort, nor the compensation, that I so sorely needed.

It was ten o'clock. The neighbours arrived for their regular Sunday night pub crawl. They made it quite clear that I was expected to accompany them. A young girl from the neighbourhood was summoned to baby-sit.

Soon we were striding along wet pavements towards the centre of town, about a seven minute walk. I was glad of my fleece-lined jacket and woollen scarf as the driving rain stung my face. Every bone in my body was cold. I had not expected the weather in October to be this chilly. No one carried an umbrella and by the time we reached Sheahan's Pub in William Street we were all soaked to the skin.

A babble of boozy voices and alcoholic smells hit me as we fought our way through the noisy crowd in the public bar to the relatively quiet lounge bar. I'd hardly sat down in front of a blazing fireplace when a huge glass of Guinness, topped with a splash of blackcurrant juice, was plonked down in front of me.

'There, that's the same drink that Ayshe always had when she came here,' Kelly smiled. 'You must taste some while you're here.'

'Cheers,' everyone chorused, 'and welcome to Ireland.' I was beginning to feel warm and relatively relaxed.

Later, Anna Sheahan, the publican, came over to greet me.

'Mother of Mercy, Tina, I'm so pleased to meet you. Your mum used to come and help with the cooking and housekeeping during the September races. She was a hard worker right to the end. A real lady that she was, quietly spoken and with a lovely foreign accent. You look like her too, that you do.'

Uncontrolled tears rolled down my cheeks as I listened to this woman talking so earnestly of the mother I wish I also knew. There, in front of Kelly and her friends, and a roomful of strangers, I was overtaken with unconstrained emotion. Kelly said with a sympathetic smile, 'Don't worry about the tears, let it all out. There'll be plenty more to come.'

Anna Sheahan gently patted me on the back and offered me some tissues. 'It's so sad that you didn't know her, she was such a good woman,' she continued compassionately, causing more tears to roll unchecked into my schooner of Guinness.

It was more than I could bear to hear kind things said of my mother, especially from a woman who knew her closely, and the realisation that I was sitting in the very building where she had worked touched me deeply. I tried to gulp down the tears with each mouthful of Guinness, but they just wouldn't stop flowing.

It was past midnight when I slid between the Irish linen sheets and gratefully sank my spinning head onto the soft pillow. Wearing a scarf around my neck and bed socks to thaw my icy feet, I hugged a hot water bottle, and eventually drifted into sporadic sleep.

Chapter Twelve

St Mary's Church

It was still dark at six o'clock the next morning when I crept down the creaky wooden stairs. There was no sound from the back room where the crying baby had kept me awake most of the night. I assumed they were all catching up on lost sleep, but there was no way I could linger any longer in that icy-cold room.

Downstairs in the kitchen it wasn't much warmer because the fire had gone out. Shivering, I wrapped my dressing gown around me and filled the jug. After I drew back the curtains and looked through the grimy window out to the backyard I noticed the long line of washing standing stiffly to attention in the sharp frosty air.

The cold silence of the kitchen created an inhospitable atmosphere and I waited for some sign of movement from upstairs, for I was impatient to do some exploring in town and to look inside St Mary's Church. Ever since Kelly told me 'her mam' had been a deeply believing Catholic, after converting from her Muslim faith, I could hardly wait to see her church.

When Kelly eventually emerged she announced she would have to cycle to work every morning and would I mind looking around the town on my own? Would I mind indeed! It was an arrangement I was more than happy with as I much preferred to take in the sights and sounds of Listowel on my own, without the distracting company of a woman who, through no fault of her own, was a virtual stranger. I wanted to soak up the atmosphere of the township, and look through every nook and cranny of the town my mother settled in and made her home.

It was almost eleven o'clock when I pulled the scarf up over my nose and walked into the face of a biting northerly wind. What a relief it was to get out into the fresh air and start some real exploring.

On reaching the grotto by the crossroads, my gaze shifted further down the street, towards the end of the cul-de-sac, to the house where my mother had lived. I walked slowly towards the block of four differently painted terraced houses, and stopped outside No. 41, the white house at the end. As I took in every detail of my mother's small, plain home, I realised that my deepest wish had come true, for at last I had found out where she had been living all those years I was looking for her. I suppose, seeing it at last did fill a vacuum of sorts. But my sense of loss was agonising, because she was not living there any more and I had failed to find her while she was still alive. I fought hard to grapple with the depressing reality that she had lived here with her husband and niece's daughter all the years that I was bringing up my own young family oceans away in New Zealand.

All that was left for me to do was to stare at this minute monument to her existence, and to dream of what our lives might have been had we known each other. Her house, now occupied by strangers, stood mockingly before me, cold and unwelcoming, its front door shut tight. I knew that I would have to steel myself to see inside it before too long.

Time was arrested for me in that moment. Out there, on the cold, wet pavement, in a fog of confusion, I grieved for the mother I never had the chance to know. I cried as I'd never cried before; the tears just wouldn't stop.

Suddenly I felt chilled to the bone and I realised I would have to take a hold of myself. I turned my back on the ghostly house and stepped up my pace towards the centre of town, not bothering to wipe away the tears that continued to course down my face. But I felt better for having been able to unleash my emotions unimpeded.

Half a kilometre further on I entered William Street and spotted Sheahan's pub wedged in the middle of a long row of shops, all painted in various vibrant colours. Anna was busy serving a customer, as, like most pubs in Listowel, hers also served as a grocery store. She smiled and waved to me as I passed by. I noticed that for every four shops there was a public house and was not in the least bit surprised when I learned later that there were fifty pubs in Listowel with a population of only four thousand. It didn't take much working out that there were eighty people for every pub.

I was drawn like a magnet to my mother's regular place of worship, and easily found my way to St Mary's Church just before the rain pelted down. St Mary's was the only Catholic church in the town. An imposing grey Gothic building, it dominated the market square, standing alongside the ruins of a sixteenth-century castle.

I reached the porch just as a large group of mourners streamed out of the church. My visit coincided with a funeral Mass which was just finishing. I watched the mourners carrying the coffin through the open door and immediately perceived this to be my mother's funeral. Once inside the church the power left my limbs and I was dragged down by some invisible and enormous force. I noticed there were still a few stragglers left inside. I sat in the oak pew at the back and watched a headscarfed woman genuflecting towards the striking crucifix over the main altar. So this was the magnificent church, with its soaring white pillars and limestone Gothic arches, where my mother had found solace from the world outside.

But now she was dead. My body shook with uncontrolled grief. The silence that had hung over my entire life erupted into a torrent of tears. The minutes flashed by in a jumble of despair and hopelessness.

Sorrow, for myself and for my mother, for fifty-two misplaced years, bore down on me to the extent that I could hardly breathe. My bereavement was amazingly palpable and, struggling with all kinds of tangled emotions, my gut-wrenching sobs echoed around the huge, and now empty, interior.

This was the first Roman Catholic church I had entered, and in the fading light of its majestic interior it seemed the right place to reach out to my mother. I was possessed by a strong conviction that her spirit was with me that day.

Through blurred vision I noticed the flickering circle of white candles either side of the altar, and imagined my mother lighting each one. Perhaps she had lit one for me and offered a prayer for her long-lost daughter. Though by now I had turned away from religion, I had a strong impulse to perform the Catholic rite of lighting a candle for my mother, and perhaps saying a prayer for her. But I knew I couldn't do it, however much I wanted to. The very thought of acting out the meaningful and emotionally-charged ritual turned the taps on again, and I knew I had neither the capacity nor the courage to do it.

Inside her place of worship I became aware of an angry presence that sprang from my unconscious past, and suddenly I was full of outrage to her God. What right had she to give all her love and devotion to Him instead of to me, her deserted daughter?

Dozens of unanswered questions consumed my mind. Why hadn't she tried to look for me? Even though she was so young when I was born, she could have made an effort to search for me, her only daughter, once she became an adult. We were both bereft of an acceptable quota of relatives. Our lives had followed similar paths in that we were both handed over to the care of complete strangers – she to the Turkish Consul General and me to Dr Barnardo homes. Neither of us had any family whatsoever – we were both the quintessential orphan, and fate decreed that we would end up living thousands of miles from each other.

Once I had acknowledged that she was dead, while I remained alive, I would have to find ways of living with that loss. I'm convinced that the strength of will within each of us had helped us both in our struggle to survive alone. With the help and support of my family I knew I could last the distance, but in the meantime I had to get through the next few harrowing days on my own.

A church official appeared from nowhere. I was the last person left and he wanted to lock up. 'Are you all right?' he enquired, seeing my tears. In between blowing my nose and dabbing my eyes, I tried to explain how I had come from New Zealand to find out about my mother who had died in 1981. 'Let's go into the sacristy and see if her name is in our records,' he suggested.

Once inside the sacristy, I waited in a tearing anguish of suspense as he skimmed through the register of deaths. A moment later he found the page which recorded my mother's death. Staring up at me again was the name: 'AYSHE O'CONNOR', DIED 6/6/81'. Under the columns 'Parents' and 'Age', inexplicably there were only blank spaces. Surely her husband would have been able to fill in the details of her parents and her age when she died?

When I saw her name in print again, the memory from thirty years before flooded back to the day I managed to sight her marriage certificate in London. All these years I had held on to it in the vain hope that some day that official piece of paper might, by some miracle, bring us together. But here was the official proof now, as if I needed it, that she was no longer living. Quickly curbing any desire to dissolve into more sobbing, I knew I would need to talk coherently with this polite stranger and regain my composure.

Kelly had already told me that my mother had been baptised as an adult at St Mary's Church, but she wasn't sure which year. I asked the clerk if he would look up the baptismal records, but he had to lock up and suggested I come back another day when he had more time.

Involuntarily, I walked out of the church into the real, rainy world of Listowel. I breathed in deeply, filling my lungs with air as though to drive out the tension. I felt a small measure of satisfaction that I had sighted the official church record of her death, and had personally experienced being inside my mother's place of worship – her haven of rest.

The unexpected funeral also helped to provide a catharsis as it forced me to acknowledge her death, even though I still could not bring myself to accept it. Little did I know when I entered St Mary's Church that I would be touched by such a deep chord of emotion, such a tidal wave of grief. On looking back, I believe that this was the start of an imperative grieving process that had been set into motion the minute I landed in my mother's adopted country.

Chapter Thirteen

Seeking Answers

During the days that followed I was grateful for the freedom to move about the district on my own.

Stormy rain clouds were again threatening as I set off the next morning on my trek around the neighbourhood. My obsessive need to learn the slightest shred of information relating to my mother propelled me to pound the pavements of the estate in a mechanical haze. A wrenching loneliness began to set in as, zombie-like, I walked the streets of her little corner of the world, following the same path that she would have trod. I could feel myself succumbing in slow degrees to an onslaught of negative emotions. The pain inside! The torment and the aching despair of knowing that we had missed each other. She wasn't here for me. What was the sense in being here? Big, scalding tears blinded me. But I needed to know everything there was to know about the lost mother whom I had idealised all my life. I conjured up all sorts of cosy scenes in my mind – of her coming out of her house with her little basket to go shopping, of her stopping and chatting to the neighbours… My imagination knew no bounds. But I knew I had to pull myself together if I wanted to find out information from the people who lived close to her, and I made a valiant effort to suppress the rising emotions that threatened to choke me.

It didn't take long to find out that nobody had been told about me. My sudden appearance on the scene was quite a surprise to many. My mother had well and truly kept my birth a secret.

I kept wishing I'd had the foresight to pack a pair of gloves, but at least I had the umbrella Anna had lent me. It looked as if I might need it again today. Since arriving in Listowel I seemed to be in a state of permanent coldness. Out of the corner of my eye I noticed a few curtains being pulled back as I went from door to door, making the same request.

'Would you mind sharing with me your memories of my mother, Ayshe O'Connor?'

Some doors remained steadfastly closed. There were one or two neighbours who seemed embarrassed as they kept me waiting outside. They mumbled a few shy words about her being 'a real lady', but that they didn't know her very well. Some refused to open their homes to this stranger who was wandering into their territory, boldly banging on every door in their street. But that day I was in no mood to give up. My mind flashed back to Kilburn and to Istanbul and Ankara, when I had to knock on the doors of strangers in my inexorable quest. Here I was again, seeking answers from people I didn't know, about a woman I desperately wanted to know.

The insatiable curiosity I had about my mother had never left me, but at least now I didn't have to grope in the dark, indulging in flights of fantasy as to what type of person she was, where in the world she might be living, or whether indeed she was still in the world. At least here was the evidence that she had been a warm human being, apparently well-loved by many people.

I was given the name Liz Keenan as someone who would be able to tell me something of my mother. Her house stood behind the grotto of the Virgin Mary at the crossroads. I walked up to the front door in a positive frame of mind, though when I glimpsed a face peering behind the curtain I hesitated for a brief second before forcing myself to rap on the door knocker.

A young man opened the door and ushered me into the bedroom of the elderly and bedridden neighbour who sat propped up in bed. A knitted shawl was draped around her shoulders, her white hair gripped in curlers. She was just finishing her lunch and at first appeared embarrassed, but as soon as her son confirmed who I was her milky face wrinkled into smiles.

At her bidding, I squatted on the edge of the bed, and apologised for calling at a bad time. 'I heard you were in town. News travels fast round here,' she laughed.

'Oh my God, you resemble her all right. It's the eyes. She never said anything about you. People don't. She was a very nice person. A real saint. She'd do anything for you.' She looked around the room waving her hand. 'She papered this bedroom for me, some years ago now. She was a great little worker.'

I looked at the pink-flowered wallpaper which covered all four walls of the small room, and was enthralled to be confronted with something tangible, work she had done with her own hands. With an overwhelming impulse to touch the paper and place my hands where my mother's had once been, all I could do was to sit and study the wall. I could almost picture her now, the mother of my imagination working alone in that room, palette and paste by the stepladder, scissors in her hand cutting the paper to size. I thought of the many times I had helped Ray wallpaper every room of our first home. I began to gain a clearer picture of my mother. In that room I could almost see her ghost. If only we'd had just one year together, I was thinking... I'd have even settled for one month, even a few hours, just to behold her face.

Swamped with sadness, I listened to Liz Keenan intoning from her bed, totally oblivious to my private agony, and I needed to tap into all my resources to avoid breaking down altogether. The feelings I had in that room were so profound that I can hardly express them even now.

'They thought the world of Kelly,' she continued, insensitive to my sorrows, 'they were mad about her. Is it a long time since you saw Ayshe?'

Obviously, she had no idea that I had never met my mother, and again I felt wounded by her innocent remarks.

'I have never set eyes on my mother.' It hurt me just to utter the words.

'Oh my God. What a pity. She would have been so delighted. The feeling would have been there, the love would have been there, to be sure.'

It was all too much. A huge lump appeared in my throat, choking me up. I gazed out of the window at the rain-washed sky, struggling to take control of my emotions.

Happy to have someone to chat to, this simple countrywoman gabbled on, unaware of how she was touching the very depths of my soul every time she mentioned my mother's name. And yet, I fervently wished that she could go on talking about her.

She then started questioning me about my own family in New Zealand, and, although it was the last thing I wanted to do, I explained briefly how I came to be in Listowel. I was here to ask the questions, and I carefully steered the conversation back to where I could control it.

'Do you feel she fitted in around here?' It was a question I needed to ask because everyone's comments about my mother being a 'grand lady' convinced me that this sad-looking council estate was not the sort of place where a woman of her class should have lived. I could certainly never imagine myself living there, now that I had seen for myself what a struggle life would have been, where half the population was on government benefit, and where the little money they had was spent on booze and cigarettes.

'She fitted in with everyone, God have mercy on her soul. She was a lovely little lady. Your eyes remind me of her now. Your looks too.' She smiled at me innocently. 'Ayshe would wave to me every time she passed this window.'

Her bland responses were not nearly detailed enough for me but I felt a strong affinity with this kindly soul who spoke with such fondness of my mother, and whose ingenuous words warmed my heart. I could have lingered at her bedside and listened to her reminiscences all afternoon, but there were others to see.

At the garden gate it was not me, but my mother who was giving her customary wave as she passed by her neighbour's window.

Word soon spread around the neighbourhood that Ayshe's daughter was in town, and wherever I went I had to give the same explanations about who I was and why I was here. Everyone expressed surprise that Ayshe had a 'real' daughter. Without exception, the people who were willing to talk painted a picture of a hard-working, virtuous woman who helped anyone in need and who could put her hand to anything, such as housekeeping, cooking, paper-hanging and clothing alterations.

The mother of my dreams was now being made real for me by seeing the place where she lived and by talking with those who knew her well. The same sentiments about her being kind and gentle and a 'grand lady' were voiced time and again. I almost wished she hadn't sounded so appealing, then I wouldn't have felt that I had 'missed something special', as one neighbour unthinkingly blurted. I admit to feeling jealous that Kelly had replaced me as my mother's daughter, and every time someone made a comment about how my mother 'doted on Kelly', or how she 'gave her life for Kelly', I hated hearing it. Of course, I was in a position of vulnerability merely by being in Listowel and asking so many questions, the answers to which were liable to hurt me.

The one revelation that caused me real distress was that, in the very same year I was bound for Australia – 1968 – my mother, aged forty-three, accepted her husband's niece's baby into her life, without doubt as a permanent replacement for me. At the age of twenty-eight I was still disconnected, restless and without a relative in the world. I had given up my search for the time being – I had to get on with living my own life – and I had turned my back on my friends and made the decision to start a new life in Australia. Unwittingly, I had gone as far away as possible from the country in which my mother lived. Fate had separated us from each other in the cruellest of ways.

With Kelly working most of the time, we saw very little of each other, and although I was happy exploring the town on my own, the situation was not conducive for either of us to get to know each other. The burden of coping with my own grief and jealousy and a host of other emotions probably got in the way of forging any sort of friendship. Our personalities and social backgrounds were so different that we might have been born on different planets. It probably didn't help matters that I could barely understand Kelly's strong Kerry dialect. As soon as she spied my little cassette recorder that I tried to use to record conversations, she immediately clamed up, with the result that I can only remember a few of our conversations. Luckily, many people from around the estate did agree to speak into the recorder, and as most of them gabbled incomprehensibly it was very helpful being able to play back the conversations afterwards.

I revelled in the freedom of wandering around on my own, and in the process wore out a lot of shoe leather trekking around the neighbourhood. Not once did I see a bus in the town, and as no one on the estate had transport I had no option other than to walk.

A picture was starting to emerge of my mother. She had never really taken any form for me before, although none of those I spoke to knew her intimately, so it was still a rather fuzzy picture. The names of others who might be of help were passed on to me, so that by the end of the week I had quite a long list of people to visit. Hardly anyone on the estate was on the phone so I had to take my chances and go door-knocking, but invariably some folk were not at home when I called, or if they were I had to wait while they searched their memories. Sometimes I had to push them further in case they had anything new to say. Some folk were apparently too busy to talk. It amazed me how so many people I tried to speak to about my mother were short of that precious commodity – time.

I learned from one neighbour whose mother lived in the same London suburb as Michael and Ayshe during the war years, that they met each other at the local pub in Kilburn, where she used to go with a group of Irish friends from her place of work at the munitions factory. As I listened to her talking, I ruefully reflected how twenty-five years earlier I had called at the address in Kilburn looking for my mother, but nobody there had heard of her or Michael. I argued with myself, if only I had gone to the local pub in the Kilburn area, or to the Catholic church, someone there might, just might, have remembered them. If only…

One couple who lived close to Kelly's house offered to let me use their shower when they heard that I had to wash down at the kitchen sink. So, each evening, brandishing my brolly and armed with towel and sponge bag, I would trudge the short distance to their house for a deliciously hot shower.

A lot of my time was spent retracing my footsteps if people weren't home, and when I did manage to linger briefly at their doorstep, some of them had no concept of what I really needed.

'She would keep herself to herself,' was their favourite catch phrase when they could tell me nothing much about her, and I had to accept that. There were so many more personal details I wanted to know than folk were willing or able to tell me.

I tried to uncover the identity of the people whose names were printed on the bottom of my mother's marriage certificate: the two witnesses – A.M. Hannon and M. Casey. I had no idea whether they were men or women, if they were friends of Michael and Ayshe or if they were just innocent bystanders dragged off the street to be witnesses for my mother's registry office wedding in Kilburn.

Kelly identified the first one as Anne-Marie Hannon, now a woman in her eighties, who was 'funny in the head'. Apparently, an ex-flat mate of my mother's in Kilburn, she would now be no earthly help to me whatsoever.

The other witness, I found out, was Mary Casey, who married and stayed in London, but unbelievably she too had dementia. This news hit me like an avalanche that nearly buried me in its impact. It really was the last straw as only a day earlier I met a woman who had been a very close friend of my mother but could not tell me a thing because she had Alzheimer's disease. Once more, it seemed the people who could have helped me with information were either dead or of unsound mind.

When I look back on my visit to Listowel and think about the friends of my mother who had died in the past few years, I can't help feeling angry, because they could have told me so much more about her than the residue of neighbours and acquaintances who were left and who had mostly been on nodding acquaintance with her.

Another woman who had since died was Nan Coppinger, who Kelly told me, was my mother's best friend. 'They were inseparable,' I was told. When I learned that my mother used to cut Nan's toenails and tend to her bunions, I realised that they must indeed have been 'close'. Here again was another person who could have given me an invaluable insight into what sort of person my mother had been.

Chasing the ghost of my mother was proving to be a difficult task, and the fact that Barnardo's had only now offered to look for her was causing a festering resentment here in Listowel. If their offer had been made even five years earlier, I might have had the chance to meet one or two of her more intimate friends. The passing years had taken their toll around the neighbourhood. Moreover, if Barnardo's had changed their rigid rules even earlier, I might have had the chance to be reunited with my mother when she was alive and well. That they stonewalled me for such a length of time and withheld information that might lead to a reunion, meant that tragically it was all too late, not just for my mother, but for me and for countless other boys and girls whose efforts to trace their families had failed.

I had spent many hours romanticising how my mother would have welcomed me into her home, even though Barnardo's thought she would not want it. I felt in my heart that I could have won her over as soon as she set eyes on me. She would not have failed to notice how alike we were. We would have got to know each other after all these years, and perhaps I could have looked after her during the time when she was so ill. How I would love to have brought her over to New Zealand, or anywhere, for a holiday. These, and other thoughts, rolled around in my mind.

I asked Kelly if she had any photos of Ayshe or any small souvenir that belonged to Ayshe that I could take home with me. From her reactions I knew immediately that I had stirred up a hornet's nest. She drew deeply on her cigarette, and exclaimed in a tone of undisguised resentment, 'That photo I sent you was the only one I have. All me mam's things disappeared when the house was sold.' Her eyes were blazing.

Her voice was now shaking. 'Everything went to Rhona.'

How I wished I hadn't brought up the subject of souvenirs. The last thing I wanted was to be drawn into a family feud, and I could foresee worrisome mental battles ahead.

Chapter Fourteen

My Mother's House

The day came at last when I was allowed to look through my mother's house at No. 41 O'Connells Avenue. Each house in the block of four was painted a different colour, and my mother's modest, two-storey house at the end was freshly painted white. The present occupiers, a young couple fairly new to the district, agreed to let us look through when Kelly bumped into them earlier in the week. They had bought the house just three years earlier. They had never met Ayshe or Michael, though they had heard about them.

Kelly and I walked together up the front path, once more sharing the same umbrella which we struggled to hold firm against the buffeting wind on another bitterly cold day. I could hardly suppress the tide of anticipation that began to well up inside me at the prospect of being within the very walls of the place my mother called 'home'. My mind spun with expectations of what I would find. I would have preferred to have been on my own but I needed Kelly to introduce me around the neighbourhood, where she was well known. I sensed that she too would be interested to see inside the house where she spent most of her childhood, and I was forced to accept her presence. I managed to conceal my own high-pitched nervous excitement, the conflict of anticipation and trepidation successfully contained within me.

As we made our way towards the front door, which was actually at the side of the house, I noticed the long, unmown grass in a somewhat ramshackle garden, though bigger than most I had seen around the estate. I paused briefly to study a bunch of flowers struggling through the undergrowth, and it took a lot of imagination on my part when Kelly told me what a lovely garden her mam used to keep.

The owners answered our knock on the door and led us straight into the kitchen. With the four of us huddled together in the middle of the room, we were cramped for space. I stood rooted to the spot, marvelling over the fact that I was standing in the modest house where my mother had put down her roots and where she lived for thirty years. She was a newly-wed bride when she first moved in to it, and apparently had to share it for a few years with Michael's parents. How on earth did they have the space? I gave an involuntary exclamation of wonder at the smallness of it all and the spartan surroundings. I looked at the large dustbin filled with peat collected from the bog, which stood in front of the Aga, the old-fashioned range, identical to all the others I had seen.

For a moment I stood in my mother's shoes, in her kitchen – the hub of her life, cooking meals for the three of them and boiling up the kettle for a pot of tea. I'd been told she was a splendid cook, skills she no doubt picked up during her time as a maidservant with the consul general's family. I imagined her busy little figure bustling over the hot stove cooking pot roasts and baking Irish soda bread.

A surge of sadness overtook me when I thought of her living here and the huge disparity between our respective lives. My home in New Zealand seemed luxurious in comparison with this. The sanitation was basic, and only now was a bathroom being added. I asked myself, was this really the twentieth century we were living in, in this wind-swept backwater of southern Ireland? Yet, as I looked with my mother's eyes, I sensed that this kitchen would have been the focal point of her existence, the private place where she felt comfortable and where she could entertain her friends.

Striving to absorb everything in the short time that was available, and feeling like a voyeur, an intruder, I quickly scrutinised every nook and cranny in that kitchen. I took a photo of the ubiquitous clothes horse that was full of wet clothes in front of the Aga – no washing machine here. My vision travelled upwards towards the smoke-stained wallpaper above the fireplace. My tears, always quick to well up, blurred the heavy pattern as I pondered whether it was another of Ayshe's do-it-yourself jobs.

Kelly walked two steps towards the family living room, and, pointing to a large window that looked out on to the grotto at the crossroads, said, 'Me dad made this into one big room when me mam was bedridden, so she could see the neighbours as they passed by.'

Thinking of my mother's life, I was overcome with mixed feelings. I had to dig deep within myself to find the strength not to cry – just as I had needed to during the low periods in my life, for this, without doubt, was one.

And then I thought about Kelly also living there as a child. Unanswered anger began to rise up as I thought of the words of the neighbour, that 'they were mad about Kelly'. I could see my mother then, cuddling Kelly and telling her stories, dressing her in pretty clothes, and over-indulging her. I know it was not Kelly's fault that she had become the recipient of my mother's devotion, for she, like me, was an illegitimate baby. We had both lived in an era when having a baby out of wedlock was almost as bad as committing murder. In Catholic Ireland abortion was illegal. Still, I fought the conviction that it should have been me living in that house instead of Kelly, but even as I looked out of the window at the dreary neighbourhood I tried to console myself with the knowledge that I was better off materially in the orphanage.

The owners led us upstairs where there were two good-sized bedrooms. That was all. There was no bathroom. I walked over the bare floorboards to look out of the small window of the back bedroom where the long grass in the garden broadened into open country. Kelly joined me by the window and explained that her mam slept in that bedroom because it was bigger than the front one and she liked the view of her church. I squinted through the small pane. Across the green fields of rural Listowel I gazed fixedly at the tall, distant spire of St Mary's, silhouetted against banks of cloud. Shivers went up my spine. Uncannily, I was my mother, looking out across the meadows to her church and standing on the bare boards of the back bedroom.

I stood riveted to the spot where she had stood. Her presence was heavy in that room. I felt her silent strength. I was so close to her then. I saw everything through her eyes and tried to feel everything with her heart. It wasn't that I could feel her invisible presence, as I had in her church. Now I was her. It was all so weird, so unreal.

In my heart, I cried out to her, 'Why did you leave me so alone? Why did I have to go through fifty-two long, silent years without knowing where you were? Why did I have to live in the unloved, sterile environment of a children's home?' Why, why?

I tortured myself by reflecting on the long, lonely stretches in my past. I felt a great sense of removal from everything – a tremendous loneliness that welled up out of some deep longing inside me. Absolutely nobody had taken her place. How could I relate to anybody in the community without the most fundamental human right – an identity?

As I trod carefully, step by step, down the wooden stairs, dozens of unanswered questions smothered me. I felt loathe to leave the house that held the soul of my mother. My feelings during the next few minutes were acute. Because I was in the company of others, I was unable to surrender to the shattering pain I felt while I stood inside her house.

Outside, a few large drops of rain fell from the darkening sky. I took a long, deep breath and, having thanked the owners and said goodbye, walked arm in arm with Kelly down the garden path. At least my curiosity had been satisfied. I had broken through the veil of the unknown and seen the interior of my mother's home. It had been for me a strange, poignant experience. My heart was crying, my head spinning.

Chapter Fifteen
Bridget

The name of a neighbour that was added to my ever growing list of people to visit was Bridget Canty, who lived at No. 37 and who was a widow, about the same age as my mother. She was, by all accounts, the best person to ask when my mother moved to the street, and when she might have been baptised.

After my habitual evening shower, instead of staying for a cup of tea and a chat, I went next door in the hope that Bridget would be home. And she was. I found myself drinking a rum and coke in her living room, a nice change from the compulsory cups of tea I was invariably offered. Bridget had a natural cheerfulness and directness about her and she immediately put me at ease.

We spent a relaxed and happy evening chatting, oblivious of the time. Two hours flew by. It was a great relief to hear that the approximate date my mother would have been baptised was between 1950 and 1956, soon after she started working for the headmaster's family, who encouraged her to renounce her Muslim faith and become a Catholic. This was good news. Now I could return to the church and get a copy of her baptismal certificate.

'They were both very poor in the early years,' Bridget said as she filled up my glass with rum and coke, and went on to describe how Michael was a builder's labourer, but because of his bad back Ayshe had to work hard to keep him as there was no social welfare then.

'Ayshe and Mikey seemed happy enough together, even though he was drinking her hard-earned money. The hardships she had to endure probably drove her to the church. Anyone less strong would have turned to drink. She did smoke, but everyone round here does.'

She told me how Michael was known as 'Mikey Bawney', a figure of affection, well-known for his heavy drinking and smoking, and that the nickname, 'Bawney' means 'white', so named because of his white hair. Ayshe was sometimes called 'Ayshe Bawney'.

I asked if she knew if my mother was musical.

'Heavens above, Tina, there wouldn't have been the opportunity for her to do anything like that here – but she was very good with her hands – very creative, she was that.'

I understood only too well what she meant by 'lack of opportunity' now that I had seen for myself the tough, working class community in which she had lived.

In answer to my questions, Bridget told me that my mother had an English accent with a slightly foreign twang, although she used some Irish idioms too.

'She was always very quiet and composed, and rarely spoke unless you spoke to her. She was a refined lady – a very private person – quite a bit smaller than you, Tina, with a very fine bone structure. Her eyes were lovely and big and brown and her skin was a golden colour. Everyone loved her, Tina. You missed something special, dear, but you have a mother to be proud of.'

As she voiced these appealing sentiments about my mother, there arose in me a wave of pain, but I desperately needed to hear absolutely everything there was to know about her.

'I wish I had known her,' was all I could weakly say as I felt my stomach twist. I begrudged her neighbours their long and close association with this wonderful, kindly, exotic woman whom they all loved and who also happened to be my mother. I felt the deprivation of my motherless state stronger than ever.

So, much of the mystery of my origins was manifesting itself here in Listowel, and especially in Bridget's living room. I was pleased to hear that, apart from looking alike, we were both quiet, with a tendency to hide our true feelings. I felt buoyed by this new knowledge, whether it was due to our common childhood conditioning or to heredity. It didn't matter much, but it helped me to understand myself better – to find a sense of self.

I was thankful that the two of us were on our own and that Bridget was prepared to acknowledge that it was *my* mother we were talking about, for Kelly's continual use of those two words, 'me mam', was beginning to grate. I knew already that we were at opposite poles, and it was not difficult to understand the reason why she was unable to bring herself to acknowledge her mam as my mother, and me as the blood daughter, and I was convinced she felt threatened by me. Like me, she would have to learn to adjust to the new circumstances in her life.

My mother's life began to take shape, and I sat back in the comfortable chair feeling more relaxed than I had since arriving in Listowel.

The rum and coke had loosened Bridget's tongue. She was talking freely now.

She recalled how in the early years my mother moved into an upstairs room at No. 35 for a few weeks to get away from her bitchy mother-in-law who was so cruel and used to call her 'the old Turk'.

'I think she was jealous of Ayshe in a way because Mikey was her only son and she didn't like having to share him. Life became a little easier for Ayshe when they both died.'

What a pleasant change it was to hear someone look me straight in the eye and talk openly and honestly. My instincts told me there must be more, much more about the life of my mother that others had been unwilling or unable to share with me, and I wondered if they were prepared to only divulge what they thought I should hear. Although Bridget admitted that she didn't really know my mother intimately, I appreciated her refreshing candidness.

'When your mother became ill she lost control of Kelly who ran wild and more or less did as she pleased. In later months the priest came to her when she was bedridden, and she had her own altar with a crucifix and holy water font, set up at the foot of her bed. She once went with a group of sick people to Lourdes.'

'I expect she was hoping for a miracle cure,' I ventured.

By now I felt relaxed enough to ask Bridget more personal questions, such as if she knew why my mother had no more children after me.

'Well dear, Ayshe implied she couldn't have any children, and I never questioned her any more about it because she seemed to me to be a very private person, and I felt it was a subject she didn't want to pursue.'

When she went into the kitchen to boil up a jug for some coffee I closed my eyes for a few moments' respite. A mental picture flashed before me of my first visit to the gynaecologist to find out why I hadn't conceived after four years of trying. He hadn't been able to explain the reason I was not ovulating. Could the problem have been the same for my mother? It made me realise how lucky I was that we had the financial means to pay for specialist treatment, a privilege no doubt denied her. Was it possible that she was unable to conceive after giving birth to me at such a young age? Or perhaps the reason was psychological. Had she become infertile after my birth? Maybe her husband had been infertile. Or was it just possible that they didn't want any children of their own – and then it was too late. I pinned my hope on her doctor being able to give me some answers, and I planned to call on him and the priest as soon as possible.

The stark reality that my mother had no more children after me continued to ferment in my mind because at the centre of my misery was the fact that if only she had had one more baby after me how different everything would have been. For a start, I would at least have inherited a relative, someone who could have given me an identity and extended my family. The discovery of my mother's adopted homeland had not delivered to me or my family any extra relatives. Although my boys had a small number of relatives on Ray's side, I know we would all have loved an extension to our tiny family unit.

The void I felt concerning my roots and about my mother was slowly being filled here in Bridget's living room, as she struggled to tap into her memory bank.

I had always assumed that my mother had never made any effort to track me down, and when I put this assertion to Bridget she could only hazard a guess.

'She would have made a life for herself here, Tina, and I'm sure she thought of you often, but the facilities would not have been here in this little town for her to start looking for you, even if she had wanted to.'

The more I thought about it the more convinced I was our lives had run parallel. She would have thought of her own mother who died giving birth to her, and of her father who had to give her away. The consul general's family had allowed the child they brought up as their own to slip so easily from their guardianship, never to be seen by them again. Had she tried to make contact with them? Had she felt deserted and forgotten, as I had? In spite of everything, I'm certain she grieved for the loss of her only child – perhaps in the seclusion of her church, or perhaps when she

saw another's baby. Would she not have felt a compulsion
to cuddle it and dream of her very own flesh and blood
baby she was forced to give away? Surely the need must
have been there. That's why she took a replacement baby
for herself. For myself, the belief that my mother had
abandoned and then rejected me continued to hang over me
like a dark shadow, which would not pass.

Before I left for the evening, Bridget told me she had a
daughter who lived in Auckland, and she asked if I would
look her up on my return. I was only too happy to oblige.

I didn't know it then but I was able to welcome Bridget
into my own home exactly one year later when she visited
her daughter.

I'll never forget the fearful racing in my heart the
moment she crossed herself as she stepped through the
front door of our home and with tears in her eyes, said,
'Jesus bless this house. Your dear mother would love to
have seen it too.' Her words left me feeling incredibly
heartbroken.

I felt choked up too when she met Ray and the boys and
said, 'Ayshe would so love to have met her grandsons. How
proud she would have been to see what grand boys they
have grown up to be.'

Chapter Sixteen

The Grave

A rough wind drove cold rain on our faces as Kelly and I passed a cluster of dreary looking houses and trudged through the long prickly grass around the perimeter of the cemetery. We were trying to locate 'our' mother's grave. Eventually we found it, and side by side we stood together, again under the borrowed umbrella, looking down at the unmarked grave. The inclement conditions seemed mournfully appropriate for such a sad scene.

I needed Kelly to show me the location of the grave, but she could never have sensed my need to be alone with my mother, so that I could meditate on what might have been. I saw its pristine condition, just a bare patch of stubby grass that Jeff had recently mown. When I saw that there was no nameplate or physical marker to acknowledge my mother's existence on earth I was hit by a stunning blow of disbelief bordering on anger. Nor was there any name for Michael O'Connor.

Since hearing of her death back in New Zealand, in my mind's eye I had imagined her grave set amongst others in the picturesque backdrop of rural Listowel, with her epitaph engraved on her tomb. I would have felt a measure of satisfaction in placing some flowers on her grave and in reading her name, AYSHE O'CONNOR. But there was no endearing epithet, no 'IN LOVING MEMORY OF...' Not one word marked the site where she was laid to rest. I needed to see her name on her grave, to help to validate her death for me and also her life. It would have been a fitting testimonial to the life of a good woman who happened to also be my mother. Nothing. Something snapped deep inside me. I felt as though I was swimming in a sea of sorrows. There was so much grief and so little time to absorb it all.

Who is there left in her family to care about such a vital detail that is important to no one but me? Couldn't a relative from Michael's family have placed some sort of plaque to at least commemorate their marriage?

I asked Kelly to tell me the names of the O'Connor family so I might ask to put a small plaque on the site. Most of them are dead, she told me, some buried in this very grave, or the one adjacent to it.

Who'd have believed my own mother is buried in a general grave that is unmarked, amongst relatives she probably didn't know? Does she matter so little to everyone else? Even in death she was deprived of the dignity she deserved.

It was difficult controlling the umbrella against the oncoming autumn wind as heavy drops of rain skidded off the rim. It made standing a chilly business. Frozen to the bone though I was, I didn't want to leave the grave. The longer I stood there the more confused and angry I became. My mind raced back to the time when I was twenty-one, when I thought I might die. I had imagined my own epitaph: 'TINA SULEYMAN BELONGED TO NOBODY.' Now, unbelievably, it seemed that the same appendage could so easily have been applied to my mother. She was born into abject poverty and seemed to die in it. She too was nobody's child.

In many ways our lives had run parallel – both of us were orphans, our childhood marked by isolation from normal humanity. I thought of her early years when she was handed over as an eight year old to well-meaning strangers.

At the same age, my own childhood, though relatively secure, concealed my own deep-seated despair in the sheer volume of other children. My biological needs had been met. I had food, water, shelter and clothes. But my other basic needs had not – the need for love and security, warmth and understanding, of emotional give and take. The only mother figure I had was a cold, despotic matron whom I had to call 'Mother'. There was never anyone to offer me motherly love. Then I was a child in mourning for my phantom mother. Nothing had changed – she was still a phantom mother. Yet now I felt so close to her, and I loved her with a fiercely burning love as I pondered on the unhappy circumstances of her difficult life. I thought of how the two of us had overcome the odds. I felt sad, but conversely proud that each of us had stood against the world alone.

Time stood still as I could not stop myself dwelling on the cruel fate that kept us apart, and the vicious disease that took her comparatively young life at the age of fifty-six.

I still bore the scars of the emotional wounds that Barnardo's past policies had inflicted upon me. The damage to my spirit from a very early age had not had the chance to heal, for I had never been restored to my mother, or to any members of my family. Barnardo's vested interest in me, one of thousands of shunned illegitimates, had been purely for my physical well-being whilst in their care. My mental and social welfare after leaving them was left entirely to fate. Standing in this graveyard, I seethed with rage and resentment towards the bureaucrats who deliberately denied me an identity – denied me access to the sole member of my family, now dead and buried in this pauper's grave. Yet, I knew the impracticalities of searching when I had lived twelve thousand miles away for half my life. I had so desperately wanted her to be alive for me. I had to be content only with the token crumbs of other people's recollections of her.

At the same time, though, I did find some peace of mind that I had finally found out where she was. The link with her could only come about from contact with the citizens of Listowel. Cut adrift from my family for all my life, here was my opportunity to find a connection with my past – to find an identity. I was determined to make the most of my time here so that I could piece together more of the jigsaw in the days that were left.

I tried to put on a stoical front with Kelly beside me. I shut her out emotionally presuming she had her own burden of grief to bear, but inside me raged a simmering storm of frustration and hopelessness.

Mum, how can I possibly say goodbye when I have never been allowed to say hello? I have never even seen your face.

In dazed repetition the questions kept beating through my brain.

I studied the bare ground where Ayshe lay alongside her husband, and pondered the fragility of human life. Their marriage lasted thirty-seven years and yet there was nothing to show for it. I hoped with all my heart that theirs was a loving and happy union, as Ray's and mine still is.

The only thing that helped to temper my grief was the certitude of my husband's unconditional love.

My thoughts reached across the sea to him, wishing he could be here to share my grief.

If only I could have received some of the love that my mother shared around. Just as the neighbour said so poignantly, I would have loved her. Standing next to Kelly, I thought of how she was able to give my mother the affection that I never could and I thought of the joy they would have given each other, especially in the early years.

I ask myself, Why have I taken my mother's death so hard when I did not know her? Has she not always been dead to me?

As I tried to come to terms with this vexing question, I think I now know the answer, for since her death all my hopes and dreams of finding her went with her to the grave. I thought of the poverty of her early life and the lack of love in her childhood – she was barely more than a child herself when I was born.

In my quest to reclaim my mother, by learning about her, I have captured some of the love she shared around and gained an insight into her deep spirituality. I think about her life and how she was cut off from her Turkish roots and her Muslim faith, and then I think of how she embraced the Catholicism that was her life support – and then I think of her untimely death, and the ache in my heart grows deeper.

As we walked slowly back to town, following the silver thread of the river Feale, the rain had stopped and the light began to fade in the still watery sky. But somehow it only showed how grey everything seemed. We talked of the salmon fishing in the river and how Kelly used to swim under the bridge when she was a girl. 'I used to come down and watch Jeff play soccer in that park,' she told me. We talked about everything except what was really on our minds.

I tried hard to see things from her perspective, to understand the hurt in her own heart. Sadly, no bonding had occurred between us up to that time. Neither of us was willing to show each other our true feelings. Perhaps it was just as well, for my needs were so much greater than Kelly was, understandably, able to fulfil. I felt sure that my arrival in Listowel could only have been a sad reminder to her of the mam she loved.

She made the offer to have 'our' mother's name engraved on a small plaque. But how could we agree on suitable wording? 'IN LOVING MEMORY OF MY MOTHER'? What memory? Whose mother? After mulling it over I decided to leave things as they were for the time being, vowing to return one day with my own family to place flowers on her grave and to put my own words on a plaque.

For the rest of the evening I stumbled alone in a darkness which no drinking session at the local pub could lighten, however much Kelly's friends tried.

Chapter Seventeen

Out and About

Baptismal Certificate

With the new information under my belt on the approximate date of my mother's baptism, I felt confident enough to make my third visit to St Mary's. I walked the short distance through the main thoroughfare towards the church, a path now familiar to me, and it seemed that I was following the footsteps of my mother and treading the same path she trod every Sunday. It was weird how close I felt to her. It seemed as though she touched me on the shoulder every time I looked over at her house. Now too, as I headed towards her church, I sensed her invisible presence beside me.

I explained to the clerk that I wanted to search through the register again now that I had a better idea of the date of my mother's baptism. He nodded his head, in reluctant concurrence, looking for all the world as though he resented the intrusion by this teary-eyed New Zealand woman into his well-ordered life. He moved slowly towards the cupboard and lifted the heavy volume that contained the register of baptisms.

'I'll have a quick search if you like,' he tutted.

I stood by his side, looking over his shoulder and trying to keep myself in check while he determinedly turned the pages himself. Ten minutes went by and still he hadn't found the name of Ayshe O'Connor. To hurry things along, I offered to look through the records as, being a fast reader myself, I was getting impatient with his laborious turning of the pages. I also sensed from his defensive body positioning that he didn't like me looking over his shoulder. But he turned down my offer and continued slowly turning the pages.

After what seemed an age, he looked up and said conclusively, 'No, I can't find it. You did say you thought the date of her baptism was between 1950 and 1956?' I nodded. I was ready to give up.

At that moment, by some miracle, the hand of God intervened, and the clerk was called away for a couple of minutes.

I quickly saw my opportunity, and after going back to the beginning and turning just two pages, I found it. What the clerk had so easily missed, I spotted. Half way down the left-hand page I saw the name SUSANNA AYSHE O'CONNOR – BAPTISED ON 1ST NOVEMBER, 1954. AGED TWENTY-NINE.

Instead of being cross with me for going through the register in his absence, the clerk actually looked relieved when he returned and saw that I had found the name.

He explained that Susanna was the Christian name of Ayshe's employer, Mrs Sheehy, who with her husband Frank, the school's headmaster, had encouraged my mother to change religions. It is the custom when being baptised into the Catholic church to use a given name. Susanna Sheehy and her husband, Frank, were recorded as being the two witnesses. They were two more residents of Listowel who had known my mother well and who had since died.

Under the heading 'Parents' I saw the names MUSTAFA SULEYMAN, FATHER, and FATIMA SULEYMAN, MOTHER. I thought to myself, how odd that my own birth name should be written down there. And then it hit me, like an arrow straight to the heart – she had named me after her own mother. For a moment I was dumbstruck. To think I had the very same name as my grandmother. The shame I suffered as a child because of my un-English and anti-Christian name was ameliorated in that instant. Suddenly everything made sense, for my child-mother, at the age of fourteen years and ten months, had named me after the mother she also never knew just as I had wanted to name any daughter of mine after her.

With that knowledge came relief and understanding. All the years of hating my name instantly evaporated. In my mother's place of worship, where she derived spiritual comfort, I forgave her there and then.

When I walked out of St Mary's, I felt a certain contentment that I could not explain to myself. I had found a connection, an identification with my family. For the rest of the day, and for many days after, I continually reflected on the fact that I was named after my grandmother. My heart was a little lighter. And it probably helped that, at last, the sun was shining.

Ballybunion

The wild west coast of Ballybunion was, according to many of the neighbours, a favourite haunt of my mother's, and when Peter, Kelly's brother-in-law, offered to drive me there I jumped at the chance. I would have liked Kelly to come with me to point out any places of interest, but she had to go to work. It didn't matter though, because Peter turned out to be an excellent companion and surprised me with a running commentary. He seemed amused by my English/New Zealand twang and as soon as we set off on Sunday morning along the R553, his words poured out like a raging river as he pointed out the landmarks and peppered me with questions about life in New Zealand.

For a while, we followed the curve of the river Feale in a south-westerly direction, along narrow rustic lanes until Peter suddenly decided to divert the car up a winding hill. He wanted to show me the view from the top. The rain was beating heavily against the window, driven by a loud-moaning wind, the sort of day which would be better spent sitting in front of a roaring fire. Instead, we sat in the freezing interior of the car while Peter pointed out the distant mountain ranges of Macgillycuddy's Reeks at the start of the Ring of Kerry, a popular tourist route.

The country roads, some of them rutted, were virtually empty during the ten kilometre journey. We picked up a local girl who was thumbing a lift at a bus stop. Peter said he often picked up hitchhikers while delivering mail around the rural districts, as the bus service was so erratic. How lucky I was that my driver happened to be a countryman who knew every turn of the roads in this corner of Ireland.

Rain continued to pelt down as we approached the famous international golf course of Ballybunion, on the southern end of the beach. The view to the north was over a wide arc of sand dunes where very high cliffs rose up from the ocean. The ruin of an old castle perched precariously on the edge of the cliff looked as though the gale force winds could blow it off any moment. We parked the car and walked briskly past a cluster of sturdy, unpretentious cottages, downhill towards the beach.

I looked at the astonishingly beautiful scene. There was a rough grey sea, with white breakers stretching along the wild, rocky shoreline. The screeching seagulls and the roar of the gale made it impossible to talk, blowing fine, stinging sand into our faces. The atrocious conditions somehow seemed to match my own inner turmoil. I felt dispirited and lonely. While I strode along the vast stretch of shell-covered sand, battling the elements, I visualised my mother strolling in the sunshine, perhaps having a pleasant paddle, and then eating a packed lunch with a friend under the shade of a tree. With every step I took in the wet, crunching sand, I allowed myself to be overwhelmed by the unrealistic notion that her kindred spirit was with me during that wild, wind-blown walk.

My mother permeated my thoughts, and for a few seconds I became her, returning from a trip to the seaside.

With great reluctance I turned my back against the on-shore wind as it propelled me towards the car park. By the time we arrived back at the car, my hands and face were numbed to the marrow, my eyes streaming. Every part of my body was shaking from the arctic conditions.

The thought came to me that this place was the home of her heart, and I wished I had the time to visit Ballybunion beach a second time, in sunnier conditions.

Although overcome with feelings of sadness, I did feel satisfied that I had seen her favourite stretch of coastline, and I seized and held the memory of where our spirits were fused as one.

The Priest

When I realised there were only four more days left for me in Ireland I was shocked, for the time had slipped by unnoticed. I was eager to meet the priest who had offered my mother her last rites, and who was now Monsignor in the parish of Castle Island, not far from Tralee. Again, Peter came to the rescue with the offer to drive me there. The next day, Kelly and I walked round to his house in the adjoining street from where our journey would start. I couldn't wait to go for a spin in the country, and to have the chance to see another part of Ireland. It would be a welcome change from the rigors of extracting hard-to-get information from the townsfolk.

Castle Island was not an island as one might think, but a small town forty-five minutes south of Listowel, and we were going there on the off-chance that the Monsignor would be home.

I settled back as we drove out of the now familiar town centre, with all its signposts written first in the Irish language then underneath in English. Peter explained that Irish was the first official language which many people spoke in this region. Soon we were speeding through lowland farming landscape with lush green fields either side of a road which ran almost as straight as a die from north to south. There wasn't an apparent speed limit on the open road, but a feeling of space with the only other vehicles on the road being farm tractors.

Peter screeched the car to a sudden shuddering halt by a muddy ditch, so that he could show me his own patch of peat bog. He explained how each field was divided up by the government and shared, without any cost, to selected families in the district.

Huge piles of peat could be seen stretching for miles across the dead flat wasteland, all drying out and ready to be taken away.

Rain began to splatter as we reached the small town of Castle Island. Following Kelly's instructions, Peter took the second turning on the left until we came across a large, newly built house befitting a Monsignor. The big residence looked unoccupied because everything was so new, and even the landscape garden in the front was unfinished. A small woman opened the beautifully panelled front door. We asked if we could speak to the Monsignor and were guided into an elegantly furnished dining room and told to wait. Peter didn't come in with us; he preferred to wait in the car.

Two minutes later, the tall, full figure of Monsignor Mahony, or Father Mahony as Kelly remembered him, walked into the room with a look of recognition on his face as he shook hands with Kelly.

We were directed to sit on the wooden chairs around the oblong table. Kelly then gave him a brief account of who I was and the reason we were here.

'What a remarkable story,' he said at the end of it all, looking across the table at me with a serious expression on his face.

'I believe you gave my mother her last rites,' I ploughed in, not wanting to waste time with niceties.

'Yes, I remember attending her when she was sick – in 1979 was it – and giving her Communion. I knew her for only two years.'

With my recorder positioned on the dining room table, I explained how the Salvation Army only recently agreed to look for her and that I had been searching for most of my life.

'You knew you had a mother somewhere.'

Was that a statement or a question?

'*Everyone* has a mother somewhere.' I laughed nervously in his presence. I'd never prattled away to a priest before, let alone a Monsignor, and I felt rather in awe of him.

'Yes, yes of course. What I meant was, were you adopted or in a foster home or something?'

'No, I was brought up in a children's home.'

Kelly chipped in. 'Tina's been looking for years and years for Ayshe (even now she couldn't say "her mother"), and it was only about three months ago that I got a letter from the Salvation Army, addressed to me mam. Tina and I have been writing to each other since then.'

'Well, well.' I suspected he was struggling to come to grips with what was, after all, a rather muddled story. 'So you'd be half-sisters, is that it?'

'Well…' We looked at each other, stifling an embarrassed giggle, 'more or less.' I think we both knew by then that the idea of being sisters was a preposterous one.

Monsignor Mahony continued. 'You know, she was a lovely, gentle little person. Your smile is like hers, but you're a bigger, taller person altogether.'

The next question blurted impetuously from my lips.

'Did she ever make any deathbed confessions to you about me?'

He thought about it momentarily, but didn't blink an eyelid.

'No, we'd have a chat about her life at home and that sort of thing, but the majority of people wouldn't tell you anything they didn't want you to know.'

'I would have thought, if she needed to confide in anyone about her dark secret,' I muttered, realising I'd bitten off more than I could chew, 'she'd have talked to a priest.'

'Yes, she would have done that years ago, soon after being baptised into the church probably, but even if she had told me in confidence I wouldn't be able to tell you anything. Absolutely not… But she didn't anyway.' He was quite adamant about it.

There was nothing for me to do than to accept his word that my mother did not make any dramatic deathbed confession. It was something I had romanticised about ever since setting foot on Irish soil. Had a movie been made of my mother's life, I felt positive that a last-minute confession about her abandoned baby would have been in the script.

As we shook hands and said our goodbyes, I felt a certain sense of accomplishment that I'd managed to meet the man who attended to my mother's spiritual needs in her last hours on earth – even though little more had been revealed about her.

The Doctor

I sat in the doctor's surgery the day before I was due to leave Listowel, waiting with all the other patients to see one of the two doctors on duty that day. The receptionist had told me I must take my turn with all the other patients before I could go in and talk to Dr McGuire, my mother's doctor. Feeling rather smug at knowing that my own health was excellent, I looked around the stuffy, crowded room that was full of genuinely sick people. I felt strange sitting among the local people, and out of place, prominent, for I was not one of them. It was easy to imagine my mother sitting there, flicking through one of the magazines and waiting her turn.

I went there hoping to find out from the doctor his medical opinion about my mother's health, for instance, if he knew whether she was unable to bear any more children and whether she had the Thalassaemia which I had supposedly inherited from her. I also wanted medical details of the cancer which caused her death at the age of fifty-six.

After forty-five minutes I'd read all the magazines which were on the table. I gave in to my desire to nudge the woman sitting next to me and say, 'Did you know Ayshe O'Connor? She was my mother.' I told her briefly why I was waiting to see the doctor. The name didn't ring a bell, but to my amazement, she informed me that her husband and Michael O'Connor used to work on the same building site many years earlier. Listowel was a small town and I guess it was natural that everyone should know each other.

Nearly an hour had passed before I was called to go in. Dr McGuire greeted me with the disappointing news that he was unable to give me my mother's records as they were all destroyed after a period of ten years. I was one year too late.

I said to him, 'I have spent most of my life in a desperate drive to find out where my mother has been living. I am Ayshe's illegitimate daughter who no one knew about, and I'm staying with Kelly, her niece's daughter who was brought up by my mother.'

He looked at me, and after a brief pause, said, 'Well, I do remember her now. I think she died of cancer of the colon. I remember signing the death certificate. I attended her and her husband for twenty years since 1962. She was very ladylike, good-hearted and loveable. She was slightly built and was always very, very kind to everyone. The neighbours loved her. She never interfered with anyone and was always very polite.'

'I wish I had known her. She sounds like a wonderful person, so angelic.' I didn't feel as calm as I might have sounded.

'That is the word I would use; she was angelic. She never complained even though she didn't have it easy at times, and towards the end she was in a lot of pain.'

His dramatic words brought home to me the unique qualities of this woman who was my mother, who had apparently endeared herself to so many people in the township. Yet it was sheer torture having to sit and listen to yet another person singing her praises. The supreme effort needed in trying to suppress my rising emotions caused all the blood to be drained from my body. I felt quite faint when I heard the doctor call my mother an angel and, again, it made me long to know her. If I was going to have a funny turn, which well I might, at least, I thought, I'm in the right place.

All I wanted to do now was to break down and weep aloud, to let the tears flow freely, but as usual I had to force myself to keep my feelings in check.

It was hard to hear about my mother's brave suffering when she was seriously ill. I could almost feel her pain. So many people had spoken to me about her, and brought her alive for me, that it was almost as if she was still a warm, living person.

The doctor gave me a sympathetic glance across his desk, and while I sat waiting, he phoned the Killarney Registry and arranged for the death certificate to be forwarded to me in New Zealand.

He could give me no satisfactory explanation as to why my mother didn't have any children in Ireland. He couldn't remember her having a hysterectomy. 'Maybe something went wrong after your birth – perhaps she had some damage when delivering you at such a young age.'

He was plucking probabilities out of thin air. And when I asked about the Thalassaemia, he had no knowledge of that either. From his expression I don't think he really knew what it was, and considering it is a Mediterranean blood disease, that is entirely understandable.

I left the surgery with the doctor's words ringing in my head. 'Your mother was angelic,' he had said quite spontaneously. There was no doubt in my mind that she was now in heaven – a fitting place for an angel. She had to be. Now as I walked back to Kelly's house I thought to myself, how many real saints, or angels, does one meet in a lifetime? My mother was one – and I never met her. If only I had...

Chapter Eighteen

Kelly's Assertions

Nine days had passed since I had been staying in Kelly's home and we had never really had the chance to have a good heart-to-heart talk. It became obvious that we were opposite in our outlook and temperament, and as she was almost half my age there was a big generation gap. But that evening, after I helped her wash up the dinner dishes, she looked at me, unsmiling, and said, 'Tina, there's something important I want to talk to you about.' I felt a stirring of anticipation what it might be, and I sat on the kitchen chair, my body primed to receive whatever was about to be thrown at me. My instincts told me that Kelly had not been entirely open with me over the few days that I had made her acquaintance.

She made her usual Irish coffee, nervously dragged on a cigarette, and launched into a seemingly rehearsed speech.

'Tina, when I told you I had nothing left that belonged to me mam I wasn't telling you the truth.'

As she uttered the word 'truth', she lifted her head and we made eye contact for the first time.

'What is the truth, Kelly?' I tried not to show in my face the deep concern I felt at this new turn of events.

'Well, up in Dublin they have me mam's wedding ring, and some other stuff that belonged to her. When she and me dad died they got the house and everything. I didn't get a cent.'

Her voice was shaking, barely discernible.

'Who do you mean by "they"?' I asked, in feigned ignorance, even though I knew it must be her mother's family.

Reluctantly, she confessed it was Rhona, her mother, whom she had previously refused to discuss. I had to pinch myself at this late, shock admission, but in the same instant, I felt thrilled to hear this positive news.

'They also have me mam's prayer book.'

'Oh Kelly.' The impassive face I had tried to maintain involuntarily changed to one of unabashed anger because she had withheld this vital information from me until this late time. 'Why on earth didn't you tell me all this sooner? You know I'm flying to England tomorrow.'

For a brief second she hesitated, then the words tumbled out. 'Because I know she would tell you a pack of lies about me. They all hate me up in Dublin because I caused a lot of trouble up there when I had to go and live with them when me mam died.'

'Look Kelly,' I implored earnestly. 'It doesn't concern me what went on in your life years ago. It's in the past and none of it's my business. But for my sake, please give me Rhona's phone number so I can make a quick phone call to Dublin.'

'No, it's impossible. She has an unlisted number.'

Normally I'm not a forceful person but now I needed to act incisively. The adrenalin was flowing and I vehemently insisted if she couldn't give me her mother's phone number at least she should give me her address. I knew it would be impossible to arrange to travel to Dublin, a distance of about two hundred and fifty kilometres, with only one more day in Ireland, especially as there was no telephone link. My mind went into overdrive as I tried to think quickly. I decided to put pen to paper and there and then, in front of Kelly, I wrote a hurried letter to her mother, explaining who I was, and requesting her to phone me at Janet's house in East Grinstead, Sussex, where I planned to stay for the next few days prior to returning to New Zealand. The main thrust of the letter included details of myself – that I was Ayshe's long-lost daughter – and how dearly I would love to take home with me anything that belonged to my mother. I showed Kelly the letter, as I wanted her to see I had nothing to hide. Things were moving so fast now that I had to shift my brain into second gear to keep up with the tide of events.

The air in the stuffy, smoky kitchen was electric while Kelly continued talking about her past. We swallowed several cups of Irish coffee as the evening wore on into the night.

In caustic tones, refusing to succumb to tears, she told me how her five half-sisters made it obvious they didn't want her living with them. She recounted how she missed her mam and her dad and hadn't wanted to move away from Listowel. But the untimely death of the couple whom she had fondly thought of as her own mother and father threw her into a completely new environment where she couldn't settle. She was only thirteen and didn't know where she belonged and became terribly unhappy and consequently rebellious.

I sat silently in stunned amazement as, in a voice raw with emotion, Kelly went on to tell me the things that happened during her unhappy five years in Dublin, and it became clear that the rift between herself and her family was very deep. She was angry and embittered, and from that bitterness sprang allegations not only about her family, but also about my mother. She claimed that my birth was as a result of rape and that my father could have been one of the sons of the Turkish Consul General. I was shattered. The sympathy I had begun to feel for Kelly when she had to return to her family immediately dissolved when I heard her astounding statements about my own parentage. My mother raped by one of the sons of the Turkish Consul! It all seemed so surreal to me. Absolutely preposterous.

By the time I slowly walked up the stairs to sleep for the last time in Kelly's house, I realised she had intentionally sown a seed of doubt in my mind, which over the next few weeks would grow and fester. I had to find out the real truth from Vahide. But my journey was at an end. I needed to get to the bottom of it, and in my mind, I made plans for another trip – this time to Turkey perhaps next year. A cold numbness had taken hold of my heart. I scribbled into my diary: 'I cannot believe these assertions of Kelly's. Why is she trying to hurt me?'

I came to the realisation that, for reasons I could not fathom, Kelly was endeavouring to get back at me – perhaps because I was her mam's flesh and blood daughter who had come to Listowel and spoiled her memories. Our tenuous friendship, in that moment, took a step back. I was still in a spasm of shock when I tried to sleep that night, for my mind was in utter confusion.

Chapter Nineteen

Rhona

With a huge sense of relief I flew out of Ireland. As I looked down from the plane at my last vision of my mother's adopted country, it seemed that I'd been in Listowel for ten weeks rather than just ten days.

My departure from Kelly's house was awkward, even icy. We had stiffly embraced each other, just as we had when we first met, and I found it hard to believe that this was the same person who had expressed the desire to be my half-sister. No bond had been established, nor any chord struck between us during my stay in her home. Since her disturbing late-night disclosures, my mind was in a whirl.

As the plane flew over the Irish Sea towards England, I had plenty of time for reflection. I thought, if Kelly wanted to put doubts in my mind, she'd certainly succeeded. I shuddered as I remembered her breathtaking charges, for although the circumstances of my birth were of no consequence to me now, the name Harold Kirton was lodged immovably in my mind as being my English father. I eminently preferred to think that I was born out of a love match rather than any violent relationship. Was I to believe the speculative ramblings of an embittered surrogate daughter, or should I trust my instinct and continue accepting the word of the consul general's family that Harold Kirton, an employee of theirs, was my father? Maybe it was all a lie to protect their own son. I decided to put the vexing question on hold until I had the chance to talk to Vahide myself, hopefully in her home in Istanbul. It didn't bear thinking about. My present world was confused enough without worrying about another overseas trip.

I remembered how I felt when I landed at Shannon Airport. Then my mind was open, intensely curious about what I might see and hear. Now the door was closed and many gaps had been filled. I had a good understanding about the sort of existence my mother had led, and what type of person she was. Hers had been a tough life, full of poverty and in her later years, pain, yet, by all accounts, she seems to have made the best of what life had to offer. I came away with a picture in my mind of a hard-working, gentle angel loved by everyone with whom she came into contact. It seems odd when I write of her now to say that, in a strange way, I loved her too. It wasn't that I missed her, because of course I'd never known her, so therefore held no memories of her in my heart. All the lovely things that had been said about her somehow brought her close to me and made me want to know her as a person, let alone a mother. If nothing else, going to Ireland helped to lighten the darkness of doubt I had always had about her and fill in most of the missing pieces. More than ever though, it made me wish I had known her.

Two days later I was flying back to Ireland from England. This time, though, it was to Dublin – and to Rhona. In her phone call to me at Janet's house, she said how surprised she was to have heard from me. She told me that my mother spoke just once, on her deathbed, about the baby she had to give away, and that she assumed I had been happily adopted by a loving couple.

Rhona insisted that I visit her and her family before returning to New Zealand. I couldn't help seeing the irony of returning to Ireland within the space of three days. Up until then I hadn't flown in a plane for sixteen years. I was certainly making up for lost time.

In spite of Kelly's bewildering, scandalous claims, I felt enormously grateful to her for having the courage in the end to speak out on my last evening with her, even though it was almost too late. I wanted to meet Kelly's mother, Rhona, a woman who must have been so close to my mother that she trusted her to bring up her own illegitimate baby.

I informed Rhona I would wear a red coat and that she should look out for a taller version of Ayshe. As I walked down the gangway at Dublin Airport, worriedly looking into the sea of expectant faces, I experienced a feeling of *déjà vu*, having been through the procedure of seeking the face of a stranger in a crowd only two weeks previously. Rhona and her husband, Jimmy, recognised me easily, and like everyone else down in Listowel, they couldn't get over the resemblance I had to my mother.

During the journey to Ballybrack, a suburb south of Dublin, Rhona couldn't take her eyes off me and immediately started throwing questions at me. Not wanting to wait until we arrived home, she even brought along some photos to show me.

Rhona didn't look like her daughter. She was taller, with dark hair, and her pale face seemed lit with a keen curiosity. I felt the attraction of her warm personality in that first meeting and I took an instant liking to her. I could understand how my mother would have taken to her.

We had hardly stepped through the front door of her home in a run-down council estate when Rhona abruptly urged Siobhan, her nineteen year old daughter, to hand over my mother's wedding ring. In a touching gesture, with her two sisters looking on, Siobhan slipped off the ring she had worn on her finger in the eleven years since her Aunty

Ayshe had died and placed it on mine. Half-blinded by a rush of tears, I kissed her on the cheek.

'There, it's yours now,' Rhona spoke for her daughter. 'You have it with our blessing in memory of your "mudder".'

Kelly had made it very plain to me that she considered the ring to be her property, as well as any other keepsakes of her mam. I had such mixed feelings. But then the rage and sense of injustice that had been trapped inside me for so long showed its full face, and I thought, why shouldn't I have it? It is all I have. I'm her real daughter. I craved to have something that belonged to my mother.

As I swallowed the lump in my throat, I tried to put the troublesome thoughts out of my mind. I was far too choked up to talk. It all seemed so unreal, unbelievable. To think that I was now the owner of my mother's most precious heirloom – her ring, the physical symbol of love worn on her finger through thirty years of marriage. I rubbed it with disbelief, feeling an inexplicable bond between us. It didn't fit my obviously fatter finger, but I managed to push it on my little finger where it stayed until I was able to have it enlarged.

'She's watching us, you know,' said Rhona, crossing herself and glancing upwards. 'May God rest her soul. She can see what's happening down here in this kitchen.'

As we walked up the stairs, I listened, fascinated, but barely understanding her effusive Irish idioms. 'I've put you in Siobhan's bedroom. It's the same room where your "mudder" used to sleep whenever she came up to stay. In fact, this is the very bed that she slept in.'

Amazingly, that very night I had a vivid dream of a wispy figure, clad in white, wafting into the room. The ephemeral form pulled back the bedclothes, stepped gently out of the same bed where I was sleeping, and then walked away slowly, seemingly with great reluctance. Never in my life had I experienced anything similar. On waking, I knew instantly that it was my mother. The spectral figure that visited our 'shared' bed, where we had both rested our heads, *had* to be my mother. Looking back, I can see that her appearance to me in that bedroom two nights before I was due to leave Ireland suggested a tie that existed between us, not only in the sharing of the same bed, but inferred also an inexplicable, ethereal kinship.

I had conjured up mental pictures of my mother almost on a daily basis throughout my sojourn in Ireland, and my senses were now filled to the brim with acute longing for her. But never before had her apparition appeared with such clarity in my dreams. So many had told me she was an angel. I perceived her appearance, like an angel from heaven, to mean that she was making room for me and was signalling goodbye. It seemed to be a good omen.

So deep was the impression the dream left that it gave me a flicker of comfort knowing that we had made a connection – we were truly kindred spirits.

Downstairs, I told Rhona that my mother appeared like a phantom in my dream that night.

'Holy divine God,' she shrieked, her eyes like saucers. 'Didn't I tell you she's watching you, she knows you're here.'

She looked at me with a grin on her face, obviously pleased with herself that she had managed to persuade me to come and stay.

I spent three days with Rhona and Jimmy and I met all their five daughters, and other members of the family. Whenever she could, Rhona talked into my tape-recorder and told me as much as she could remember about her favourite Aunty, whom she loved dearly. She said that even if my mother had wanted to communicate with me, she would not have been able to because she wasn't able to write English, and Michael had to write everything for her.

All she could do was to sign her name. I was stunned to hear that my mother was illiterate. Had she not received an education when she was living in England under the care of the Turkish Consul General?

I learned much more about my mother from Rhona. She told me that most people in Ireland were very badly off years ago, and that my mother worked for everybody and anybody to make ends meet.

'You've got to believe me Tina when I tell ya, I idolised your mudder. I t'ink she was the most wonderful woman on earth – I absolutely loved her.'

I concentrated hard while Rhona's diatribe went on through the evening. I listened while she described the problems they had when Kelly came up to live with them once Ayshe had died. I did not wish to hear any of it, as I had realised when I was down in Listowel that she and her daughter were alienated from each other but I was trapped in the bowels of her kitchen and had no choice in the matter. She gave me a torrid account of my mother's last days on earth, and how she fought to stay alive.

'She thought you were happily adopted and living as someone else's daughter. She was crying, as you are crying now, and she said, "I had my own little baby girl and I had to give her away."'

It was clear that Rhona was very fond of her Aunty Ayshe. When she told me things about my mother I believed her, but I suspected she indulged in a bit of Irish blarney. I guessed she was simply trying to make me feel better.

Before I left, Rhona retrieved from her attic a small box of my mother's keepsakes. It had been there, untouched, since my mother died eleven years before. They were the physical, pathetic remnants of my mother's religion, scant testimony of her strong faith. They included her Mass Communion kit, consisting of a crucifix and her holy water bowl, her prayer book and rosary beads, two religious pictures, a few slides of her visit to Lourdes, as well as a necklace and her purse.

I opened the prayer book tenderly, noticing the folded corners of the page which perhaps denoted a favourite scripture. A few prayer cards were tucked in the back. For the first time I saw her handwriting – her signature, and I was filled with awe as I looked at the small, flowery writing. Also hand-written on the front page was a prayer, obviously copied and misspelled in many places. Goose bumps pricked my arms as I studied the touching fragments of her faith. I fondled the brown rosary beads, and as I turned them over in my hand I could feel the value of them to her. Her treasures were now my treasures. I had a strong need for them.

Rhona also managed to find a total of thirty photos of my mother. And so, wearing my mother's precious ring and with her worthless knickknacks stacked in my suitcase, I flew home to my family. Although none of them are of any intrinsic value, to me they are priceless.

My joyful homecoming was tempered by the knowledge that I had not found any vital blood ties that I so yearned. Rhona, bless her heart, tried to make me feel better by saying that we two were cousins, and we shook hands on it. The few days with her had been tough going. The stress of listening to her talking endlessly about my mother was emotionally draining.

But it was not a journey wasted. After twenty-four hours of flying, I felt as if I had emerged from a vale of darkness, unburdened from the heavy weight of my ignorant past. My mother had come alive for me. At last I had been able to piece together the major part of my mother's life which had always been a mystery. With the knowledge came a sense of connection. For the first time in my life, I got a sense of what my mother was like as a real, warm human being. Yet I had to face the fact that she was dead.

Chapter Twenty

Visit to Vahide

Returning home to New Zealand, my adopted country, I gave myself up wholly to my family. Life was busy and full of purpose. Our vocal quartet sang at various senior citizen's clubs on the North Shore. Ray and I played tennis at our local tennis club, and the boys were having tennis and soccer coaching. Nigel was by now passionate about the trumpet and he knew he wanted to do a music degree in trumpet performance.

But beneath the veneer of raising our children, a cauldron of emotions bubbled away ready to spill over at any time. After seeing my mother's home environment I gleaned a real sense of her presence and her personality. But in order to piece together and give meaning to all the revelations that had surfaced from my pilgrimage to Ireland I needed to put them down on paper. So I joined a creative writing class run by Joan Rosier-Jones. Writing, I discovered, was a wonderful release. It helped to cast off some of the heavy emotional baggage I've been carrying around inside me all my life. Week by week, as I unburdened myself in the class by reading aloud more and more of my written pages, I began to feel lighter. Joan persuaded me to send my story to the New Zealand *Woman's Weekly*, where it was subsequently published in the May edition of 1993.

And so started the wonderful healing process of writing. After years of sublimation and denial, I was able to set things right in my head by putting down my muddled thoughts on paper. My true self started to emerge. And a book of my life was conceived.

In my first couple of brain-storming drafts all the bitterness and tears poured out. I was still attempting to complete the book three years later. But an important chapter had to be verified, and I would need to go to Turkey before I could complete my story and close the book once and for all.

A few of my closest friends knew the real reason for a trip away from home for the third time in as many years but most knew only the barest facts. Ray understood why I needed to make yet another odyssey – to piece together the fragments of my mother's early life. Ever since Kelly had made the breathtaking charges about my father being one of the consul's sons, I had to find out the truth for myself. Here was the opportunity to blow away once and for all the seeds of doubt about my parentage that Kelly had so cruelly sown in Ireland.

Laurence and Nigel, now fifteen and sixteen, two tall, good-looking lads, were preparing for exams at their local high school and, knowing that we would be in regular contact by telephone, seemed unperturbed that Mum was fleeing the nest again.

As the taxi sped north towards the suburb of Teşvikiye, memories of 1964 came flooding back, when Istanbul first put a spell on me. Amazingly, some things had not changed in this city of ten million people. A *hamel* (porter), carrying a huge load on his bent back, shuffled across the busy sidewalk. But there would be no time to savour the sights and sounds of the city I used to love.

I had already written and told Vahide, the Consul General's daughter, about my mother's early death from cancer, and there were still questions that I needed to ask about her early years that she alone would, hopefully, remember. Now a widow approaching the age of seventy, her health poorly and her memory fading, Vahide agreed that I could stay with her for a few days. It was twenty-one years since I had visited her, with Ray, in her Bebek apartment.

All too soon I found myself standing in a seedy back street, and as I glanced upwards towards the third floor of Vahide's apartment, I could not help thinking about her change in fortune since she moved to Teşvikiye. I lugged my suitcase up three flights of stairs and rang the doorbell. What a relief to see Vahide's smiling face appear at the door. She ushered me into her heavily furnished lounge and introduced me to her fifty-two year old son, Osman.

There was barely enough room to swing a cat in the cramped sitting room, but it was the stray cats and barking dogs on the street below which kept me awake for most of that first steamy night.

A bed was made up for me on the floor of the lounge, squeezed between the armchair and the dining table.

Next morning the high, shrill voice of the muezzin calling the faithful to prayer by means of a loudspeaker, abruptly woke me.

We ate a typical Turkish breakfast of feta cheese and olives, swilled down with aromatic tea. Even at this early hour the air was stifling. I absorbed the surroundings through the senses rather than the brain, for my sleepless night had left me bleary-eyed. Vahide spoke in halting English, her dark, twinkling eyes full of laughter, and we quickly warmed to each other.

What little I had been told about my mother's life with the Akcer family had faded with the passage of time. And I knew even less about her earlier life. There were so many questions I wanted to ask.

'Why did my mother live in Romania even though she was Turkish?' I asked, launching into my long list of written questions and placing the cassette recorder on the table.

Vahide explained how the ethnic Turks came to be living in Romania. The Ottoman Empire had extended across the middle of Europe and over the centuries people of Turkish origin settled in the European region of Romania and inter-married. Later on, after the First World War there was an uprising against the Muslims and many families were made homeless and became refugees – just as they have in modern-day Bosnia.

Vahide's father, the consul general at that time in Constanza, an historic Black Sea port on the coast of Romania, had the job of arranging the transportation of many Turkish families. My mother was the last of a family of many children, maybe eight or ten. They were perishing with hunger, living in terrible conditions, and the local people took pity on the children and asked the consul general to take care of them.

Vahide confirmed that the tall, sturdy old man in the photo was definitely Ayshe's father, Mustafa Suleyman, my grandfather. He looked about ninety years old, but was probably about seventy-five when he brought his youngest daughter to them, because his wife died shortly after giving birth to Ayshe. He pleaded with her family to take Ayshe into their household as he was destitute and no longer had a home of his own. It was the custom in those days for a benevolent, wealthy family to help out poorer families and find appropriate husbands for the girls, as well as giving them a dowry. Vahide hesitated before continuing.

'Do you know, Tina, when she came to us we had to shave her head like a monk because her hair was full of lice. We didn't know what her life was like before, but she must have been very poor because she told us she had never tasted bread until she came to us.'

She was warming to the subject now, her English improving markedly. 'My mother told me Ayshe used to eat certain types of grass to stay alive.'

Her words shocked me beyond measure. I listened spellbound to Vahide's torrid account of my forbears, absolutely horrified by the images she portrayed of their struggle to survive.

I asked, 'Were there any other servants in your household?'

'Yes, there was another girl called Selime, a bit older, whom we took in about the same time as Ayshe, and they became good friends. In Constanza we had other maids, a cook and a butler in the house. Your mother learned the traditional Turkish etiquette, sewing and cooking. But during the war when we were moved to London, it wasn't so easy to get staff and Ayshe had to do extra work.'

I was flabbergasted at the revelations that my mother was not the close-knit member of the family I had always imagined, and that she and the other maid worked together, not as 'daughters' as I had supposed, but purely as housemaids, serving at the table doing the housework and eating their meals in the kitchen.

When Vahide told me that Ayshe called her parents 'My Lady' and 'Sir' and, worse, that she never ever went to school in Romania, Turkey or England, I gave an audible gasp. Tears welled up in my eyes as I thought of my poor mother being a maid with no opportunity to have a decent education.

These new disclosures corroborated the information that I found out in Ireland – that my mother couldn't write English, and it confirmed what Barnardo's had stated on my admission form that she didn't speak a word of English. And she had lived in England for over a year before I was born.

Vahide said, 'Although Ayshe spoke only a few words of English she could explain herself. She was very clever you know, she had a good aptitude to learn. We were usually speaking in French and she quickly picked up what we were saying. Apart from her native Turkish, I believe she also spoke Romanian.'

Starved for more details, I listened avidly as Vahide went on to say how fond her family had been of Ayshe. 'She was extremely introverted you know. Both the girls were fortunate to be accepted into a good home. We took them with us on picnics, to the seashore, on outings. Who knows what would have happened to them if it wasn't for my parents' generosity? They probably would have perished.'

I heard everything she was saying with increasing hypersensitivity. I sipped the coffee that her son offered to us. It was difficult concentrating on what Vahide was saying against the background of the street noises drifting up from the open window, and the music from her son's radio.

I thought to myself, no wonder no bond was formed between my mother and the consul general's family. It is easy to understand now why she had no more contact with them after leaving their service.

Intensely keen to know if my mother had ever lived in Turkey, because my love affair with the country stemmed from the belief that she originated from that country, I asked Vahide how long she had lived in Turkey.

'Only for about a year and a half. First she lived with us in Constanza, Romania for a few years. We left there in 1937, then went to Ankara, in Turkey, and in late 1938 we travelled by ship to England and stayed in London during the whole of the war.'

Vahide passed her hand over her head. I sensed she was tiring, and I suggested we had a break. After tea and sandwiches, she continued with her story.

'We lived in a Georgian three-storey apartment in Lower Sloane Street, Chelsea. The shelter was in the basement and during the air-raids we all used to go there to spend the night on mattresses. The girls had their own quarters on the top floor. The family lived on the second floor and the ground floor was used as offices.'

I plucked up the courage to bring up the subject of how my mother met my father. What Barnardo's had told me of my father was that he was a thirty-year old porter at the Turkish Consul General's office in London, and his name was Harold Kirton.

'Well Tina,' Vahide said, almost in a whisper, 'Harold lived in his own room in the basement. It was easy for him to meet Ayshe as they lived in the same building. I suppose they must have met in the evenings.'

I reminded Vahide that when I first visited her in Istanbul in 1964 her mother told me that Harold was tall with fair hair and glasses. I have it written in my diary for that year, and have carried his image in my head. Whenever I look at my first-born, Nigel, I think of my father as he fits the same description, whereas Laurence is the image of Ray.

Taking a deep breath, and trying not to sound as embarrassed as I felt, I brought up the subject of how my father broke the law by having sexual relations with an underage girl.

'I understood your family wanted to keep things quiet.'

I showed Vahide my admission form, which stated: 'For diplomatic reasons the consul did not wish the police to be approached, and admission to a residential home would relieve the members of the consulate of an embarrassing situation.'

'Yes, it's true,' she admitted. 'The reason was that any future marriage would have been ruined for her. Harold was called to the British Expeditionary Forces, and had to quit his work. He had already gone when we found out she was pregnant.'

The words tumbled out of my mouth.

'Barnardo's state that he was my putative (assumed) father. What proof is there that he was the only man she slept with?'

In lowered tones, Vahide said, 'I don't know if there were other men, but apparently Ayshe, who was only fourteen at the time, told my parents, and the doctor, that Harold was the father. That is how Barnardo's were informed.'

It took my breath away to hear such things said about the mother whom I thought to be nothing less than a saint, and I could not bring myself to say what was really on my mind. It occurred to me that she was a young, orphaned girl, in a foreign land, without a family of her own, and it was patently obvious that she was merely looking for love. If anyone could have recognised the aching longing for a physical relationship, it was me.

With tongue in cheek, I told Vahide about Kelly's allegations that one of her brothers was my father. She laughed at that. 'Who is this girl that she is trying to make such mischief? I was the only one living at home during the time when you would have been conceived. Muammer, my younger brother, would have been just thirteen, and Faruk was having private tutoring in Scotland.'

Ashamed to have brought up such a scandalous indictment of her obviously innocent brothers, but satisfied with her adamant denials, I quickly changed the subject.

'Do you remember when I was born?'

'Yes, they had to call the ambulance. You were in a hurry to come into this world.'

'I can't think why,' I grinned, adding, 'Do you know how long my mother kept me as a baby?'

'I think she fed you for about a month but I couldn't swear to it. She didn't bring you back with her. She was too young to keep you and my parents took the responsibility of putting you in the care of the authorities.' We both agreed there was nothing else that could have been done in the circumstances.

Vahide continued. 'Ayshe stayed with us for a year or two after you were born, but she wanted her independence, so my parents reluctantly gave her some money and some clothing in place of her dowry, and apart from a brief visit to our home a few months later to collect her birth certificate, we heard nothing more from her since.'

She explained that her parents were Ayshe's 'unofficial' guardians, with no legal contract.

We had been talking for nearly three hours. In the comfort of a small living room in Istanbul I felt protective towards my mother. What consuming love I felt for her then, now that I understood her unloved and impoverished background.

My own fundamental needs had now been met by finding out more about my mother – and father. I had been made aware of my own history and origins by knowing more of my mother's background. I still yearn for what I never had – a living mother, but more importantly some last, vital pieces of the puzzle had been rapidly filled in Vahide's sitting room.

Before I left Turkey I made one last visit – to Hilkat Bey's office, where he was still working, with the help of his umpteenth secretary. He gave me a few black and white photos taken of me thirty years ago. He had already had two heart attacks, and at the age of seventy-five he knew his days were numbered. Three weeks after I returned to my home in New Zealand he was dead. Kismet had played a hand in the meeting up of the two of us again.

Epilogue

July 1995, Listowel

I sit at the back of the church. I am alone. It feels oddly appropriate to be sitting in almost the same spot in the oak pew that I sat in three years ago during my first cathartic visit, three years almost to the day when I watched the funeral procession, deeming it to be my mother's. Being here in her church reminds me that I am still going through the mourning process, still mourning for the loss of my dreams that were shattered once I knew she was dead. Like a homing pigeon, I have again been drawn to her home town and to her haven of rest, the place where she sought comfort. And now I seek it.

I sit alone, silently sobbing. The feelings that I have stored inside me slowly unfold revealing a fusion of compassion and love, pain and anger.

Just as I had three years ago, I want to enact the symbolic ritual of lighting a candle for my mother but again I am incapable. It is no doubt a simple act, but I do not have the confidence to walk up to the circle and perform the ceremony.

I feel so alone, but there is no one to share these feelings with me. I need someone to hold me until I stop crying. I am a child again needing adult comfort. It's my mother I need. But she is not here.

Three years have passed when I have shed tears of shame and sadness as I try to grasp the truth that she is dead – that

I will never meet her. She has continued to saturate my imagination. She died at the much-too-young age of fifty-six. As I approach with dread the age my mother died I am acutely aware of my own mortality.

The reality of my mother's life has imprinted itself on my mind. I now know as much as I can ever hope to know about the woman who gave me the precious gift of life. I have discovered that she was an 'angel'; she had compassion and warmth, a child-mother who grew into a courageous woman of quiet determination and strong faith. I can look at her life now as a finished story.

After a lifetime of being an orphan, seeking knowledge of a family, searching for a mother, I have made a connection. Yet, at the age of fifty-five, incredibly, I still do not know any blood relation, and to this day remain an orphan. It is easy to understand why my poor child-mother had to put me into an orphanage, for I know she was too young to bring me up. Yet I am trying to deal with the pain still buried deep inside me of being separated from her.

In the last three years, explosions of pain have erupted whenever I have thought about her life, and then her death. My mind has wandered back to Listowel, to my mother's house, her grave and her church. Jealousy has swept over me whenever I have thought of how my own needs were not met and I had to face up to the reality that my mother gave unconditional love to another child, who happened to be in the right place at the right time.

My compliant nature has prevented me from expressing long-suppressed anger and pain. Yet I do not bear any malice towards Barnardo's, my parental guardians, because I am aware that the laws in the past were designed to protect us from being hurt. Nevertheless, I have been hurt by being kept away from my only blood relative who lived somewhere on this earth.

In the three years I have again returned to Europe and visited Barnardo's in England, taking the opportunity to view my personal files for the first time. I have attended the 150th birthday celebrations of Thomas Barnardo, the founder, when two thousand old boys and girls gathered at Barkingside for a grand reunion. I have laughed and joked with my old friends in shared reminiscences when I have once again been called Fatima Suleyman.

I have found out that I was by no means the only one hurt by the lack of love in our institutionalised upbringing. Many of us still rail against the well-meaning but misguided practices of the past, when little attention was given to the needs of the individual. There was no welfare state in the Forties, and it was thought best to remove children from any family that might exist. Only a few were real orphans. Some were adopted. Others, like myself, were placed in large, regimented homes run by authoritarian matrons. Thankfully, these homes are now a thing of the past and today much of Barnardo's work is involved alongside families.

The head of after-care admitted in a recent issue of *The Barnardo Guild Messenger*: 'In those days the organisation believed that children should have the chance of a new life and that contacts from relatives might be unsettling for them. "Look to the future" many were told, and "forget about the past".'

Barnardo's are now bending over backwards to strengthen family bonds and to repair any past damage by adopting a more open policy. They have increased four-fold their after-care staff to offer counselling and help to those who need it.

I appreciate the skilled care and education that I received, but when my thoughts turn back I do feel a sense of injustice for the lack of love in the homes, and the scant assistance that I was given in my adult search for a family.

Because I was one of the few real orphans where my need for family connections was so essential to the discovery of my true identity, their past policies remain hard to forgive.

The process of writing has been emotionally gruelling right from the first page, but its therapeutic process has helped me to see my way clear through the foggy gloom of my past. As well, it has helped me to come out, in the sense that I have allowed myself to talk openly to strangers about my origins, and about my lack of a mother-figure. It has brought a real sense of cleansing anger and has enabled me to understand the depths of my suppressed bitterness, something which I can no longer deny.

First, I have wanted to write for myself, and then for my children. I want to explain to them their Turkish/English origins and the reasons they have never had any grandparents, aunties, uncles or cousins on my side. My focus now is to explore my genealogy on the Internet, for there is the fascinating prospect of finding information about my father, Harold Kirton, and his family in England. And you never know, someone on the World Wide Web might be able to locate the Suleyman family in Romania.

Whenever I used to be questioned about my family, my embarrassment was always patently obvious. Now, at last, in middle age, I have something palpable to grasp hold of. I can positively refer to my mother in the past tense. 'Oh yes,' I am able to say, without any shadow of doubt, 'I did have a mother who was Turkish, and she lived in Ireland for thirty years, but she's dead now.' A sad fact, but at least I can now say, in all honesty, that it's true.

As I take stock of my life with my three wonderful men and our extended family, it occurs to me that I am fortunate that I live in one of the most beautiful cities in the world, that I am healthy in mind and body and that I am surrounded by true friends.

For twenty-seven years my love with Ray has helped to give my life meaning and shape, for I now know the intense delights of being loved and having an actual family.

Watching my sons grow to maturity has given me untold pleasure. I now have the family I missed in early life, and I am loved by them. Still, I can almost feel the pain my own mother would have felt at giving away her only child, and the unspoken longing at times such as Christmases and birthdays.

Now I can better understand my history. At last I have an identity. To know my mother, in my heart at least, is to know myself. I want to tell my sons, and the whole world, about her and my lifelong search for her.

Now I'm part of the human race; I feel secure in the knowledge that I have a close-knit family with whom I can share the highs and lows of life. I want to fill my life with the things I love – forming friendships in the local walking group, playing tennis at the Northcote Tennis Club and singing with the North Shore Ladies' Choir. But most of all, I just want to be with my own flesh and blood.

My quest is over. There are still gaps in the story, but I have answers to many questions.

And so I stand at the back of the church to where I am drawn towards the mother whose indomitable spirit touched the lives of so many – except me. She was 'someone special'. Although I will never know her I am grateful to have come this close. I like to think she has passed on to me some of her qualities, her kind nature and her courage in the face of adversity. I thank her for it.

As I sit gazing at the light shining through the coloured glass of the windows, a woman approaches. Her face triggers an array of feelings. I recognise her from my previous visit. My mother did her housekeeping.

'Would you like to light a candle for your mother?'

I look at her, tears brimming my eyes, for I see instead my mother, smiling with wistful longing for what might have been.

With arms outstretched she takes my hand and together we light a candle. I am acutely aware that this single flame glows for me alone, and in the beacon of light I have renewed hope, for I am linked for ever with the spirit of my mother. Now I am in tune with my past. The years of frustration and grief have led me here to a new beginning – out of the darkness into the light.

Goodbye, Mum. I'm sorry I missed you, but thank you for giving me life.